D0385430

JUDAEA WEEPING

JUDAEA WEEPING

*The Jewish Struggle Against Rome from Pompey
to Masada, 63 B.C. to A.D. 73*

GEORGE C. BRAUER, JR.

Thomas Y. Crowell Company   New York

Established 1834

Title page photograph courtesy of American Numismatic Society.
Map by Donald T. Pitcher

Designed by Virginia Smith

Manufactured in the United States of America
L. C. Card 79-106583
1 2 3 4 5 6 7 8 9 10

PREFACE

In A.D. 70, Jerusalem fell to the Roman general Titus, climaxing four years of Jewish revolt against Roman rule. To celebrate the victory Titus' father, the emperor Vespasian, had coins struck showing a Jewess seated under a palm tree and weeping. She personified her country.

The revolt was the product of a Jewish antipathy toward Rome that had its beginning in 63 B.C., when Pompey ended Jewish independence, and continued with mounting tension through the reign of the Romanizing Herod the Great, the reigns of his descendants, and the administrations of Roman governors such as Pontius Pilate. The fall of Jerusalem was, in other words, many decades in the making, and Judaea had been tearful a long time. The events and leading figures in Judaea during the period from 63 B.C. to A.D. 73 are the subject of this book.

CONTENTS

I

BEFORE POMPEY

Pompey the Great stood in the Sanctuary of the Temple at Jerusalem. At the time, 63 B.C., he was the most highly regarded and politically important general in the Roman Empire. Having been granted enormous military powers on land and sea by the senate, he had recently cleared out the pirates that infested the Mediterranean, defeated Rome's inveterate enemy, the king of Pontus, and turned Syria into a Roman province. Now he had overcome the soldiers of Aristobulus, king of the Jews. Of those in Jerusalem, some may have guessed that Jewish independence was ended. But this must have distressed them much less than the realization that Pompey stood in the Sanctuary, where his presence was a gross offense against God.

Curiosity, it seems, was his main motivation. He looked around at the seven-branched lampstand of gold, the gold altar, the holy gold vessels, and the enormous amount of money that had been contributed by Jews from all over the Mediterranean area. Although he left the money untouched, his lack of avarice did not reduce the horror of his intrusion. Only priests of the Jewish faith were allowed inside the Sanctuary.

Pompey may have penetrated even farther, into the Holy of Holies itself—where emptiness confronted him. Just as the Temple constituted the house of God among His people, so the Holy of Holies was

God's inmost dwelling place. No one except the high priest himself could ever enter the Holy of Holies. If the Roman stood there, what was to follow?

The independence to which Pompey put an end had been achieved by the Jews only after centuries of belonging to other nations: to Babylonia, Persia, Egypt, and then Syria. The Seleucids, the Macedonian Greek family that ruled Syria after the conquests of Alexander the Great, had won Israel from Egypt about 200 B.C.

Antiochus III, the Seleucid who sat on the Syrian throne in 200 B.C., was not harsh toward his newly acquired subjects. He officially recognized Judaism as their religion and granted them the right to live according to the Law of God as handed down by Moses in the Torah, or the first five books of the Bible. Under Antiochus III the Jews could preserve inviolate their jealously guarded customs and beliefs. They could rest from work on the Sabbath day and let the land lie fallow throughout the Sabbatical year, neither sowing nor reaping nor gathering fruit. They could follow the principle of "eye for eye, tooth for tooth, hand for hand, foot for foot," and even "life for life"; they could observe the divine regulations governing marriage and divorce and could apply the punishments that God had ordained for stealing sheep or oxen, practicing witchcraft, and committing adultery. They could kill the man who lay with a female animal or the woman who lay with a male animal. They could be careful to avoid eating unclean beasts, such as the camel and the pig, or unclean birds, such as the vulture and the owl, or unclean creeping things, such as the lizard, the mouse, and the weasel. Parents could have a son stoned to death for being egregiously disobedient; husbands could have their wives stoned to death for saying falsely that they had been virgins before marriage. The priests could without hindrance perform the rituals requisite for the Day of Atonement and for the feasts of Passover, Pentecost, and Tabernacles, could sacrifice unblemished lambs at the altar of burnt offerings, and could adore God as God had instructed them to do. Everyone could refrain from following the gods of the Gentiles—those deities that inspired unspeakable fertility rites, the embarrassingly anthropomorphic pantheon of Greece. The Jews could lead their own lives in a closely knit, religiously oriented, xenophobic society—undisturbed by outside forces, at liberty to do what God had commanded, free from foreign interference.

But a subtle kind of interference was already at work. This was the influence of Greek culture, which Alexander the Great and his successors had spread all over the eastern Mediterranean region and which, in fact, reached from northern Africa to central Asia. The Jews were nearly surrounded by Greek-style cities. Although there were none in Judaea itself, there were many in Syria, on the Phoenician coast, and south in the direction of Egypt: metropolitan centers such as Syrian Antioch and Laodicaea, and smaller places clinging proudly to an imported heritage. Most of these Graeco-Oriental communities had been founded by Seleucid or Ptolemaic monarchs; some, such as Tyre and Berytus and Ake-Ptolemais, had originated much earlier but had recently undergone Hellenization. Their citizens of Greek or Macedonian descent mingled with the native Syrians, Phoenicians, or Arabs, superimposing Greek modes of thought and action on the non-Greek populations and in many cases successfully fusing two cultures into one.

In these hybrid cities and towns on the periphery of Israel rose many-columned temples to the Greek gods, or to Oriental deities who had become identified with Greek gods or goddesses. Gymnasiums were built so that young men could engage in Greek athletics and learn to run, wrestle, and jump naked in the Hellenic fashion. Institutions common to most of the Greek city-states were provided if possible—the council, for instance, and the assembly of citizens. Greek plays were performed in the theaters; Greek scientific theories and philosophical systems were submitted to eager discussion; statues suggesting the softness of flesh or the folds of a Greek garment decorated public buildings, marketplaces, and elegant homes. Men of education, even if they were not of Greek descent, wrote scholarly Greek; and a more popular form of the language was used as the common tongue in the shops and on the roads.

It was inevitable that all this neighboring Hellenism should affect the little land of the Jews. Greek customs, assumptions, and preferences were brought in by the representatives of the Ptolemaic or Seleucid governments, by merchants and other visitors to the Greek or Graecized cities, and by soldiers who had been on duty away from home. Many residents of Judaea had relatives living in nearby Hellenic towns or in more distant centers of Hellenism, such as Alexandria in Egypt or ancient Ephesus on the Ionian coast; and the Jews learned new approaches to life from them. Some Jews enjoyed stories

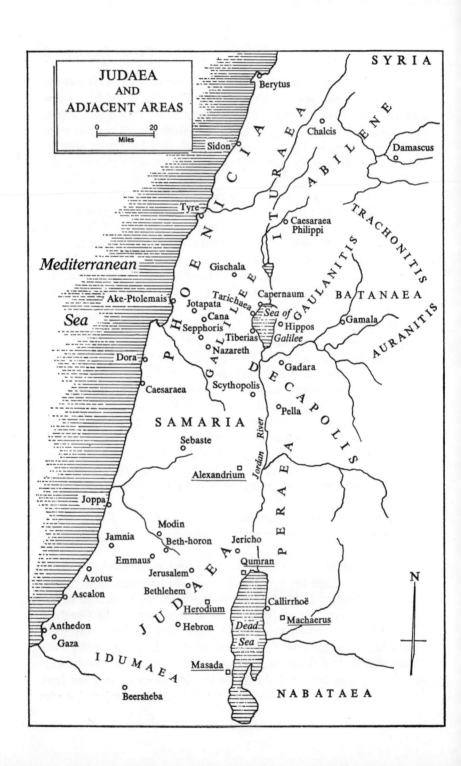

JUDAEA
AND
ADJACENT AREAS

0   20
Miles

SYRIA

Berytus

Chalcis

Damascus

Sidon

Tyre

Caesaraea
Philippi

Mediterranean

Gischala

Ake-Ptolemais

Tarichaea

Capernaum

BATANAEA

Jotapata

Sea of

Sea

Cana

Sephoris

Galilee

Hippos

Gamala

Tiberias

Galilee

Nazareth

AURANITIS

Dora

Gadara

Caesaraea

Scythopolis

Pella

SAMARIA

Sebaste

Alexandrium

Joppa

Modin

Jericho

Jamnia

Beth-horon

Emmaus

Qumran

Azotus

Jerusalem

Bethlehem

Callirrhoë

Ascalon

Herodium

Machaerus

Anthedon

Hebron

Dead

Gaza

Sea

IDUMAEA

Masada

NABATAEA

Beersheba

PHOENICIA

ITURAEA

ABILENE

TRACHONITIS

GALILEE

GAULANITIS

DECAPOLIS

Jordan River

PERAEA

JUDAEA

N

about the naked gods and revealingly draped goddesses of the Greeks
—of their powers, their gifts to man, and their highly human love affairs. A few Jews discovered the pleasures of rational, skeptical discussion and suspected that it, like the Law as recorded in the Torah,
might be a source of right conduct. Most Jews remained inflexible in
the faith of their fathers, but enough were swayed—especially among
the aristocrats—so that the old way of life was in danger.

About 170 B.C., not more than thirty years after the Seleucids took
over Judaea from Egypt, the high priest Jesus—who had adopted the
heroic Greek name Jason—proposed that Jerusalem be turned into a
city of Hellenic type to be called Antioch, like several other cities in
the Asiatic Greek world. Although the center of Judaism continued to
be known as Jerusalem by most people, the place did in some respects take on a superficially Hellenic appearance. With Jason's encouragement an ephebeion was built: an establishment where the
teen-age sons of the Jewish aristocracy could perform military exer-
cises like young Greeks. A gymnasium invited male Jews to participate in the physical training that their more conservative compatriots
could only regard as a glorification of the body and, consequently, a
horror. Jewish youths, it appears, took to wearing the petasos—the
broad-brimmed hat of the god Hermes (or Mercury), which had become the distinctive apparel of young Greeks because Hermes was
the patron of those approaching manhood. God had declared in the
Torah: "The uncircumcised male child, whose flesh of his foreskin is
not circumcised, that soul shall be cut off from his people: he hath
broken My covenant." But when nude Greeks and nude Jews practiced Greek sports in common, the fact that the Jews were circumcised made the Greeks laugh and point; and in order to avoid such
humiliation, Jews who were too weak to obey the Law underwent an
operation known as uncircumcision, which made them look like other
men and not like the children of Israel.

Jason urged the priests themselves to indulge in Greek athletics,
even if this obliged them to slight their religious duties; and he dispatched a group to represent the newly Hellenized Jerusalem at a
great festival honoring the Baal of Tyre, a Phoenician god equated
with Hercules. As the more orthodox Jews watched all these things, it
would not have been difficult for them to predict that trouble would
soon break out.

The king of Seleucid Syria during Jason's high priesthood was Antiochus IV, surnamed the God Manifest. He had been brought up at Rome and, just before coming to the Syrian throne in 175 B.C., had spent some time at Athens—still the heart of Hellenism even though its greatest days were memories. Antiochus was a brilliant man, a determined ruler, a student of philosophy, a creature of whim, a perpetrator of theatrical effects, and a champion of Greek culture. In his own opinion he was also a god. He had strong precedent for such an opinion, since Alexander the Great had regarded himself as a deity and since the association of divinity with kingship was deeply rooted in Asia. Besides, from a political standpoint the divinity of kings was an excellent idea to cultivate. Seleucid Syria, which encompassed a vast area, contained people of widely diverse cultures who adored a profusion of different gods. King-worship served to concentrate the inconsistent religious feelings of Syria's multitudes on a single figure and thereby to unify the country. In addition, it helped to provide a tyrannically inclined monarch with a justification for tyranny. Antiochus IV even tried to identify himself with Zeus, king of the Greek gods. Whether he went so far as to believe in this particular identification we do not know, but he must have realized its practical value.

Just as king-worship was a unifying factor in Syria, so was the Hellenistic culture that Antiochus so dearly loved. If Greek ideals and practices could be made to prevail throughout all of Syria, his dominions would be more nearly one nation and would be strengthened a great deal. Among Antiochus' subjects the only real opponents to Hellenization were the Jewish conservatives. The initial steps in the Hellenization of the Jews had of course been taken by some of the Jews themselves, but the orthodox masses that resisted the new order bothered Antiochus. They did not look on him as divine, since their uncompromising monotheism admitted only one Divinity. Many of them also did not feel very enthusiastic about his government, since they were governed by the Torah. The king apparently decided that Hellenization was proceeding too slowly under its Jewish instigators. He learned besides that Jerusalem had been disloyal to him while he was waging war against Egypt.

Therefore he visited Jerusalem on the way back from Egypt and slaughtered a number of disaffected Jews. Like Pompey more than a century later, he also introduced his profane self into the Temple. There is no record of what this god in fleshly form thought as he contemplated the silent, empty inmost chamber of the God of the Jews; possibly he experienced a sense of his own superiority. He left Jerusalem soon after, taking along some gold and silver vessels from the Sanctuary.

In 169 B.C., Egypt again occupied Antiochus' attention; but in 168 he sent his general Apollonius to Jerusalem. The result was a massacre and the military occupation of the city. A fortress, the Akra, was built to remind the people that the god-king was in control. Meanwhile Antiochus tried to obliterate Judaism by means of Apollonius and the troops. He seems to have reasoned that if the Jews' own religion was destroyed, there would be enough room for the Olympian gods and goddesses and for the whole beautiful Hellenistic culture that had already fascinated the less stubborn citizens. What he unleashed against the Jews was not intended as a persecution but as a conversion.

The Temple, the sole center of Judaism, was rededicated to Zeus. A statue of Zeus was set up there, and it seems likely that the face on the statue looked very much like Antiochus'. An altar to Zeus (the "Abomination of Desolation," as it was called in the Book of Daniel) was built over the altar of burnt offerings. Pigs were sacrificed at it, and the broth concocted from their unclean flesh dripped onto the sacred floor. It was made a mortal crime to possess a copy of the Torah; all copies must be surrendered to the authorities, to be ripped to pieces and burned. Observance of the Sabbath was also made a crime punishable by death. So was the celebration of Jewish religious festivals; so was the circumcision of male children. Jews were forced to take part in a ceremony in honor of Bacchus, walking in procession with wreaths of ivy on their heads.

The severity of Antiochus' measures brought about some apostasy; there were defections from the God of Israel to the gods of the Greeks. But there was resistance too—not all of it secretive. About twenty-five miles northwest of Jerusalem, in a town called Modin, lived a priest named Mattathias, member of an aristocratic house which is usually called the Hasmonaeans, after one of his ancestors. According to the story, when the Syrian royal commissioner came to Modin to demand pagan sacrifices from its inhabitants, Mattathias watched with scorn as a renegade Jew approached to obey the order —and then in sudden, overwhelming disgust he struck the renegade dead. He proceeded to kill the Syrian commissioner too, and to tear down the Syrian altar. The revolt against the God Manifest had begun.

Mattathias had five sons already grown to manhood; with these he fled into the wilderness, where Jews hungry for rebellion rushed to join them. Most of the rebels were farmers or herdsmen, since the land of Israel was largely given to agriculture and stockbreeding, and since the peasants were the least receptive to the sophisticated Hellenism that came out of the cities. Mattathias himself died before the resistance was really organized, but his five sons inherited both his vigor and his hatred for things Hellenic. Shortly before his death he designated the third son, Judas, as military leader of the revolt. The other sons would help in somewhat less important capacities; but all were in a sense leaders, and all were able to work in brotherly harmony toward a common goal. The rebellion was a Hasmonaean family affair.

Around Judas the infuriated and bloodthirsty peasants rallied, wild with ardor to fight for their God and His Law. Judas turned out to be a second Joshua: a good strategist and a gallant general. He carried on guerrilla warfare against the might of Seleucid Syria, conducting surprise raids and retiring swiftly to the hills, inspiring his fanatical rabble of followers with deadly devotion. Outnumbered, his forces met the troops of Apollonius on the field and massacred them. He appropriated for his use Apollonius' own sword—since the Syrian general, having died in the battle, would no longer need to wield it. Sweeping out of the yellow desert with his band of pious patriots, he spread terror. With the harshness necessary to his form of heroism, he killed all Syrians and Hellenizers that could not escape him—sometimes, it seems, the entire male population of a town. More than nineteen centuries later the composer Handel would write a glorious oratorio named after him and containing the chorus "See, the Conqu'ring Hero Comes!" It is a just tribute to a warrior of the strength and rage of Judas Maccabaeus.

The Syrian governor even allowed Judas to enter Jerusalem in triumph with his men and to reinstitute the worship of God at the Temple. The rebels did not receive an entirely hearty welcome in Jerusalem, since there were still Hellenizers in the city and since Syrian troops still occupied the Akra—the fortress that Apollonius had built three years before. But most of the citizens gave themselves up to a joy they had almost forgotten how to feel. The altar to Zeus was destroyed, and his image was disposed of. A new altar was built, in careful conformity to the prescriptions of the Torah; the Temple was purified of the pagan presence; and in December 164 B.C.—three years after it had been submitted to unmentionable rites in a ceremony honoring the sun—the holy building was dedicated again to the God of the Jews.

But peace was not achieved in Jerusalem. Even during the cleansing of the Temple, Judas' soldiers apparently had to hold the Syrian soldiers at bay. In opposition to the Akra, Judas fortified the hill of the Temple itself, so that Jerusalem was now a military base for both the Syrian faction and the Jewish nationalist faction. The two forces frequently skirmished and clashed within the city. Outside Jerusalem, too, the war was not over. Although news came that Antiochus had died on campaign in Parthia, Jews still fought Syrians in Judaea.

Judas' brother Eleazar, the second-youngest of the five Hasmonaeans, earned fame for himself in one of the battles. The Syrian army was supplied with thirty-two war elephants, and Eleazar thought that one of these probably carried the new Seleucid king, a nine-year-old boy. The elephant he singled out was bigger than the others, had a large tower on its back, and was caparisoned with gold. Eleazar was a different kind of hero from Judas; some might call him more foolhardy than inspired. Rushing ahead of his own troops, he slashed his way through the enemy until he was under the elephant, where he could stab the beast in its unprotected belly. He succeeded in wounding it mortally, but it squashed him to death as it fell. The tower on its back did not contain the boy king after all.

Syria finally made a new compromise with the Jews, according to which the Jews would be allowed to practice their religion uncontaminated by Greek polytheism, so long as the ceremonies included a sacrifice for the Syrian ruler. The Jewish fortress in Jerusalem would have to be taken down, and the hated Akra would continue to quarter Syrian soldiers; but as a consolation the current high priest, who was an unprincipled Hellenizer detested by the Hasmonaean faction, would be put on trial in Syria. A little later the Hasmonaeans felt encouraged when they heard that this renegade high priest had been thrown into a fiery furnace.

But the war resumed. The new high priest, who had adopted the

Greek name Alcimus, proved as repugnant to the Hasmonaeans as the former one. They therefore kept him from fulfilling his proper duties in the Temple, and the Syrians sent soldiers to force him down their throats. Judas and his brothers reorganized the rebel forces in the grainfields and the desert. They crushed a Syrian general whose name, Nicanor, meant "Victor"; then they cut off Nicanor's head and his sword arm, carried them into Jerusalem, and hung them up in the Temple to please God. Following this they challenged another Syrian general—but this time the result was less glorious. Most of the Jews, outnumbered perhaps seven to one by the Syrians, deserted. The few who stayed faithful fought fanatically and died. When the battle had ended, Judas also lay on the field.

Judas' brothers did not let the war die with him, however; and in the next few years, as dynastic disputes convulsed Syria, the Jewish rebels grew strong. In 152 B.C. a contender for the Syrian throne offered the high priesthood to one of the brothers, Jonathan, in return for his support. As a descendant of Aaron, whom God had named the founder of the priestly order, Jonathan the Hasmonaean was entitled by the Law to hold the office. In October of 152 he began performing his high-priestly duties at the Temple.

After fifteen years of struggle and suffering, hunger and heroism, the Hasmonaean house was the great power in Israel; and during the next decade, with the help of his brother Simon, Jonathan consolidated and extended its gains. In the meantime Syria wore herself out in a snarling, suicidal series of civil wars for the throne. When Jonathan died in 143 or 142 B.C., the high priesthood went to Simon—the only one of the five brothers still alive. Simon made the people love him by starving into surrender the demoralized Akra, last remnant of Syrian overlordship in Judaea. In 140 a popular assembly named Simon hereditary high priest and prince of the People of God. Israel was now an independent nation—a theocracy with a Hasmonaean high priest for ruler. The Jews would later look back on Simon's administration as an idyllic age. "Then did they till their ground in peace," the First Book of Maccabees says joyfully, "and the earth gave her increase, and the trees of the field their fruit. The ancient men sat all in the streets, communing together of good things. . . ."

When Simon died, about 135, his son John Hyrcanus succeeded to his offices. In addition to handing the Syrians another defeat, he con-

THE PRINCIPAL HASMONAEANS

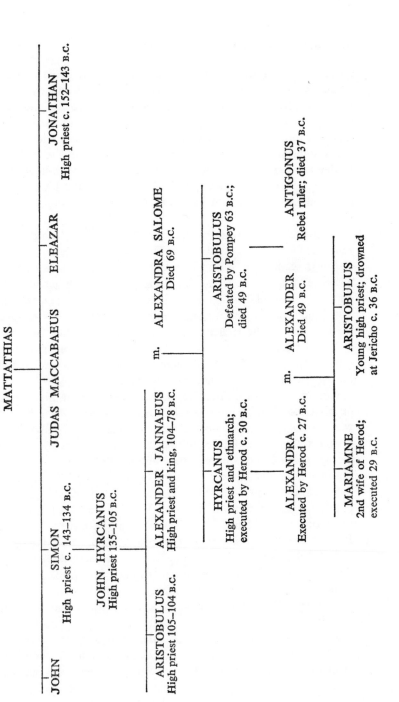

quered the Idumaeans (anciently the Edomites), fierce Arabs living in the limestone hill and desert country south of Judaea. The Jews were now more than defenders of their own way of life: they were invaders of other cultures. Just as Antiochus IV had tried to convert the Jews forcibly to Hellenic religion, John Hyrcanus tried to convert the Idumaeans forcibly to Judaism—but he was more effectual. Under his stern regime these Arabs were made to follow the Law, and their males were circumcised. The fact that the Idumaeans were nominally Jews from then on was to have important consequences for Israel.

Although Judaea wore a relatively untroubled surface during those years, problems grew underneath. The ideals of the lean, hard, sacrificial days seemed to be forgotten. John Hyrcanus was something of a tyrant, and the conversion of the Idumaeans was an act of downright oppression. Besides, in spite of his tendency to Judaize others, John was in no sense an enthusiastic enemy of Hellenism. His court copied the manners of the Hellenistic palaces. His army, like the armies of Hellenistic monarchs, consisted partly of foreign mercenaries fighting for pay rather than for the freedom of Israel and the love of Yahweh. He even bestowed Greek names on his sons.

One of these sons, Aristobulus, who assumed the high priesthood on his father's death in 105, exhibited even more affection for Greek ways, so that his subjects called him "Friend of the Greeks." By clapping his mother and three of his brothers into prison (where his mother starved to death) and then murdering the only brother he had not jailed, he demonstrated that the family unity of his ancestors was dead. He did, however, follow his father's nationalistic policy of expansion, making war on the wild Ituraeans who lived in the hills north of Israel. When he had beaten them, he forced them to adopt Judaism like the Idumaeans and, of course, circumcised the males.

But Aristobulus fell ill and died before he could do any more conquering; and in 104 the power went to one of his brothers, Alexander Jannaeus—who, in addition to becoming high priest, assumed the title "king." The ruler of the Jews now had equal rank with the Hellenistic rulers. An ambitious, unquiet man, greedy for battle and blood, exulting over his enemies, Alexander Jannaeus filled his long reign with war. He fought cities across the Jordan, cities on the coast, Arabs and Egyptians and Graeco-Syrians. Sometimes he lost—but

more often he conquered, pushing his kingdom outward in all directions until it was just about as large as the kingdom of David had
been many centuries before, and covered just about the same territory. It extended south to the border of Egypt, far east of the Dead
Sea and the Jordan, far east and north of the Sea of Galilee.

But David's people had been much happier under their king than
Alexander Jannaeus' people were under theirs. Some of his subjects
gradually grew tired of his savage militarism; some held that he was
not a real king since he did not belong to the house of David—the
only house whose members could legitimately sit on the Jewish
throne. Many considered him too close in spirit to the Greeks and not
sufficiently impressed by the Law. During his reign a great deal was
heard from the Pharisees. These were devout traditionalists, unflinching in their insistence that the commands contained in the Torah—
the commands given by God to Moses and by Moses to Israel—must
be obeyed. The Pharisees felt that Alexander Jannaeus, so often away
at war, was shamefully neglecting his sacred duties. To have a soldier
for high priest was, in their opinion, intolerable.

They drew most of their support from the common people rather
than the aristocrats, and they had a large following. One year, when
the king was officiating at the Feast of Tabernacles in the Temple, the
people heaved at him the citrus fruits that they had brought along for
the ritual, which was a ceremony of thanksgiving for the gathering in
of the crops. He retaliated by massacring several hundred of the in-
surgents—but that did not end the resistance. In fact, for six years
the Jewish people, led by the Pharisees, carried on a rebellion against
Alexander Jannaeus. The role of this Hasmonaean resembled that of
the Syrian kings of an earlier generation: he was the tyrant, the menace to ancient Judaism, the enemy who must be overcome.

But he triumphed. There is a story that one day Alexander Jannaeus had eight hundred Jewish rebels crucified at the same time. As
they hung, dying slowly, on the crosses, it is said that he let them
watch their wives and children being butchered below—while he
himself, reclining at ease and drinking wine, looked on at the scene
from among his concubines.

Alexander Jannaeus died on campaign in 78 B.C., and his widow,
Alexandra Salome, took over the government. On her death in 69,

her sons imitated the royal family of Syria by engaging in a civil war for the throne. The older brother, Hyrcanus, was king by right of seniority; but he appears to have been a quiet, mild-mannered, almost self-effacing kind of person who did not care a great deal whether he was king so long as he held the office of high priest, which he had assumed during his mother's reign. His brother Aristobulus, on the other hand, had inherited their father's aggressiveness. At a battle near Jericho the majority of Hyrcanus' men deserted to Aristobulus, probably because they considered him the likeliest candidate for the kingship. Shortly afterward the brothers reached an agreement: Aristobulus would be king. He may have let Hyrcanus retain the high priesthood—although it is probable that he confiscated this too, and that Hyrcanus simply retired to private life.

The situation seemed to be settled; but a stronger and more clever man than either of the brothers intervened.

This was Antipater, an Arab from Idumaea, the land south of Judaea that had been converted to Judaism at swordpoint half a century before. Antipater was an opulent chieftain, profiting from huge flocks of sheep and gaining great wealth from the caravan trade. His father had governed Idumaea under Alexander Jannaeus. He himself had married a noble lady named Cypros from the kingdom of the Nabataean Arabs. Still a young man, Antipater already possessed much power through his riches; but he wanted more power—and he thought he could achieve it by means of the weak Hyrcanus. He began by persuading Hyrcanus to rouse himself and seize the power that rightfully belonged to him—to defeat the usurping brother who probably intended to murder him in the near future. Once Hyrcanus was king again, Antipater could direct the government from behind the throne.

A period of military and political confusion followed—a painful period for a disenchanted Israel. Finally the great Pompey came to Syria (by now a thoroughly demoralized, shriveled kingdom) and put an end to its show of independence by making it a province of the Roman Empire. Both Hyrcanus and Aristobulus went to Pompey at Damascus in the spring of 63 B.C. to enlist his support. Antipater also went to Damascus, to speak for Hyrcanus. A delegation representing the disheartened Jewish people appeared in Damascus, too, and requested Pompey to do away with royal rule in Judaea. Most of the

Jews, the delegates said, did not want either Aristobulus or Hyrcanus as king; they wanted a return to the days when only a high priest governed the land—a time like that of Simon.

Pompey was not impressed with their arguments. Nor was he impressed with Aristobulus, who had brought along an entourage of overdressed, affected young men. Although he did not announce a decision, it was obvious that he favored Hyrcanus and Hyrcanus' backer: the efficient young Arab, Antipater.

There followed an interlude in which King Aristobulus ensconced himself in a strong hilltop citadel, from which Pompey kept making him come down for conferences. Finally Aristobulus fled to Jerusalem, where he made military preparations against Rome. In too short a time the world-renowned Pompey—victor in many wars, terror of pirates and kings—approached Jerusalem. Aristobulus, intimidated by Pompey's fame, went out toward the Roman camp to meet him. It was a frantic attempt at appeasement. The king offered Pompey money; he promised to surrender both the city and his own royal self to Pompey's discretion. And the great soldier agreed to these abject terms.

But when Pompey's officer Gabinius went to Jerusalem to collect the money, Aristobulus' overzealous adherents would not let him in. Pompey, enraged at this insult to a Roman officer, made a prisoner of Aristobulus, who had not yet left the Roman camp. Within Jerusalem, however, not everybody was for Aristobulus. A brief civil war sprang up between his supporters, who wanted to fight the Romans and rescue their king, and Hyrcanus' supporters, who wanted to open the gates to the Romans and thereby save many lives. In view of the fact that Pompey's veterans looked invincible, Aristobulus' sympathizers must have been exceptionally devoted to think of resisting at all. Many of them were evidently priests. Hyrcanus' party, much larger in size, chased them up the holy hill and into the Temple, then threw open the city gates and welcomed the Romans. The siege of the Temple was on.

It took three months to overcome the resisters, largely because a valley and a great ditch adjacent to the hill had to be filled in first. Pompey had his men work on Sabbath days, knowing that Aristobulus' soldiers would not disturb them when the Law required rest. After the valley and the ditch were filled, the Romans brought up their siege engines and slung stones and arrows at the Temple and its defenders. The priests meanwhile performed their daily sacrifices and the whole ritual of their office unperturbed; Yahweh meant more than a war. Finally the Romans forced their way in, followed by a huge crowd of Hyrcanus' adherents. The priests gave their offerings to God until the Romans and Hyrcanus' men ran swords through them at the altar.

Then Pompey entered the Sanctuary.

II

ANTIPATER AND THE ROMANS

Many Romans would not have shown as much respect for foreign ways as Pompey did. On the day after his pollution of the Sanctuary he obligingly ordered the Temple to be cleansed of his presence and permitted the rites to be renewed.

Then he reorganized the land of the Jews. He restored Hyrcanus to the high priesthood and named him ethnarch, which meant "ruler of the people" but was a lower title than that of king. Reducing the Jewish state in size, he gave to the new Roman province of Syria the Semitic and Hellenistic cities that Alexander Jannaeus and others had conquered; but he allowed the Jews to keep several territories annexed by earlier Jewish rulers. Among these was the Arab region of Idumaea, from which Antipater came. Although Pompey did not make Judaea a part of Syria, he arranged for its affairs to be supervised by the governor of that province; in other words, Hyrcanus was to rule under Roman surveillance, for Roman benefit. Finally, the Jews would pay tribute to Rome.

As for King Aristobulus, Pompey took him to Rome to be exhibited in the triumph which he was granted by the senate and which he celebrated in 61 B.C. It was a great show. Together with many other defeated Oriental dignitaries, Aristobulus had to march in humiliation before Pompey's chariot, while Romans on the sidelines howled and hooted. Three of Aristobulus' four children also took part in the procession. (The fourth had escaped from Pompey on the journey to Rome.)

Roman overlordship in Judaea was in some respects advantageous to the Jews. Now there were neither the wars of conquest that had exhausted the land under Alexander Jannaeus nor the factional broils that had recently ripped it apart. More important, there was full permission to follow the Law and to worship the God of Israel without fear of interruption from Hellenizers or anybody else—for the Romans pursued in Judaea, as in other parts of the Empire, the policy of religious toleration. Rome did not even station troops in Judaea; when soldiers were needed they had to be sent from nearby regions such as Syria.

We do not know much about the activities of Antipater during these years. In a sense he had achieved his objectives. Although he had not made Hyrcanus king, he had made him ethnarch and had obtained considerable power for himself. He stayed close to the center of things in Judaea, occasionally pulling strings, while in other parts of the world gigantic figures such as Pompey, Caesar, Cicero, and Crassus affected the lives of millions.

Crassus himself came to the East in 54 B.C. as governor of Syria. He did not injure his reputation as one of the richest and greediest men in the world when he proceeded to plunder the Temple. The enormous amount of money that Pompey had left untouched—money contributed for religious purposes by Jews living not only in Judaea itself but in Alexandria, Rome, the cities of Asia Minor, and other parts of the Mediterranean world—now went into Crassus' bags. In addition to confiscating the sacred treasury, Crassus appropriated sacred objects worth perhaps four times as much as the coins. A great deal of this wealth could be put to good use in a war he planned to wage on Rome's behalf against the vast mid-Asian kingdom of Parthia. But the Jews sat back in horror, powerless to do anything, wondering whether the Syrian tyranny had been any worse than the Roman. They rejoiced the following year when news came that Crassus had died in Parthia.

The fragile peace that had existed among the leaders of the Roman world was shattered in 49 B.C., when Caesar crossed the Rubicon to wage war on Pompey. He knew that much of the East was on Pompey's side; certainly Eastern men of power such as Antipater had no reason to be disloyal to Pompey. Caesar therefore released King Aristobulus, who had been languishing in prison at Rome, and put him at the head of two legions for the purpose of winning over Syria and Judaea. Caesar probably could not have found a man more eager than Aristobulus to fight Pompey's forces, to fight Hyrcanus, to fight the wily Antipater. But Aristobulus did not get started. Some of Pompey's supporters, having heard rumors of the scheme, fed him poison. For a long time the body of this Hasmonaean did not even lie in what had briefly been his kingdom; it lay embalmed in honey, until Mark Antony sent it back to the Jews.

When the once-feared general Pompey, in flight from Caesar, was murdered on arrival in Egypt, Antipater changed sides. There was no point in staying loyal to a dead man—or to a dead man's followers, if any remained. Presented with the opportunity to prove his devotion to Caesar, and being an astute opportunist anyway, Antipater experienced no difficulty in making the shift.

Caesar was in Egypt, beginning to enjoy the company of the young Cleopatra. She happened to be fighting her teen-age brother Ptolemy XIV for the throne; and Caesar, who had intended to adjudicate their differences in an impartial Roman manner, soon found himself enthusiastically on Cleopatra's side. Her brother's army laid siege to the palace, where Caesar had established himself. The force that Caesar had brought along to Egypt was too small to be effective. For a general who had just achieved control of the whole Roman world, this was an embarrassing situation. Antipater decided to rescue him from it.

The Arab was a brave warrior as well as a shrewd politician. Mustering a desert army, he fought his way into Egypt, taking with him some valuable reinforcements which Caesar had been expecting but which had been afraid to enter Egypt by themselves. Antipater did not try to stay out of battle but risked his life dramatically for Caesar, since that was the only way to make a good impression. Whenever cunning could be more useful than valor, however, he chose cunning. The Jews living in Egypt were loyal to Cleopatra's brother; but Antipater persuaded them to join his own side rather than fight against him—since it would not be right for Jews to kill Jews.

In this manner Antipater endeared himself to Caesar, who completed the defeat of Ptolemy in short order. Caesar sent his new ally on other enterprises, and he served his Roman master faithfully and courageously. He did not have to wait long for his reward.

The first part of it was Roman citizenship. Soon after Antipater had received this coveted gift, King Aristobulus' son Antigonus apparently complained to Caesar. The gist of the complaint was that Caesar was rewarding Antipater undeservedly—that Antipater had after all been one of Pompey's most trusted adherents only a short time before, and that he was still not a true friend to Caesar. In answer Antipater took off his clothes, remarking that the wounds he had received in battle for Caesar's cause spoke for him. In case the wounds had not said enough, he also reminded Caesar that Antigonus was the son of a rebel and the heir of sedition.

Caesar now made Antipater the procurator, or governor, of all Judaea. He recognized Hyrcanus as ethnarch, or ruler of the people; but Hyrcanus was still a puppet, since the powers granted to Antipater as governor were extensive. The Idumaean was in fact the actual ruler of Judaea for the next several years—subject to the governor of Syria, of course, but with enough independence of action to satisfy his political ambitions. Caesar must have expected that he would do a good job and would administer for the benefit of Rome; and Antipater proved Caesar's expectations correct. He was the most capable administrator that Judaea had seen in a long time.

Many of the Jews, however, felt dissatisfied. Most of those in the upper classes were grateful for the stability of Antipater's regime and, on the whole, did not object to Roman suzerainty, which looked benevolently on trade and manufacture. But it was also from the upper classes that most of the Temple priests came; and some of these men, guardians of the ritual of Israel, could not accept the fact that the country was governed by an Arab. It made little difference to them, or to other conservative Jews, that the Idumaeans had been converted to Judaism: the Idumaeans were still Arabs, sons not of Jacob but of Esau, and their ancestors had not taken part in the Exodus from Egypt to the Promised Land in the heroic days of Moses.

Antipater had made himself greater than his father, who had governed only the small territory of Idumaea. He wished his four sons to be greater than he—or at any rate as great. For the furtherance of his paternal ambitions he put the oldest, named Phasael, in charge of Jerusalem, and the second oldest, Herod, in charge of the northern part of the Jewish state: the pleasant land of Galilee. There may have been more than fatherly pride in these appointments; Antipater may have reasoned that he could trust his own sons more than other deputies. In any event the second son, Herod, proved not only trustworthy but potentially a leader far greater than Antipater.

Herod was about twenty-six at the time—a strong, athletic, handsome man, descendant of desert sheikhs, brave in war like his father and, also like his father, most astute. Religiously he was of course a Jew. In fact his early education had been conducted by a member of the Essenes, an extraordinarily pious Judaic sect; but he had apparently not taken to heart the saintly disregard for worldly considerations that characterized that group. His bent was not only materialistic but very practical.

Jewish patriots were overrunning Herod's district of Galilee. They were probably close in spirit to the guerrilla bands of Judas Maccabaeus, except that their enemies were Romans and Romanizers rather than Graeco-Syrians and Hellenizers. The Roman administration viewed them as bandits. It did not take Herod long to realize that he would do himself a very good turn by getting rid of them. He therefore chased them into their retreats and had many of them killed, including their leader.

The upper-class Jews who disliked Antipater's administration were delighted. It looked as if Herod had unwittingly furnished them with a weapon to use against the whole Idumaean regime. They went to Hyrcanus—who, although he possessed little actual strength, could at least exercise certain rights as high priest and ethnarch—and suggested that it was time he assert himself. They said that Antipater and his sons had usurped his authority and had made themselves masters of the land; that these Arabs must be stopped; that Herod had been so flagrant as to kill the patriot leader and many other patriots in Galilee without permission from the ethnarch. Herod should therefore be brought to trial at Jerusalem before the Sanhedrin—the Jewish court and parliament, consisting of seventy aristocratic members plus the high priest.

Either Hyrcanus felt an unfamiliar upsurge of independence or, more likely, he was persuaded by the large number of those who cried out against Herod and Antipater. Even the mothers of the murdered Galileans came to him at the Temple, begging him to make Herod stand trial. Consequently he summoned the young man to Jerusalem.

Herod's appearance before the august legislative body of Judaea was the first really dramatic act in what was to be a dramatic life. Instead of putting on the expected show of humility (or at least respect) for the Sanhedrin, instead of giving the impression that he wished modestly to claim the rightness of his actions, he came in pride and wrath, surrounded by his well-equipped troops. The aristocrats of the Sanhedrin were intimidated. Besides, Caesar's kinsman, the governor of Syria, had written Hyrcanus a strong letter to the effect that Herod must not be found guilty of anything. Herod was found not guilty.

It seems that soon afterward he was called before the Sanhedrin again, and that—either because he considered this second summons an insufferable insult or simply because his rage against Hyrcanus had not burned itself out—he marched with an army to Jerusalem, determined to throw Hyrcanus out of the office of ethnarch, if not to end the man's life. But Antipater, older and wiser, met his son outside the city and pointed out that if he started a civil war, Rome would not approve. This argument convinced Herod and saved Hyrcanus from much trouble.

When Caesar was assassinated in 44 B.C., the problem before Antipater was whether to remain loyal to the Caesarian party—now headed by the ambitious Mark Antony—or to join the party of the assassins. One of the most influential of the assassins, Cassius, soon came to Syria to gather an army for the oncoming war against the Caesarians. Antipater decided that Cassius was the man to support.

The Idumaean soon had a chance to demonstrate that he could be as useful to the assassins as he had been to Caesar. Cassius needed a great deal of money for his campaign against the Caesarian whom the senate had put in charge of Syria, and for the greater conflict with Antony. Part of this money, he announced, was to be collected from the Jews. Antipater was expected to furnish him with 700 talents. ("Talent" was a designation of weight. If these talents were of silver, they would have equaled, very roughly, about $1,400,000. If they were of gold, as is more probable, they would have equaled—again very roughly—$22,000,000, which was a staggering amount to squeeze suddenly out of the population of Judaea.)

Antipater thought that the best way to go about this assignment was to let his sons and his enemies share it. His sons, he hoped, would do a good job of collecting the money; that would redound to his own credit and to theirs. His enemies, he hoped, would react against the onerous duty and not collect their full share; that would put them in bad repute.

He charged Herod with the responsibility of supplying 100 talents. Herod somehow forced this much out of the farmers and artisans of Galilee, turning the money over to Cassius before anybody else was able to turn over his portion. We do not know what means he resorted to in order to get the money, but it is a safe guess that he proceeded mercilessly. Cassius was most favorably impressed.

Toward areas less generous than Galilee, Cassius himself could be merciless. He sold the inhabitants of four reluctant cities as slaves; that recourse both punished the cities and supplied the money that they had felt they could not afford. The most unenergetic of the money collectors was a man named Malichus, who had hated and feared Antipater for a long time. Apparently he did not turn anything in. Cassius was so angry at Malichus that he would probably have killed him if Hyrcanus had not intervened. Perhaps the mild Hyrcanus did not like to see people killed; perhaps, if the intimations of his courtiers and priests still rankled, he was particularly averse to the killing of one of Antipater's enemies. Since the ethnarch made up the 100-talent deficit out of his own fortune, Cassius was appeased and let Malichus live.

That was unfortunate for Antipater. Malichus of course blamed Antipater for the humiliation and danger he had just suffered, and Antipater prepared for possible trouble by crossing the Jordan to recruit an army of Arabs and Jews. Malichus denied having any evil design against Antipater, however, even backing up his statements with an oath; and for once the shrewd and suspicious Idumaean seems to have been deceived. It was a fatal lapse of cynicism. Malichus paid a cupbearer to poison Antipater at a feast.

III

HOW TO BECOME A KING

Before his father was killed, Herod had been appointed military governor in Samaria and part of Syria by Cassius, and had been supplied with both foot soldiers and horsemen. He even hoped to be made king of the Jews if he performed creditably for Cassius in the war against Mark Antony; Cassius held out this possibility as a reward for loyal service. Herod's political climb may have been another reason why Malichus had arranged for Antipater's murder: the Idumaean family was getting too powerful. Malichus in fact wanted the Judaean throne for himself. Of course he disclaimed any involvement in Antipater's death.

Herod meanwhile had fallen prey to one of the passionate, unreasoning rages that swept over him from time to time—when he could think of nothing except his enemies, when he wanted nothing except revenge on them, when he longed for their deaths. Just as he had once come down to Jerusalem with an army to depose and probably kill Hyrcanus, he now came against Malichus with an army; and this time there was no wise old Antipater to cool his wrath with reason. But his older brother Phasael took their father's role, explaining that if Herod attacked Malichus, the Romans would be angry. Cassius in particular would not like to see Judaea split with civil war, when his own civil war against Antony was his most pressing problem. It was possible besides that Malichus would escalate a fight against Herod into a struggle to further his private ambition for the throne.

Herod became rational again. He did not give up the idea of vengeance: his father's murderer must die. But he remembered that there are subtler, more dependable modes of revenge than battle. For the time being he pretended to be convinced that Malichus had not really been instrumental in Antipater's death. Malichus probably believed his offer of friendship as much as Herod himself believed Malichus' protestations of innocence.

Since Cassius thought so much of him—and so little of Malichus, recalling the man's reluctance to collect the 100 talents and fearing he might take advantage of the Roman civil war to crown himself king of the Jews—Herod wrote to Cassius for aid. Cassius gave him free rein to wreak revenge and even ordered the Roman officers to help him if they were needed.

Malichus had gone with Hyrcanus to Tyre—the great port and caravan terminus on the Phoenician coast of Syria, famous through many centuries for its purple dyestuffs. As military commander for Cassius in that part of Syria, Herod was in Tyre too. He invited both Malichus and Hyrcanus to a dinner which, he said, he would feel honored to provide; and they politely accepted—although Malichus probably made a mental note that he would have to be careful about being poisoned during the meal.

As it turned out, however, Malichus was not even able to come. Before evening he walked on the beach with Hyrcanus. Herod had sent a servant to inform the Roman officers that it was time for them to execute Cassius' orders. Hurrying to the seashore, they mobbed Malichus and drove their daggers into him. Hyrcanus got so upset that he fainted.

When Hyrcanus after some difficulty was revived, he inquired who had been responsible for Malichus' murder. Very likely he suspected that Herod was at the root of it, and he may have feared that he himself would be next. But when a soldier said that Cassius had ordered the killing, Hyrcanus appeared relieved, remarking that Malichus had been a menace to Judaea and to his own office of ethnarch, and that Cassius had done a very good thing. Perhaps Hyrcanus really felt happy to be liberated from yet another strong and dangerous politician, or perhaps he felt the need to get on the good side of Cassius—

the potential lord of the Roman East, and too close a friend to Herod.

The times were torn with war. Cassius left Syria to fight for his life against the friends and heirs of Caesar; and in Judaea another revolt began. This was the attempt of a Hasmonaean to drive out the establishment and, presumably, establish himself.

Aristobulus II now lay embalmed in honey; but his younger son Antigonus was commencing a career of violent activity that would embroil Judaea in periodic warfare for the next several years. Prince Antigonus had as protector the ruler of the Ituraeans—the Arab people north of Judaea who had now been converts to Judaism for quite some time. It was with the encouragement of the Ituraean monarch that Antigonus undertook his revolt. He also had the assistance of the Roman military commander at Damascus (whom the Ituraean ruler had bribed) and of a man named Marion, whom Cassius had installed as tyrant at Tyre. Marion obligingly took over a number of fortresses for Antigonus. Meanwhile the Hasmonaean prince himself marched south toward Judaea. The situation looked bad—until Herod came to the rescue.

Like his father, Herod was a mighty man in battle and a clever tactician. Not bothering to lay siege to the fortresses, since he knew that they would capitulate if he could defeat the leaders of the revolt, he fought against Marion, whom he beat. Then he fought against Antigonus and made him run. The campaign had not taken long but it had been glorious, and Herod was its hero. Shining in armor, followed by his faithful men, he marched in triumph to Jerusalem. The people applauded him. Even if many of them secretly feared his forcefulness, even if many of them secretly wished that the young Prince Antigonus had made himself king and that Herod's friends the Romans would all die of the plague, the Jews recognized a fine warrior when they saw one. They could not keep from admiring Herod's prowess.

Hyrcanus could not keep from admiring it either. Besides, since Hyrcanus was part of the establishment that his nephew had tried to overthrow, he really felt grateful to Herod for chasing the ambitious young man away. If one were ethnarch and high priest, one had to be protected by somebody. Herod's father had protected Hyrcanus against Antigonus' father; it was suitable that Herod should protect

Hyrcanus against Antigonus. Aristobulus and Antigonus were two of a kind: ruthless in their compulsion to seize what belonged to others, ruthless in their urge to rule, never satisfied to be subordinate. It took a man like Antipater or this strong, young Herod to overcome people like that.

At about this time Hyrcanus apparently decided that Herod would make a good husband for his granddaughter. He had a daughter named Alexandra—an ambitious, imperious woman. Many years before, perhaps in an attempt to mend the split between the two factions in the Hasmonaean family, Alexandra had been married to her first cousin, a son of Aristobulus II himself and an older brother of the Antigonus whom Herod had just defeated. We have no record of what Alexandra's married life was like with this man whose father had fought her own father for the throne, but she gave him a son and a daughter. If the Hasmonaeans were ever to achieve harmony, it would have to be through these children, who had Hyrcanus for their maternal grandfather and his brother Aristobulus for their paternal grandfather. Their father was now dead, but Alexandra was alive and active, and she no doubt had a great deal to do with arranging her daughter's betrothal to Herod. The girl, named Mariamne, was very young but of marriageable age, and the Idumaean was obviously a leader; Alexandra could see that.

Although the marriage was not celebrated for several years, to all practical purposes Herod had now found his way into the Hasmonaean house—the house which not long ago had held kingly power in Judaea. He himself may possibly have promoted this marriage that looked so advantageous for him. The fact that he already had one wife, an Idumaean girl named Doris, made no difference, since the Law did not prescribe monogamy. Mariamne was evidently destined to be a beautiful woman, and she had high spirit; but most important, she was a Hasmonaean princess.

There was little time for courting right now, however. Affairs on the outside demanded attention. Herod's friend and supporter Cassius, whose victory over the Caesarians would have benefited him so much, went down to defeat and suicide in the autumn of 42 B.C. Mark Antony now controlled the Roman East—and it became necessary for Herod to change sides.

In this as in other things, he inherited talent from his father. The

HEROD'S IMMEDIATE RELATIVES

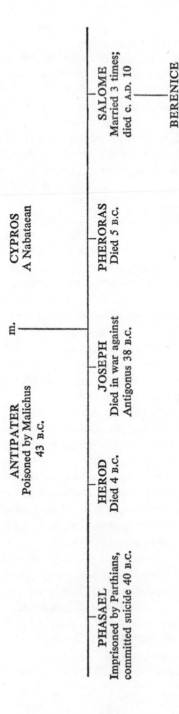

ANTIPATER
Poisoned by Malichus
43 B.C.

m.

CYPROS
A Nabataean

PHASAEL
Imprisoned by Parthians,
committed suicide 40 B.C.

HEROD
Died 4 B.C.

JOSEPH
Died in war against
Antigonus 38 B.C.

PHERORAS
Died 5 B.C.

SALOME
Married 3 times;
died c. A.D. 10

BERENICE
Married Aristobulus, son
of Herod and Mariamne I

matter was complicated, however, by the anti-Herodian faction in Judaea. In spite of the applause that Herod had received as the conqueror of Mariamne's uncle Antigonus, many Jews continued to feel toward him as they had felt toward Antipater: that as an Arab he did not deserve authority in Israel. As in the case of Antipater, the upper classes seem to have been particularly vehement in this opinion. Members of the aristocratic priestly families reasoned that although Herod had been born into the Judaic religion and trained by a pious Essene, and although he could claim a considerable knowledge of the Law, his Idumaean origin was ineradicable. It horrified these people that Hyrcanus—high priest at the Temple, descendant of Aaron, and scion of the royal house of the Hasmonaeans—had been so weak and foolish as to give his granddaughter to an Arab.

Dignitaries from all over the East were flocking to Antony, some to assure him that they had liked him all along, some to beg favors. The anti-Herodian party also dispatched dignitaries to Antony, who was holding audience in Bithynia, a province of western Asia Minor. The envoys were prepared to accuse Herod and his brother Phasael of usurping powers that belonged to Hyrcanus, and to request Antony to dismiss the Idumaeans from office. But the Roman would not listen to them: Herod had gotten to him first.

Antony went on a triumphal progress through the East. When he had traversed Asia Minor and come into Syria, he paused for a while at Daphne, the pleasure spot near Antioch. Another delegation from Herod's enemies appealed to him here; but although Antony listened to this one, he was not convinced. Herod was on hand too, of course, and so was Hyrcanus. In a move that was neither equitable nor very considerate, Antony tossed the whole matter in Hyrcanus' lap, asking the ethnarch who, in his opinion, were better suited to govern Judaea: Herod and Phasael, or members of the opposing party. Hyrcanus replied that Herod and Phasael were. In his response he may have been afraid of Herod; he may have felt that he should support the betrothed of his own granddaughter; he may have decided to utter what he knew was the truth—or he may have realized that the master of the Roman East would be displeased with any other reply. Antony, having heard what he wished, reacted by creating Herod and Phasael tetrarchs. This title had originally meant "rulers of a fourth part," but now it just implied that the status of the Idumaeans was somewhat inferior to that of a king. Hyrcanus, as ethnarch, would be their puppet superior.

The anti-Herodian delegation at Daphne had been about one hundred strong. Although they had suffered a calamity, the anti-Herodians did not give up. They sent a delegation of about a thousand representatives to Tyre, where Antony was expected soon. Perhaps the size of this body would convince Antony that most of the Jews were opposed to Herod. As a matter of fact the opposition to Herod did seem to be spreading, so that even members of the lower classes who had recently considered him a hero now thought of him as a usurper. But Herod did not need to worry that Antony would withdraw support. Partly he could rely on the fact that his father had served Antony's mentor Caesar with devotion until Caesar's death, and on the fact that Antipater had fought alongside Antony himself against Mariamne's father in 57 B.C., when that man had led a short rebellion in Judaea. Partly he could rely on the favor engendered by the money which he donated to Antony—money which the Roman badly needed. But also, Herod and Antony seem to have liked each other with more than political sincerity, respecting each other as warriors and leaders of men, as inspired opportunists, and as lovers of life's amenities.

When Antony heard that Herod's thousand enemies planned to beseech him at Tyre, he ordered the Roman commander there to send them away prior to his arrival. Herod, wishing to avoid a disagreeable incident, came to Tyre with Hyrcanus in tow. Perhaps if the high priest, their spiritual leader and the head of the Hasmonaean house, urged the anti-Herodians to withdraw, they would do so. Hyrcanus, however, did not prevail against their devotion to himself: they stayed anyway. The Roman commander sent soldiers to deal with them; the soldiers slaughtered some and took a number of prisoners. As soon as the people in Jerusalem heard about this, they cried out against Herod, tyrant and friend of the tyrant from Rome. Then Antony had the prisoners killed.

For a short time Herod and his brother Phasael ruled in peace as tetrarchs. Under the surface there was, of course, trouble; the Jewish resentment against these Arab overlords continued to grow. But the veneer at least was smooth—until Antigonus started a war.

This Hasmonaean—younger son of Aristobulus II, nephew of Hyrcanus, and uncle of Herod's betrothed, Mariamne—was unhappy with the obscurity to which Herod had relegated him after his revolt several years before. He itched to be king of the Jews. When Parthia, the great power in central Asia, invaded Roman Syria in 40 B.C., he saw his chance and made a bargain with the Parthians. If they would invade Judaea and help him become king, he would give them a thousand talents as well as five hundred beautiful women, culled from the noblest Jewish families. Antigonus cannot have been much of a diplomat, since the latter part of his offer was not designed to please his future subjects. Nonetheless there were several factors in his favor. He belonged to the royal Hasmonaean house; his Parthian allies had a reputation for military ferocity that terrified most people; and a great many Jews hated Herod.

One Parthian army marched south along the Phoenician coast toward Judaea, while another marched south through the hills east of the coast. Meanwhile Antigonus himself, with a combined expeditionary force of Parthians and insurgent Jews, marched ahead to Jerusalem. Some inhabitants of the holy city did not know how to feel toward Antigonus: they liked him because he wanted to overthrow the brother tetrarchs Herod and Phasael, but they disliked him because he wanted to overthrow Hyrcanus too. He evidently did not have any trouble entering the city, however.

A battle occurred in the marketplace between Antigonus' soldiers and Herod's—and Herod's soldiers won. Antigonus and his men were chased into the Temple, which now became their fort, just as it had once been the fort of Antigonus' father Aristobulus when Pompey besieged him there. Now Herod's forces besieged Antigonus. In addition to this there were skirmishes between Herodian sympathizers and adherents of Antigonus in Jerusalem's streets and dark, dirty alleys, with members of the two parties stabbing each other day after day in civil squabbles.

Men who had decided that they liked Antigonus probably outnumbered Herod's soldiers and supporters by far. Herod saw that he stood in danger of losing the tetrarchy he had so recently attained; and with the help of Phasael he fought the enemy in the suburbs. He comported himself gloriously as he had done when he fought Antigonus three years before, issuing orders and plying his sword in a rage, wishing for nothing except the death of his enemies. But the followers of Antigonus seemed to multiply all over.

And then a Parthian officer, Pacorus, who was also royal cup-bearer, encamped outside the city with Parthian nobles and warriors. Antigonus at this point must have either gone himself to see Herod's brother Phasael or sent envoys to Phasael. His object was to get Pacorus admitted into the city, and his argument was that Pacorus could act as a mediator between the two parties, bringing peace back to Judaea. Herod of course realized that the Parthian was not the impartial bringer of peace that Antigonus described. Phasael should have realized this too, but apparently he did not. Phasael gave permission —and into the city rode the Parthian with five hundred horsemen.

Pacorus persuaded Phasael to go with him to the Parthian general Barzapharnes, who had not yet come close to Jerusalem but was in Galilee just below the Syrian border. Herod's own opinion was that Pacorus' five hundred horsemen, and the cupbearer along with them, should be exterminated; but Phasael would not listen to him. Perhaps Phasael felt that his brother was growing too authoritative and that he could make his own decisions without Herod's help; there may even have been an incipient struggle for independence behind his resolution to go with Pacorus.

All this while, Hyrcanus had been doing little except growing older. He now agreed to go with Pacorus too; and the Parthian, leaving horsemen to watch Herod, set forth with his two victims toward Galilee.

For the moment there was quiet in Jerusalem. At the palace Herod waited. Rumors came that Phasael and Hyrcanus had been seized in Galilee. Together with Herod waited the ladies: his mother Cypros, the noble Nabataean; his sister Salome, who had attached her own ambitions to Herod's fortunes; his affianced Mariamne; and Mariamne's mother, Alexandra. Unlike her father Hyrcanus, Alexandra suspected everybody—and just now she suspected the Parthians strongly, reinforcing Herod's own sentiments. When Pacorus reappeared outside the city, saying that he brought letters for Herod and trying to tempt him to come out and read them, Herod refused, and Alexandra applauded the decision. Herod got his soldiers and the ladies ready, and at night they escaped from Jerusalem.

On their flight they were joined by Jews who favored them, but they were chased and attacked by Parthians and by Jews who despised them. It was a sad and desperate journey—the ladies weeping and shrieking, Herod and his soldiers trying to fend off their enemies,

Herod wondering (when he had time to wonder) whether his brother and Hyrcanus were still alive. Parthian soldiers meanwhile had burst into Jerusalem and were raising havoc, plundering rich residences and even the palace.

South from Jerusalem and a short distance west of the Dead Sea, in the midst of the dead, buff-colored desert, rose a rocky plateau called Masada. Judas Maccabaeus' brother Jonathan, more than a century before, had fortified the top of the plateau. The place was almost inaccessible and easily defended. Here Herod had determined to bring the ladies. If they could be safe anywhere from the Parthians and the rebellious Jews, it was at Masada. Since his army of flight had now been augmented to more than nine thousand men and since Masada could not support so great a number, he dispersed most of them, leaving them to follow their own inclinations, and came to Masada with a force of perhaps eight hundred. Among those who had joined him was his young brother Joseph, whom he now put in charge of the ladies. When his mother, his sister, his betrothed, and the shrewd Alexandra were established on the plateau, with Joseph to care for them and the eight hundred men to guard them, he set out on a quest for help. If the quest failed, he would lose his tetrarchy and probably his life.

Herod went to Petra, capital of the Nabataean Arabs, as the closest and likeliest source of help. His mother was a Nabataean; the Nabataeans had furnished his father Antipater with an army when his father was fighting Aristobulus on Hyrcanus' behalf; Antipater had given the Nabataeans a loan that was still outstanding. But their king, perhaps because of threats from the Parthians, would not receive him.

Dismissed from Nabataea, Herod set off for Egypt, where his most powerful friend, Mark Antony, was presumably whiling away the time with Cleopatra. On the way there he received word that Phasael was dead. Apparently his brother had found out that the Parthians meditated treachery but, impelled by a self-sacrificial feeling that seldom gripped members of his family, had resolved to stand by poor Hyrcanus no matter what happened. According to the story, Phasael was put in a dungeon as a preliminary to being killed; but he refused to give his enemies the pleasure of ending his life. He cracked his head open against the stone wall of his prison.

Hyrcanus was not dangerous enough to kill, but Antigonus wanted his uncle's high-priestly office as well as the throne. It was said that when Hyrcanus was brought before him as a suppliant, Antigonus gnawed off the old man's ears. A high priest had to be without bodily blemish. Hyrcanus would never be high priest again.

Antigonus delivered him over to the Parthians, who took him to their own land. There was a considerable settlement of Jews in Parthia, and perhaps Hyrcanus would be happy there.

Meanwhile Herod continued on his way to Alexandria, that glistening, Greek-styled metropolis on the coast of Egypt, surpassed only by Rome among the cities of the Mediterranean world. Antony unfortunately had already gone to Italy. Although Cleopatra offered Herod no assistance toward preserving his tetrarchy, she did receive him very well. He was, after all, potentially formidable—and far from penniless, even though he had been forced to become a fugitive. Recognizing Herod's skill at war, she suggested that he become commander of a military expedition she was getting ready; but he declined with thanks. Actually he distrusted this daughter of eight royal generations of Ptolemies, this meretricious Macedonian in an Egyptian setting, this lavishly jeweled mistress of the greatest Romans, this greedy Greek girl who remembered that her ancestors had once possessed Judaea. She had borne Caesar a son and would probably produce children for Antony; but Mariamne waited for Herod on Masada. He set sail for Italy.

When he reached Rome, Herod went immediately to Antony, who was glad to see him and kindly introduced him to the other master of the Roman world, Octavian. Herod's situation was far from that of the poor beggar with no arguments except his own sore need. His enemy Antigonus was also the enemy of Rome: a rebel against Roman authority, a tearer-down of the establishment, an inciter to riot and disorder. Antigonus' allies the Parthians were Rome's strongest rivals for supremacy in the Orient, and their defeat of Crassus' army thirteen years before had made them abhorred in the capital. Antony himself had named Herod and Phasael tetrarchs. To have one of these men killed and the other forced to flee from Jerusalem was insulting. Herod's father had been the friend of Octavian's adoptive father, Caesar; Herod himself was the friend of Antony. Besides, one had only to look at the Idumaean to see that he was competent, energetic, enterprising—a good man to keep on Rome's side. If he were in charge of things in Judaea, he could be relied on to block Rome's enemies in the East and to suppress the seditious inclinations of the Jews themselves.

Herod appeared before the senate, where two patricians and Antony spoke in his favor. The result was a foregone conclusion: unanimously the senate voted that Herod should be king of the Jews.

In the spring of 39 B.C. Herod returned to Judaea. Antigonus was in control, with the fervent support of perhaps the majority of his subjects. Even if Antigonus had disposed of Hyrcanus in a somewhat barbaric manner, he was a Jew and a Hasmonaean rather than an Arab, and his treatment of his poor old uncle could be excused as the kind of family outrage that characterized all royal houses. As for Herod, not only was he an outsider but he had been proclaimed king by the pagan Romans.

Herod's army therefore contained few Jews, except for those who came from the northern part of Palestine—from Galilee, where he had commanded under his father and where he was more popular than farther south, toward Jerusalem. Some of his soldiers were probably men who had fought under Antipater and Hyrcanus against Aristobulus II, or sons of those men. Others were mercenaries, from almost anywhere. Two Roman generals, Ventidius and Silo, who had been occupied with clearing out the Parthians, perhaps helped him a little; but Ventidius had gone to Cappadocia, and Silo, having accepted money from Antigonus, was not enthusiastic.

Herod's immediate objective was to relieve Masada, which had been under siege by Antigonus' army for quite a while, and to rescue the ladies. After taking the port of Joppa he marched southeast, passing south of unfriendly Jerusalem into the desert region by the Dead Sea where Masada stood. He had no trouble there; Antigonus' forces hastened to abandon the siege, and the ladies could come down from their high plateau.

Jerusalem, however, was another matter. Herod knew that his arrival outside the city stimulated little rejoicing within the walls. Although by no means all of the inhabitants viewed him as a tyrant, few considered him a liberator. The Idumaean Arabs who had recently added themselves to his army did not help his image, and the presence of the dreaded Romans in his forces was more than embarrassing. Some of the citizens did come out and join his troops, but probably more from fear of his power or hope of reward than from devotion to his cause. To attract as many adherents as possible, Herod issued statements to be proclaimed at the wall: that he had come for the city's benefit; that he did not seek revenge on those who followed Antigonus even though his own claim to the throne was a just one; that he was full of forgiveness and possessed a large, kind heart. While these sentiments were being broadcast, Antigonus' soldiers raised such a clamor, yelling and hooting and banging their shields, that it was difficult for anybody to hear what Herod had to say. Antigonus also issued statements: that Herod had no title to the throne; that Herod did not come from a royal family, and was an Idumaean besides; that if his own alliance with the Parthians displeased the Romans too much, he would resign from the kingship—as long as the king who replaced him was a Hasmonaean like himself and not Herod.

The Roman general Silo now demonstrated his loyalty to the bribe from Antigonus: he encouraged discontent among his soldiers. They complained about their pay, and about the paucity of life's essentials around Jerusalem, and about the dismal prospect of going into winter quarters in the outskirts of that city, where the fields had already been laid waste and there was nothing to eat. Herod knew that if the Roman soldiers withdrew to winter quarters in areas a long way from Jerusalem, there would be little left of the siege; and resourceful as usual, he led his men into the countryside—perhaps far afield where the crops were plentiful—and brought back food to stuff down the throats of the complainers. He even had grain sent from Samaria, which lay between Judaea proper and Galilee and which, like Galilee, was at least partly friendly to him. But in the end the treachery of Silo prevailed. The Roman troops went into winter quarters in pleasant, fruitful parts of the land, where they could live at ease and enjoy good things.

Herod himself spent the winter of 39/38 B.C. in the cold hills of Galilee, suppressing robber bands that were also rebel bands opposed to his authority and to Roman authority. If Galilee went against him, he would not have much left. The robber-rebels hid in caves in the cliffs, where no sizable body of men could get at them. Narrow paths led to the caves; at their side sheer precipices dropped dizzily away into valleys far below. But if the gangs thought they were safe here from Herod, they had not reckoned on his resourcefulness. He ordered big boxes to be built, filled these boxes with soldiers, and lowered them over the cliffs down to the caves. The soldiers carried long poles, to the ends of which great hooks had been affixed. They thrust these poles into the caves, hooked the rebels or the rebels' wives and children, dragged them out, and sent them plummeting down the precipices. If the rebels and their families retreated too far into the caves to be caught with the hooks, Herod's soldiers built fires at the cave mouths with material that they had brought along in the boxes. When the fugitives had been smoked out, it was easy to dispatch them.

After a while Herod sent out an invitation to the remaining robbers and their families to give themselves up. These cave dwellers, however, must have been intense patriots as well as thieves, believing that if they could no longer resist the Arab usurper who had Romans for his friends, they might as well die. Perhaps they also thought that Herod would kill them anyway. It appears that not one man capitulated to Herod; and of those whom his soldiers captured, many committed suicide.

The story of one elderly patriot, even though it may be legend, illustrates the spirit of these Galilean rebels. He, his wife, and their seven sons were attacked in their cave by Herod's forces, and knew that it was hopeless to resist. His family, evidently less intense in their patriotism than he, begged him to let them yield themselves up to the Romans, since captivity was better than death. But he stood at the mouth of the cave, where he killed each son that came out. Herod himself was close enough to watch the scene. Between killings the old man shouted insults at Herod, calling him a man of low birth, a commoner with no title to kingship. When the man's wife stepped out of the cave, he murdered her too. Having thrown the eight warm bodies over the cliff, he jumped down after them.

While Herod was clearing the rebels out of Galilee, his brothers were helping him in other areas. Joseph, the one who had guarded the ladies at Masada, secured Idumaea for him, so that at least he did not have to worry that the land of his birth would go against him. The other brother, Pheroras, was stationed at a fortress called the Alexandrium. It had been dismantled, and Pheroras rebuilt it.

Antony had ordered that two legions be sent to Herod, but their commander, a certain Macheras, proved more quarrelsome than useful. Herod put part of his army under the command of Joseph, instructing his brother to wage only a defensive war and not to attack anybody on his own. With the other portion of the army Herod proceeded north through Syria to the kingdom of Commagene, whose ruler had given help to the Parthians. Antony himself was now besieging Samosata, the ancient Commagenian capital on the Euphrates. During the march through Syria, Herod picked up troops at Antioch that were supposed to join Antony at Samosata but had been afraid to cross the hostile Commagenian countryside by themselves; with Herod's army to protect them, they were now ready to make the journey.

Herod's objectives in going to Samosata were to make another favorable impression on Antony and to obtain more Roman support for his own enterprise. He succeeded in both these objectives. Antony was delighted that Herod had brought the troops from Antioch; with their aid the siege of Samosata, which had not been going very well, was soon over. Once again a conqueror, Antony told his general Sosius, the newly appointed governor of Syria, to devote the whole Roman army to Herod's cause.

On the return march to Judaea Herod stopped at Antioch, where he received the message that his brother Joseph had disobeyed orders and had waged an offensive war in the vicinity of Jericho, that garden spot between Jerusalem and the Jordan. With Herod as far away as Commagene, Joseph had probably felt free to do as he wished; and being an energetic member of an energetic family, he did not wish to act entirely on the defensive. But his independent move had proved calamitous. His men, together with the Roman soldiers whom Herod had left with him, were sliced up by Antigonus' army. Joseph himself was dead—the second brother of Herod to die in this war. Pheroras, the only brother left alive, asked sentimentally for Joseph's body and offered a great deal of money for it, but Antigonus slaked his fury against the corpse by having the head hewn off.

Galilee, which Herod had so recently subdued, was again in chaos. Apparently the majority of the Galileans, who certainly were loyal to Herod if anybody was, had been demoralized by Joseph's defeat at Jericho; and the partisans of Antigonus—not all of whom had been thrown over precipices in the mountain warfare of the winter—felt strong again. Their number was perhaps augmented by renegades from the Herodian party. They seized the Herodian leaders, took them to the Sea of Galilee, and drowned them. As for Judaea proper, it was more entrenched than ever in its hatred of Herod, who was coming down with his army of Arabs and Romans to drive the royal Hasmonaean out of the land. Herod had to take Jerusalem this time. It was the third year since the Roman senate had declared him king, and he did not yet have a people to rule. Unless he conquered the capital now, he was lost.

Before the siege of Jerusalem began, there was a battle in which Antigonus' general Pappus was killed. Herod (perhaps rightly) believed it was Pappus that had cut off Joseph's head for Antigonus. In poetic justice Herod had Pappus' head cut off and sent to Pheroras.

At Jerusalem Herod encamped outside the north wall of the Temple, which was also the north wall of the city and its most vulnerable spot. Having ordered the construction of earthworks leading up to the wall and topped by siege towers, he departed for the town of Samaria —which had once been the principal city of the land between Judaea proper and Galilee, and had shone as the capital of the northern kingdom of Israel long ago under Ahab and his queen Jezebel. There, on the verge of either victory or ruin, Herod celebrated his marriage to Mariamne. The Hasmonaean princess was now close to twenty, and more beautiful than she had been several years before. If Herod did conquer Jerusalem, and if he did become king of the Jews in fact as well as in title, having Mariamne as his queen would give him much joy. She would be more than just a political asset.

Actually it would have surprised Herod at this point to lose the war. Antony's general Sosius, governor of Syria, had joined him at Samaria with many more Roman soldiers than Herod himself had brought from Commagene. He now had eleven Roman legions at his service—a force of at least fifty thousand footmen. He also had six thousand cavalrymen, plus a great many native Syrian auxiliaries, plus his own army of faithful Galileans and Idumaeans and mercenaries—together amounting to perhaps another thirty thousand troops. It was a large city that camped outside Jerusalem after Herod's marriage at Samaria.

But inside Jerusalem the Jews were fevered with fanaticism: resistance to Herod was their religious duty, and it would be glorious to die for Antigonus the Hasmonaean—rightful ruler of Judaea, descendant of Judas Maccabaeus. People said that Yahweh would not allow the city to be taken by Herod, that He would not allow His Temple to be desecrated again. It was a Sabbatical year—the one year out of every seven when, according to the Torah, the land must lie fallow.

Many of the citizens were therefore starving; but to starve in a holy cause was almost a pleasure. The Romans set up siege engines to batter the city with stones, and the Jews sallied out and burned them. The Romans undermined the walls, and the Jews swarmed into the tunnels and killed the intruders. Week after week went by, and still Herod was outside the City of David.

In time Herod's soldiers managed to penetrate certain portions of Jerusalem, but the siege was not nearly over. About five months passed before picked men from Herod's army surmounted the inner wall and descended upon the citizens. Romans followed, and so did slaughter, with the Herodian Jews taking revenge on the now helpless party that they hated and the Romans taking vengeance on the citizens for having protracted the siege so long. The invaders made use of the traditional privileges of invaders, raping the women and looting the houses as well as killing their recent opponents. Out of the buildings they carried money, precious objects, and women. Fugitive Jews ran down dark streets and crowded together in alleys, while the enemy came after them with drawn swords and daggers. Some of the Jews retreated to the Temple—where they would be safe if they could be safe anywhere.

By the supremacy of his position and the force of his personality Herod prevented the Roman soldiers from entering the Temple and committing the sacrilege of Pompey and Crassus. Either he was pious enough in his Judaism to feel horror at the thought of pagans penetrating the mysteries, or he knew that now was the time to make the best possible impression on the people who were to be his subjects. From the second motive he even tried to stop the pillaging of the city, asking the Roman Sosius sarcastically whether he was to be king over a desert. Sosius very reasonably replied that soldiers had always pillaged: that loot was the soldier's legitimate reward, that it was loot that attracted a man to a military life, and that after a siege as lengthy as this one the troops deserved whatever they could grab. Herod, however, offered to give every soldier a generous donative out of his own purse if the looting ceased. That saved the city from further depredation.

Antigonus came crying to Sosius and fell at the feet of the Roman, striking the approved attitude for the conquered. But Sosius addressed him as "Antigona" (the feminine form of his name) and brought him in chains to Antioch to plead before Mark Antony. At first Antony thought he might let Antigonus live, but Herod persuaded him otherwise. Antigonus' death, like his appeal to Sosius, was a humiliation. The deposed ruler was tied to a cross and whipped, then beheaded.

Herod, without a rival, now reigned as king of the Jews.

IV

SOME PROBLEMS OF BEING A KING

Ten years earlier, when Herod as governor of Galilee had been called before the Sanhedrin at Jerusalem to answer the charge of killing Galileans without authority, his demeanor had been not humble but haughty. Far haughtier now, he exacted retribution for the ten-year-old insult. The Sanhedrin at Jerusalem contained seventy-one members; the corpses of forty-five were carried out of the city to be buried.

In addition to satisfying his hunger for revenge by means of this purge of the Sanhedrin, Herod had demonstrated to his people that he would stand for no opposition—that he would exterminate all who offended him. The forty-five dead aristocrats had offended him by being partisans of Antigonus; they were replaced by forty-five aristocrats who would say yes to his wishes. Herod intended to be a strong monarch—even a ruthless one—ruling through fear. His conception of a king (which could have been acquired from almost anywhere in the East) was that of a despot living in golden splendor and dealing death to his enemies. Through too much mildness Hyrcanus had lost his throne long ago; then he had lost his high priesthood and ethnarchy and had been taken to live in his enemies' land. Herod, in contrast, would act like a king. The moral question of whether a certain man deserved to die was irrelevant to kingship: if the man was a threat to his monarch, he died. That was a simple fact; and the

[42]

sooner the Jews learned it, the sooner Herod would sit firmly on his throne.

But if a king was to reign successfully, the right and power to terrorize his subjects must be combined with the ability to deal shrewdly with other rulers. In Herod's case the most important other ruler was not a king but the Roman citizen Mark Antony, who was governing the Eastern half of the Empire. Notwithstanding the seemingly benevolent attempt to save Jerusalem from being plundered by the Romans, Herod did not scruple to confiscate silver and gold that belonged to the richer inhabitants. He sent this treasure to Antony and Antony's friends so that they would not forget to treat him well.

Antony's closest friend, and a far more powerful ruler than the master of the little Jewish kingdom, was of course Cleopatra. She was also a remarkably intelligent woman, whose linguistic proficiency might have qualified her for rank as a scholar. Unfortunately for others in the East, she devoted much of her intelligence to the satisfaction of her acquisitive instincts. She loved money and property almost as passionately as she loved men, and she maneuvered cleverly to get all three. In these days she looked longingly toward Judaea—not because Herod interested her very much (he was, after all, small game) but because he possessed valuable property that her ancestors had owned less than two centuries ago.

The queen of Egypt would have liked all of Judaea, but since Herod was ruling it for Rome and with Rome's approval, she would have to be happy with less. The most desirable part of Herod's kingdom, in her opinion, was the aromatic and lucrative balsam groves near Jericho. The milk-white juice from the shrubs or trees was made into costly perfumes and into rare medicines believed to be excellent for curing headaches and improving eyesight. Cleopatra therefore persuaded Antony to assign to her the balsam groves. Rather than being responsible for overseeing them herself, however, she leased them to Herod, who could continue to draw the profits from them if he paid her a large annual rent for what had recently been his own. The expense and the indignity made him squirm, but he could not afford to anger Antony. As a further insult Cleopatra required Herod to guarantee the payment of another annual fee by the king of the Nabataeans—who similarly had leased from her the bitumen industry of the Dead Sea region, which had recently been his. She was a lascivious queen but a very good businesswoman.

Antony and she had been living together at Antioch; but when he set off on a new campaign against the Parthians, she returned to Egypt, passing through Judaea on the way. Evidently she was eager to inspect the balsam groves. Suppressing his dislike for her, Herod presented a polite surface. He conducted her with great ceremony to Jerusalem, and from there to Jericho, not far away, where she examined her new property.

Cleopatra now was thirty-three—very experienced, attractive by long habit, exuding a full-blown voluptuousness. Herod was a few years older, still a lean and handsome Arab. There is a story that she tried to seduce him—either because she would then be able to denounce him to Antony as a trespasser, or because she really felt drawn toward him, or because Antony was a long distance off and regular sexual relations were her way of life. The story goes on to say that Herod, outraged by her vicious lust and suspecting that she might be laying a trap for him, predicted that sooner or later she would do Antony great harm and asked his advisers whether they thought he should kill her right away. The advisers apparently cautioned him to be circumspect instead; and so he gave her presents and escorted her toward her own country.

The story, however, is almost certainly a legend—although it incorporates what one might like to think about the alluring, insatiable Cleopatra. Even if the bloom of her romance with Antony had not inspired her with any girlish constancy toward her lover, she probably realized that since Herod was only a paltry king, it would be unwise to risk Antony's anger for the chance of either denouncing him or enjoying him. As for Herod, he characteristically did not ask advisers for their opinion about anything, and he would not have seriously contemplated murdering the mistress of his most potent protector. He probably managed to treat Cleopatra with an expensive show of gallantry, even to gloss over his rage at her successful avarice. But he surely did no more.

One of Herod's worst problems was that since he was not descended from Aaron, he could not make himself high priest. The Hasmonaeans had ruled the Jews as high priests before they became kings; and in fact their assumption of the title "king" was perhaps less a hearkening back to David than an attempt to resemble the surrounding Hellenistic monarchs. All sincere Jews considered themselves to be ruled ultimately by God. The high priest, who fulfilled the prime religious functions in the nation, was God's principal repre-sentative and consequently the nation's most eminent man. The fact that old Hyrcanus had originally felt content to be high priest, and had seemed uninterested in retaining the kingship until Antipater urged him, may possibly be explained by the enormous importance of the high-priestly office. The respect that most of the Jews contin-ued to pay to this ineffectual man may indicate that they regarded even a weak spiritual ruler as more awesome than a strong secular one.

Herod saw that for his own security it would be necessary to take away as much power as possible from the high-priestly office, until he had turned this theocracy into a real monarchy. Having appropriated the prerogative of appointing the high priest, he gave the title to one of the so-called Babylonian Jews—people whose ancestors had cho-sen to remain in Babylonia (in Herod's reign part of Parthia) after Cyrus permitted the Jews to return from exile in 538 B.C. The new high priest was named Ananel. In temperament he does not seem to have been a great deal different from Hyrcanus. Certainly he was no leader, and would not pose a threat to Herod's dominion.

Meanwhile Hyrcanus himself had been living as a prisoner in Par-thia among the Babylonian Jews. In the five and a half centuries since the exile, the Babylonian Jews had prospered intellectually as well as materially. They had developed a rich culture in the alien land, retaining many of their national traditions while control of the territory shifted from the Babylonians to the Persians to the Mace-donians to the Seleucid Syrians to the Parthians. They had worshiped the God of Israel in quiet fashion, softening some of the requirements of the Law while their relatives in Jerusalem were fixing those re-quirements in rigid sharpness. Many of the Parthians seemed quite congenial in the matter of religion: they too adored one supreme God; they told stories about Abraham and Joseph and the Flood; and they hoped for a star that would herald the birth of a savior. The alien Jews were therefore fairly happy under Parthian rule—and Hyr-canus was happy too. Although the Hasmonaean was technically a prisoner of war, the Parthian king stipulated that he be treated with respect by everyone. He was certainly treated with respect by his fel-low Jews, who did not mind the absence of his ears as much as the Jews of Judaea would have, and who honored him as a wise old leader—still high priest despite the mutilation.

But when, after three years in Parthia, Hyrcanus heard that Herod had become king in Judaea, a desire to return began bothering him. He thought sentimentally about the land over which he had been ethnarch and high priest, about the holy city of Jerusalem and the great Temple which was God's house and in which he had officiated. His family, after all, had reigned among the fig and olive trees of Judaea; the Babylonian Jews who honored him so much were hardly even distant relatives. His granddaughter Mariamne was now queen of the Jews; he would like to congratulate her. And so he made it known to King Herod that he wished to come back. The Babylonian Jews tried to persuade him to stay—loaded him with favors, reminded him that his imperfect head would render him less respected in his own country than in theirs, pleaded with him tearfully to live among them; but Hyrcanus wanted to spend his final years at home.

Herod was not averse to having him back. The presence of Hyrcanus in the palace would imply consent to his own rule on the part of the chief of the Hasmonaean house, and this consent was valuable. Besides, if there should be any trouble, he wanted Hyrcanus close at hand, where he could kill him. The king of Parthia, seeing no political reason for denying the elderly prisoner permission to return, said he was free to go.

Hyrcanus was well received in his own land. The courtiers respected him as erstwhile king, ethnarch, and high priest; his Hasmonaean relatives venerated him as the head of their family and as a man who had suffered much. Herod welcomed him with a warmth that looked genuine, invited him to participate in committee meetings, accorded him the seat of honor at banquets, and called him "Father" —probably because he was Mariamne's grandfather. And even though he had had to leave the sincere, uncomplicated, nonpolitical devotion of the Babylonian Jews behind him, Hyrcanus had attained his primary objective: he was in Jerusalem again, among members of his own family and aristocrats who recalled the distinction of his ancestors. He did not of course consider resuming the high-priestly office; Ananel was the duly constituted high priest, and Ananel was whole. But to be able to live out one's days quietly and honorably at the court where his granddaughter was queen perhaps compensated for the loss of his ears.

It was not Hyrcanus but his daughter Alexandra, Herod's mother-in-law—the shrewd woman who had supported Herod's suspicions of a Parthian trap several years before—who objected to Ananel's appointment as high priest.

Alexandra was intensely aware of her own Hasmonaean lineage. Her grandfather had been the warrior king Alexander Jannaeus; her great-great-grandfather had been Simon, brother of Judas Maccabaeus himself. In her opinion Herod was a usurper, an interloper, a nobody, who reigned only because he had married her daughter Mariamne and because he possessed Rome's approval. It racked and infuriated her to think that Herod now sat on the royal throne of the Jews—and she thought of it almost constantly. Imperious by birth, she did not hesitate to communicate her sentiments to courtiers who might be inclined to share them; and she kept giving her daughter such advice as, "Always remember that you are a Hasmonaean, while he is an Arab."

Alexandra congratulated herself on having a son as well as a daughter: a youth named Aristobulus after his paternal grandfather, Hyrcanus' overambitious brother. Since there was so much opposition to Herod in Judaea, Aristobulus stood a good chance of driving Herod from the throne at some future time, especially if the Romans could be won over to his side. For the time being, if Alexandra's family could not exercise royal authority, at least it could exercise high-priestly authority. The Hasmonaeans had been high priests for more than a century; the high priesthood belonged by tradition to her son. Aristobulus was only sixteen, a little young for the office, but that was of no importance. Herod had ignored him in order to make the Babylonian Jewish nonentity Ananel high priest, and that was an insult to her family. Ananel must be replaced by Aristobulus.

Alexandra plotted and maneuvered, schemed and wheedled, but without accomplishing anything. She complained to her friends, trying to make them Herod's enemies. When she had to, she whispered; otherwise she spoke openly. She had her daughter—the young, alluring, vivacious, headstrong queen—plead on behalf of Aristobulus; but when it came to politics Herod would not listen even to Mariamne. Alexandra could not of course rely on her father Hyrcanus to help the ambitions of the family. Frustrated almost beyond bearing, she wrote to Cleopatra for assistance. Perhaps the queen of Egypt could prevail on Antony to make Herod appoint Aristobulus high priest.

Cleopatra was very willing. She welcomed any opportunity to curb Herod's authority because she still hoped to take over his kingdom someday. In addition to that, she seems to have regarded herself as a reincarnation of the mystic Egyptian mother goddess Isis, patroness of fertility and protectress of women. Perhaps even more seriously than Antiochus, the "God Manifest," had considered himself divine, Cleopatra appreciated her own divinity; and as Isis she felt duty-bound to help the woman Alexandra against the man Herod. But in this case neither Isis nor the seductive queen could move Antony. Ananel the Babylonian Jew remained high priest.

About this time a man named Quintus Dellius visited Herod's palace. He came from Antony, whom he served in various capacities, among them that of pander. Being pander to Antony was a job demanding much time and effort, since the great, coarse-faced Roman, even in his passionate enslavement to Cleopatra, needed an assortment of other people to absorb the overflow of his love. At dinner Dellius' practiced eye took in young Mariamne's physical loveliness and Aristobulus' boyish charm. He suggested that Alexandra have portraits painted of her daughter and son and that she send the pictures to the needy Antony. The suggestion should have horrified Alexandra, since she knew the Law as recorded in the Torah: "Thou shalt not make unto thee any graven image, or any likeness of any thing that is in heaven above, or that is in the earth beneath, or that is in the water under the earth." But her ambition conquered her religion, which was probably diluted by Hellenism anyway. If the portraits pleased Antony, she calculated, she could send him the originals; and in return Antony might help her against Herod. He could depose Herod—or if not that, he could force Herod to appoint Aristobulus high priest.

It would appear that neither Mariamne nor Aristobulus objected to having the portraits painted, although they like their mother must have realized the heinousness of going against the Law in this respect. Mariamne, who did not love Herod as much as he loved her, perhaps found an act of defiance attractive; and the prospective high priest at sixteen may have been too much under the domination of his forceful mother or too eager on his own part for an august title. The portraits were, at any rate, delivered, and Antony enjoyed looking at them. He decided that he had better not send for Mariamne, since there was no point in angering Herod by violating his marriage bed, or Cleopatra by introducing a rival queen into the ménage. But Antony's romantic interests were not confined to one sex; and so he sent for Aristobulus.

Herod now had to write a delicate letter, explaining in a most respectful manner that Aristobulus could not come. It would be politically unwise, he said, to send Aristobulus out of the country at a time when many of the Jews wished for a change of reign. The malcontents would claim that Herod was trying to rid himself of the strongest possible candidate for the throne: the heir of the Hasmonaeans. There would be turmoil, riot, war; the *status quo* so recently established by Rome would be overthrown. Antony seems to have seen the reasonableness of these arguments.

Not long after this, Herod dismissed Ananel from office and made Aristobulus high priest. Perhaps Mariamne's cajolery on behalf of her brother had finally taken effect, or Alexandra's relentless campaign had grown too oppressive. More likely Herod realized that it was not safe to continue offending the Hasmonaeans while so many Judaeans remembered their rule nostalgically and were poised to leap to their support in case of a rebellion. Besides, a high priest could not leave the country. Herod probably thought that Aristobulus could cause less trouble at Jerusalem—where any plot to gain the throne could be detected and snuffed out in short order—than if he traveled to a country such as Nabataea or Egypt, where he could gather an army unopposed.

The king made certain, however, that his mother-in-law would not taste the joy of pure triumph at this turn of events. He announced the new appointment at a meeting of his own supporters, and at the same time he accused Alexandra of conspiring against his government with Cleopatra—of treacherously scheming to overthrow him and get her son made king. Summoning tears easily enough, Alexandra denied these charges, although she admitted that she had tried to obtain the high-priestly office for Aristobulus. Herod was far too realistic to believe her denial. He ordered her to stay in the palace, where he deputed people to watch her closely. This humiliating supervision was perhaps the worst punishment that he could have meted out to a woman as arrogant as Alexandra. She could stand the torture for only so long; then she wrote to Cleopatra, who urged her to come to Egypt if she could manage to escape from the palace.

It did not take Alexandra long to devise a plan of escape. Two coffins were prepared: one for herself and one for Aristobulus. In these the mother and son were carried out of the palace one night as if they were ordinary people who had died. The servants bearing the coffins were ones that Alexandra could trust. Herod, however, had already been informed of the scheme, and he made sure that the coffins would not get far. Before they had left the city they were stopped, and their prone passengers returned in shame and anger to life in the palace.

Herod did not punish either Alexandra or Aristobulus for this abortive attempt to disobey his orders. He would have liked to punish Alexandra, but when he thought of Cleopatra and her influence over Antony he decided to feign forgiveness. So Alexandra continued to talk against Herod whenever she had the opportunity, to speak scornfully of Herod's mother Cypros and his sister Salome, and to laugh at his pretensions to kingship. She encouraged Mariamne to oppose him, feeding her daughter's own regal contempt for this Idumaean.

All in all Alexandra had not done badly so far. Her daughter was queen of the Jews and her son was high priest, and she could still plot toward a future in which Aristobulus figured as king. Until she had achieved that future, she could derive abundant satisfaction from the fact that he officiated in the Temple.

Seventeen years old now, and taller than most men, Aristobulus was beginning to acquire the dignity that a high priest or a king should have. His handsome face and noble bearing proclaimed him a prince of the Hasmonaean line. When lesser human beings looked at him—grave and aristocratic, resplendent in his sacred vestments—they thought spontaneously about the glories of his ancestors, about the times before Herod ruled the Jews for the Romans. Especially at the ritual of the Feast of Tabernacles, when the people came with their palm fronds and citrons to stand in the Temple court and watch him offer sacrifices to God at the altar, it was evident that he had become their idol. His presence overwhelmed the crowd, who gave him applause and love. Alexandra, when she heard about it, rejoiced. But Herod had watched the whole spectacle and had made up his mind. This offensive youth, this threat to his position, must die.

Soon afterward Alexandra entertained the court at Jericho, the lovely oasis in the dryness of southern Judaea, home of the precious balsam groves that Herod was now renting from Cleopatra. Herod seemed to be in an unusually happy mood: affectionate toward everybody, shedding the severity of kingship to have a good time, acting like a youth of seventeen or eighteen as he cavorted with young Aristobulus. Merrily he urged Aristobulus to keep on drinking. Alexandra perhaps wondered where this specious friendliness would end.

Since the day was hot, the guests strolled under the palms to a swimming pool, accompanied by servants to cater to their wants.

Some of the servants took off their clothes and jumped in, and so did some of the courtiers. Herod's court was sufficiently Graeco-Roman that the custom of swimming nude in a pool would not have seemed shocking or out of place. The king tried to persuade Aristobulus to get into the water too, but the young man demurred, either because he was modest by nature or because he realized that it would be flagrantly indecent for the high priest of the Jews to splash around naked in public. But Herod continued to urge him; and since the afternoon was suffocating, finally he went in.

As the day darkened into evening, Aristobulus laughed and shouted and swam with the other revelers, having divested himself of his priestly dignity along with his clothes. It was a noisy group and the sport was rough. They would jump on him and hold him under the water, as if in fun, while he kicked and flailed and struggled. But they had received their orders. One time they held him under so long that when they let him up, he was dead.

Even Herod cried a few unhypocritical tears as he looked at the quiet, handsome face of the youth who had been brought out of the pool. As for the women, they wailed and shrieked without respite—his sister the queen, his mother, the servant girls too. Hour after hour and day after day the lamentations rose.

Herod gave Aristobulus a funeral befitting a high priest and Hasmonaean prince, as any other kind of funeral would have been politically inadvisable. Into an elaborate sepulcher they carried the body that less than a year ago had been carried alive from the palace at Jerusalem in a coffin. All around stood people weeping. Many precious and beautiful objects were put into the tomb with Aristobulus, even though he could not see them.

The passionate sadness of the funeral, with thousands mourning, indicated to Herod how dangerous this Hasmonaean could have become in a short time. Some were murmuring against Herod even now, blaming him for the death. However, with their idol out of the way these people would soon cease to be dangerous. It was a shame to cause Mariamne so much sorrow; but Mariamne would have to reconcile herself to the tragedy, and the splendor of the funeral would perhaps help to console her. At least she would know that her brother had gone out of the world in great honor. There remained of course the mother—still a threat. Yet she was only a woman.

Alexandra was suffering a compounded grief. She had lost her only son, of whom she had been proud, but that was not all: with him she had lost her chance to regain the Jewish throne for her family. She could not be the mother of a king. She could not even be the mother of a high priest. Ananel, the Babylonian Jew, had been given back his office. Alexandra's beautiful ambitions, her hopes for glory, lay in the elaborate sepulcher with Aristobulus. There was still of course the likelihood that a son of Herod and Mariamne would eventually succeed to the throne of Israel, but such a son would be only half Hasmonaean and the eventuality was many years off. If Alexandra had not had such practical, secular instincts, she might even have given serious thought to suicide. Instead she suckled the hope of revenge.

It had probably never been so hard for Alexandra to dissemble before; in her furious grief she longed to call Herod a murderer. She realized, however, that the safest policy was to conceal her suspicions. She did not accuse Herod of contriving the death of her son, or even whisper to her friends that he was certainly guilty. But she sent a secret letter to Cleopatra, describing the horrible scene at the pool, naming Herod the man behind it, and of course asking for help. Perhaps Cleopatra could persuade Mark Antony to punish Herod for the murder.

Antony soon arrived at the Hellenistic city of Laodicaea in Syria, a rich and populous station on the great caravan route from the Euphrates. He summoned Herod to come to him there and answer the charge of devising Aristobulus' death.

As he made preparations for the journey, Herod knew that he might be going to his execution or, if not that, to his dethronement. To murder an ordinary human being was not much of a crime, but to murder a prince—the scion of the family one had displaced—could be serious. Under Cleopatra's subtle, insinuating influence, Antony might very well believe that Herod had arranged Aristobulus' drowning. On the other hand, Antony had been Herod's friend for quite a few years now. Even though Cleopatra had sucked away some of his strength, he might still possess enough character to exonerate a man whom he respected—a man to whom he had given a throne, a man who had ruled well for Rome and had caused no trouble at all, except for this little domestic incident. In any case a healthy bribe might help, and Herod supplied himself with costly gifts for Antony.

While Alexandra, Mariamne, and Herod's sister Salome waited in

Jerusalem—while the whole nation waited, some of its citizens hoping that Antony would let the king go free, many hoping that Herod's unforgivable crime against the Hasmonaean house would be his last—a rumor circulated that the Roman had ordered Herod to be tortured and then killed. All over the city one heard the story, and at the palace one heard little else. Alexandra treated it with caution, however, and before long a letter arrived from Herod containing the news that she had been dreading. The king had done well at Laodicaea. Antony, grateful for the costly gifts that Herod had brought, now liked him more than ever. When he wished, Herod could speak very convincingly, and he had been most persuasive with the Roman, until finally Antony announced that a king was not accountable to anybody for his actions and that to require explanations from a king would be an unthinkable insult. Antony evidently went so far as to reproach Cleopatra for interfering in Herod's affairs. When the king heard him issue this rebuke, he must have felt that the worry and torment of the journey had been amply repaid. His patron had humiliated his enemy: Herod ruled more securely than ever.

V

WIFE AND MOTHER-IN-LAW

After a pleasant stay in Laodicaea, dining with Antony daily and sitting at his side when he heard cases, Herod returned to Jerusalem and unhappiness. Domestic life at the palace had deteriorated since his departure. His spirited wife, heiress of the Hasmonaean hauteur, had been insulting his sister Salome chronically even before he left. She liked to insinuate that Salome's birth was undistinguished, that Salome was quite inferior to a girl of Hasmonaean blood. She had sharpened these taunts in recent weeks, and Salome (who possessed a great deal of spirit herself) replied in kind, so that by the time Herod got back, the hatred between the two women was fierce. Meanwhile Alexandra did all she could to encourage her daughter in this feud with the house into which she had married. Under Alexandra's guidance the young queen's resentment of Herod ripened into detestation; and although the king still loved his wife, there were times when he was very sorry he had taken a Hasmonaean to his bed. His Idumaean wife, Doris, now living in retirement far from the broils of the court and educating his first-born son, would have proved more tractable, meeker, quieter. Mariamne did not know a woman's place. Neither of course did her arrogant, ambitious, scornful, devious mother.

The more Alexandra schemed and maneuvered, and the more Salome counterschemed and countermaneuvered, and the more the women tried to sting each other with sarcasm, the less bearable the court became. Many of the courtiers, through sincere sympathy or hope of reward, took sides, so that the women's petty quarrels spread and reverberated. Basically it was a case of Hasmonaeans against Herodians, and this too made Herod regret having married into the displaced regal family. But the fundamental question—whether an Idumaean Arab was good enough to reign in Judaea—was complicated by many side issues, subsidiary loyalties, peripheral animosities. It had grown into a headless, tailless tangle that perhaps only the deaths of the principals could relax.

The royal residence was a new structure called the Antonia—a huge, roughly square fortress-palace with a tall tower at each corner. Herod had built it almost on the site of an old Jewish fortress called the Birah, atop the highest part of the Temple hill; there were even a couple of underground passages to connect it with the Temple itself. From its lofty position it dominated Jerusalem as the dreaded Akra had done in the days of the Syrians, reminding the Jews that Herod was king and was formidable. Although it was grimly fortified, the portions where the royal family and the courtiers carried on their quarrels were luxurious, with elegant porticoes, courtyards full of flowers, and Graeco-Roman baths. Herod was proud of this building.

He had named it the Antonia to flatter Antony—but in the year 31 B.C. the name was beginning to sound unfortunate. In the previous year Antony had divorced his patient, moral, long-suffering, and uninteresting wife Octavia, sister of Octavian, and had married Cleopatra. The senate deposed him from his command, and Octavian went to war against him. Just as Cleopatra's vision of a Greater Egypt including Judaea had never materialized, Antony's vision of an Eastern empire ruled by his new wife and himself did not materialize. The Battle of Actium was fought on September 2, 31 B.C. For Antony and Cleopatra it was the end of all visions.

By a lucky circumstance Herod had not been obliged to go into battle on the side of his waning patron; and ironically enough it was his enemy Cleopatra who relieved him of the obligation. Because she hated Herod, she did not want him to look like a hero in front of Antony at Actium; she knew that he was a fine warrior and would probably signalize himself in Antony's cause if given the chance. He had already been enrolling and equipping troops for Antony; he seemed disgustingly loyal. She therefore persuaded her husband to send him against Malchus, king of the Nabataean Arabs. Malchus had been remiss about paying tribute for property that had formerly been his but that Antony had assigned to Cleopatra several years before, so that she could lease it to Malchus himself. Since Antony had made Herod responsible for the regular payment of the tribute by Malchus, Herod had to take action. From Cleopatra's viewpoint this was splendid. There was even the possibility that he would be killed by a Nabataean soldier. In any case it would please her if Herod and Malchus exhausted each other through war.

That was how it came about that the Jewish Arab and the pagan Arab met in battle east of the Sea of Galilee. As it happened, Herod had to fight not only King Malchus but, on one occasion, a general in Cleopatra's employ who bore some grudge against the king of the Jews. Herod's superb military skill and his ability to inspire his troops won out. He besieged the Nabataean camp and made some of the Nabataeans surrender rather than die of thirst, and he slew thousands.

So Herod returned to Jerusalem in triumph, while Antony and Cleopatra went back to Egypt in defeat. Although their armies were in shreds, however, they still had some soldiers left—among them a troop of gladiators that intended to march through Syria and then through Judaea to join the Antonian forces in Egypt. The governor of Syria, however, had gone over to Octavian's side, as many other people were doing. His soldiers stopped the gladiators near Antioch, and Herod, who so far had shown no sign of defecting from Antony, forbade them to pass through Judaea. They never reached Egypt.

Either Herod objected to the idea of these unruly pagan soldiers crossing his kingdom (as he certainly had reason to do, since gladiators as a class tended toward the subhuman), or else he had decided that under the circumstances it was time for him to make a transfer of loyalty—as delicately and adroitly as possible, by using the convenient excuse that he did not wish the foreigners to violate Judaea. Like his father before him, like his own younger self when he withdrew his allegiance from the anti-Caesarian party and sought out Antony, he would side with the strongest. It was much more difficult to abandon Antony, however, than it had been to abandon Cassius' party for Antony. To begin with, Cassius was dead by the time Herod went over to Antony's cause; Antony, on the other hand, was still alive, though jaded. Cassius, it was true, had contributed a great deal to Herod's rise. But Antony was Herod's friend; Antony had made Herod tetrarch, had made him king, had declined to call him a murderer at Laodicaea, had refused to give Judaea to Cleopatra although he loved the woman, and had even chastised Cleopatra for interfering in Jewish affairs.

It was hard; but it had to be. Antony was done for, whereas Octavian represented the future. Even so, there was no guarantee that Octavian would accept the king of the Jews. This chief of the Roman state—cold and penetrating and always practical, with the emotional content of a statue—would be less easy to win over than the robust, human Antony. Herod decided to visit Octavian on the merchant island of Rhodes and state his case; there was no other course. If Octavian dethroned him or had him executed as a friend of Antony— well, at least he would have tried his best.

Before he left for Rhodes, however, there was another matter to settle. Alexandra had devised an unusually dangerous plot. Her father, old Hyrcanus, had lived quietly in Jerusalem now for several years, satisfied just to be close to Alexandra and his granddaughter the queen and the people for whom he had once been high priest. But Alexandra told him over and over that Herod was mistreating the whole Hasmonaean family, himself included, and that they must obtain help from somewhere. She suggested as the likeliest source of aid King Malchus of the Nabataean Arabs, the man whom Herod had recently defeated. She added that if Herod happened to be killed on Octavian's order, Hyrcanus was the most obvious candidate for the throne notwithstanding his age; and in this eventuality too, support from Malchus would be most helpful. Alexandra was in some ways a pitiful spectacle: still trying to advance her family in spite of miserable failures, obsessed with the memory of Hasmonaean greatness, scheming incessantly against the bitter present, resorting now to her weak old father because her son was dead.

She urged Hyrcanus to write a letter to King Malchus, explaining that he and she both longed to escape from the inimical atmosphere of Jerusalem and seek refuge in Nabataea, and requesting that Malchus be kind enough to grant them succor and asylum. Hyrcanus, no stronger toward his daughter than toward anybody else, wrote the letter. A highly trusted messenger was charged with carrying it to Malchus; but the highly trusted messenger, deciding that more was to be gained from a reigning monarch than from an old man and a king's mother-in-law, carried it to Herod instead. After reading it, Herod instructed the man to take it to Malchus and bring him Malchus' reply, which would probably be interesting.

As a matter of fact Herod found the reply incriminating. In it Malchus promised to send horsemen to conduct Hyrcanus and Alexandra to safety, and said that he would be glad to receive all other Jews who did not like the present government.

Herod did a little thinking. For a long time Hyrcanus, mild as he was, had been a potential threat simply because he was a Hasmonaean; and with young Aristobulus dead he was more a threat than ever, since he could now serve as the rallying point for all Hasmonaean sympathizers. The proposed journey to Rhodes complicated the situation. While Herod was gone, Alexandra might use Hyrcanus to get a revolt started against him. Besides, if the journey ended in the king's dethronement or execution, Hyrcanus was the logical choice for the succession, as Alexandra had pointed out; and Herod could not stand the thought of the throne's reverting to any Hasmonaean—even this antiquated and inoffensive one. He also could not stand the thought of Alexandra's insolent glee if her father became king. The correspondence with the Nabataean ruler provided an admirable justification for getting rid of old Hyrcanus, and Herod knew how to make the most of it.

He showed the letters to the Sanhedrin, whose members were of course his friends, most of them his appointees. The charge was treason—and the aged Hyrcanus was executed. In a long life he had been king (very briefly), high priest, and ethnarch. He had lost his ears. He had seen his brother and nephews defeated as rebels; had seen his granddaughter made queen, and his grandson made high priest and murdered. He had witnessed many important things but had accomplished none of them, preferring a quiet life like that he had led among the Babylonian Jews. He had been pushed many times—and now he had been pushed all the way over.

Alexandra, having caused the death of her son through her ambition, had also caused the death of her father.

Herod did not leave his family in the Antonia at Jerusalem while he was away. Afraid that Octavian might try to punish his family as well as himself, or perhaps that the Nabataeans might come seeking revenge, he had his mother Cypros, his sister Salome, and his children taken to Masada in the wilderness near the Dead Sea—the high, heavily fortified plateau where the ladies had sought refuge in the flight from Jerusalem almost ten years earlier. On that occasion

Mariamne and Alexandra had lived at Masada too, but they could not be put there this time. The Hasmonaean ladies would taunt Cypros and Salome so savagely, and Salome would fight back with such fury, that there was no telling what might develop in the confinement at the top of the buff cliff. The women must be separated while Herod was at Rhodes.

He therefore placed Alexandra and her daughter in another fortress, the remote Alexandrium, under the protection of his steward and a body of soldiers answerable to the faithful Sohemus, a converted Ituraean Arab in his service. In addition to protecting Mariamne and Alexandra, the steward and Sohemus could make sure that the mother and daughter were not carrying on any treasonable machinations. Both of them now hated him, he knew. He had almost (but not quite) come to accept the fact that Mariamne was too much under her mother's influence, and too much a Hasmonaean, ever to be able to love him. Alexandra, perhaps with Mariamne to help her, would certainly try to cause trouble again sooner or later. Hyrcanus' execution had not crushed her forever or even discouraged her; it had just made her thirsty for revenge. Herod's absence would be an excellent time to plot for the overthrow of the government—perhaps to contrive to have him assassinated if he should return. He adjured the steward and Sohemus to keep a close watch.

He also gave these two men a secret order. If Octavian imprisoned or killed him, Mariamne and Alexandra were to be murdered right away. With regard to Mariamne his motive might have been love jealousy, since he still could not conquer his passion for her even though he knew that she felt as her mother felt—even though he feared that she might turn into a conniving, contriving, quarrelsome old woman like her mother in time. But with regard to Alexandra his main motive was the prosperity of his own family. In the event of his death he wanted the kingdom to go to his one surviving brother, Pheroras, whom he put in charge of the government while he was gone. Herod had a son by his Idumaean wife Doris, and three sons by Mariamne. He wished one or more of his sons to gain the throne eventually, but they were all too young to rule for many years yet, and Alexandra would try to prevent Pheroras from ruling during their minority. Pheroras must reign if Herod could not. Otherwise there would be dissension, there would be civil war, the kingdom would decline, and the house of Antipater would have no more glory. For this

HEROD'S WIVES

Herod the Great had ten wives in all. The five more important ones

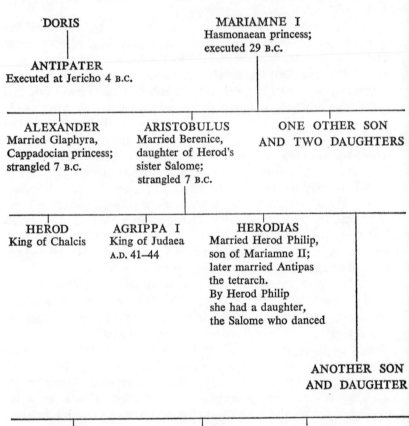

DORIS

ANTIPATER
Executed at Jericho 4 B.C.

MARIAMNE I
Hasmonaean princess;
executed 29 B.C.

ALEXANDER
Married Glaphyra,
Cappadocian princess;
strangled 7 B.C.

ARISTOBULUS
Married Berenice,
daughter of Herod's
sister Salome;
strangled 7 B.C.

ONE OTHER SON
AND TWO DAUGHTERS

HEROD
King of Chalcis

AGRIPPA I
King of Judaea
A.D. 41–44

HERODIAS
Married Herod Philip,
son of Mariamne II;
later married Antipas
the tetrarch.
By Herod Philip
she had a daughter,
the Salome who danced

ANOTHER SON
AND DAUGHTER

AGRIPPA II
King in regions northeast
of Galilee; died c. A.D. 100

BERENICE
Married 3 times;
mistress of Titus

MARIAMNE

and PRINCIPAL DESCENDANTS

and their principal progeny are as follows.

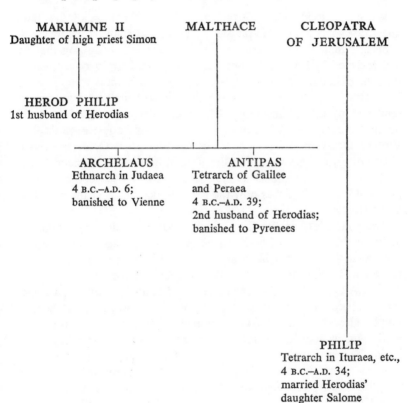

MARIAMNE II
Daughter of high priest Simon

MALTHACE

CLEOPATRA
OF JERUSALEM

HEROD PHILIP
1st husband of Herodias

ARCHELAUS
Ethnarch in Judaea
4 B.C.–A.D. 6;
banished to Vienne

ANTIPAS
Tetrarch of Galilee
and Peraea
4 B.C.–A.D. 39;
2nd husband of Herodias;
banished to Pyrenees

PHILIP
Tetrarch in Ituraea, etc.,
4 B.C.–A.D. 34;
married Herodias'
daughter Salome

DRUSILLA
Married Felix,
procurator of Judaea

reason alone, if Herod died Alexandra must die—along with her haughty, contemptuous, impressionable, beautiful daughter.

Herod therefore carried many worries with him on the journey to Rhodes.

When he stood before Octavian, however, the king of the Jews knew just what to say. He played the frank and stalwart desert chief, admitting that he had been Antony's good friend, admitting that he had received help from Antony and had given help in return—even regretting that the Nabataean war had prevented him from fighting for Antony at Actium but adding that he had at least managed to send Antony money and grain. The implication was that if he could be unflinchingly faithful to one patron, he could be just as faithful to another. Octavian understood this implication. Since Octavian needed vigorous, loyal kings to defend the Roman borders, he decided to accept this petitioner almost at face value. Herod had scored another personal triumph: he was now the honored lieutenant of the strongest living Roman.

The young lord of the Empire intended to invade Egypt immediately for the purpose of finishing off Antony and Cleopatra. It was a case of striking a final blow at a tired old bull and a limp serpent; there could be no doubt as to the outcome. Herod hastened to the port of Ake-Ptolemais, where he received Octavian almost as a victor. Heaping gifts on the great man and his friends, lodging them in one hundred fifty sumptuous apartments, the king just about smothered them in luxuries. In token of gratitude Octavian let Herod ride beside him in the military reviews. The Jewish king accompanied the Roman troops part of the way across the desert toward Egypt and supplied them plentifully with the only amenities they really appreciated just then: wine and water. Wishing Octavian well, he turned back toward Jerusalem.

Mariamne was not interested in Herod's beautiful successes. In fact she seemed displeased to hear about them. When he tried to embrace her she repulsed him with disgust, perhaps with loathing. She had probably not found another lover, but she had certainly been listening to her mother.

Well, what else could he have expected? Mariamne knew that he was responsible for her brother's murder and her grandfather's execution. Even if her mother had not been around, it would have been difficult for him to make her love him.

But while Herod's domestic affairs were going badly, at least he had politics to occupy him. When word came that Antony and Cleopatra had committed suicide, he realized it would be an excellent idea to travel to Egypt and congratulate Octavian. Getting away from his mother-in-law would be a pleasure, and his wife obviously did not want him near. Egypt would not only provide a release, it might even prove lucrative. For example, he wanted back the profitable balsam groves at Jericho that Cleopatra had taken from him.

At the time of their suicide Antony was fifty-three, Cleopatra thirty-nine: two overambitious leaders who for a while had held much of civilization in their grasp, two much-discussed lovers past their prime. They had been devoted to each other—not faithfully of course, but passionately—for more than ten years. But now they were dead, and Herod could make a profit.

Octavian, pleased to see a client king so prompt at demonstrating loyalty, received him with honor and gave him a great deal. Before Herod left Egypt he had secured for himself the balsam groves of Jericho, plus the ancient Philistine city of Gaza, plus Joppa, Anthedon, and Strato's Tower on the Mediterranean, plus the land of Samaria with its quiet old capital, where he had married Mariamne in the days of uncertainty. He also acquired a corps of four hundred soldiers from Galatia—crack military men who had been Cleopatra's bodyguard but who could not guard her against the asp. This acquisition probably delighted him almost as much as the balsam groves; both implied a sweet personal revenge on the dead enemy. In addition to the guards a Greek named Nicolaus of Damascus, who had tutored Cleopatra's bastard children, came into Herod's service at this time. Nicolaus possessed a superb intelligence and would over the years prove an indispensable helper and adviser to the king.

Herod's dominions were now almost as widespread as those of the Hasmonaean warrior ruler Alexander Jannaeus. They stretched from Dan to Beersheba, from far north of the fish-filled Sea of Galilee to the salt-filled Dead Sea in the south, from the rocky region east of the Jordan westward to the Mediterranean shores. They included Judaea proper, with its cities such as Jerusalem and Jericho, its many small towns such as Bethlehem, and its green hills and fruitful farms and the dry, thirsty areas in the south. Toward Sinai, Herod's sway embraced Idumaea with its scrub-covered limestone hills, land of Ju-daized Arabs, homeland of Herod's own family. East of the Jordan lay the wheat country and rocky wilderness of Peraea. North of Ju-daea were the sun-dried hills and valleys of Samaria and the flat, un-indented coastal strip, with the Plain of Sharon, rich in grain, grapes, olives, and forests of oak. And north of Samaria stretched lovely Gal-ilee: mountainous in the east (where Herod had cleared out the bands of rebels), gently hilly in the west, containing walled cities and many country towns, and also groves of walnut and fig trees, abun-dant vineyards, and the Sea of Galilee, swollen with fish.

Even so, however, Herod's kingdom could not be called great. The majority of its people were poor farmers, overawed by a few potent landowners. It could boast no metropolitan centers comparable to Damascus, Antioch, Tyre, or Sidon; Jerusalem itself was a religious capital rather than a sophisticated, highly cultivated, and opulent trading city. If Herod had presumed to equate himself with the "King of Kings," the ruler of Parthia, people would have laughed at him. Yet in terms of most of the monarchies of the age his domain was re-spectable; he did not want much more. Under the surveillance of the Roman government—and the protection of his newly acquired patron Octavian—he could improve what he had and could make his name famous.

But despite his satisfaction with his present fortunes and his high hopes for the future, Herod could not feel happy, since Mariamne re-sented his prosperity and treated him cruelly. When she addressed him, it was with undisguised loathing. She told him to his face that he had murdered her brother and her grandfather, that he was despica-ble, that she abhorred him. She called him a wild Arab, a barbarian. She reproached him for having shut her mother and herself in the Al-exandrium while he was at Rhodes, not so that they could be safe from marauders but so that they could be spied on. He would argue with her—yell at her in his great rages—but he did not hurt her. In the earlier years of their marriage she had borne him three sons and two daughters, and although she was now his enemy, she was still his queen.

When she did not revile him she reviled his mother Cypros and his sister Salome. In this campaign of denigration, of course, her own hard mother, Alexandra, marched by her side. Since Herod's return from Egypt the womanly war—Hasmonaean mother and daughter against Arab mother and daughter—had mounted in a screeching crescendo, until it seemed that the struggle could not go on much longer without a death. Mariamne and Alexandra, imperious and insulting, shot scorn and sarcasm at Herod's common-born relatives, partly because this was a means of attacking Herod himself. Cypros and Salome by way of retaliation hinted that Mariamne was a whore. They said that she had even sent her portrait to Antony in Egypt to stimulate his lust.

Herod had had enough of the whole thing—but he was soon to become yet more deeply involved. The subtle Salome sent a cupbearer to him with the story that Mariamne had concocted a love potion to renew his erotic interest in her. Actually the story was false. Herod partially believed it, but he suspected that the "potion" was really a poison. He seized and tortured Mariamne's favorite servant, a eunuch, to find out whether the queen was trying to kill him. The eunuch, who could probably have saved his body from agony by saying yes, stayed loyal to the queen and protested that he did not know of any attempt to devise a poison that would end Herod's reign. Perversely masochistic in his own mental torment, wanting to hear his horrible suspicion confirmed, the king subjected the eunuch to more racking and wrenching. Finally the servant, still disclaiming all knowledge of poison, offered to explain why the queen hated Herod.

It had all started, the eunuch said, when Mariamne and Alexandra were confined in the Alexandrium during Herod's visit to Octavian at Rhodes. Sohemus, the trusted Ituraean who had been deputed to watch over them, had at that time told the queen some things that infuriated her against the king.

Herod started screaming in an agony far greater than the eunuch's. Sohemus must have betrayed the secret commission to kill Mariamne and her mother if Herod did not come back from Rhodes. To break his faith so flagrantly Sohemus must have been full of rank passion for Mariamne; and Mariamne must have wormed the secret out of him by giving him her body. While the king stood before Octavian, facing possible dethronement or death, the queen high up in the fortress had been playing with his officer—sleeping with his deputy. The red rage that burned in Herod now would not subside for many days. He ordered the immediate execution of Sohemus. Mariamne would have a trial—not because there was any chance that she was innocent but only because Herod did not feel free to kill a queen until her guilt had been legally established.

She was charged with attempting to poison him. The "jury" consisted of men who would obey the king's wishes like little dogs; and by shouting uncontrollably against Mariamne during the hearing, he made those wishes clear. There is no record of Mariamne's conduct at her trial—only of Herod's fury.

She may quite possibly have been guilty of something: not of plotting to poison her husband, surely, but of carrying on a romance with Sohemus—for which she was not, however, being tried. Hating her husband more than ever for having locked her up in the Alexandrium during his absence, she may have decided to corrupt the man delegated to spy on her, and she may have fallen temporarily in love with him or made him fall in love with her. In his infatuation Sohemus may have spilled secrets before her, including Herod's covert instructions.

The historian Josephus relates the oddly parallel story that when Herod went to Laodicaea to see Antony, he secretly ordered Salome's husband Joseph (whom he had made regent during his absence) to have Mariamne killed if he did not return. Joseph, according to the tale, revealed the order to Mariamne, and when Herod found out about this he suspected his wife of having lain with Joseph. This account cannot be accepted at face value because it resembles too closely a later series of events that are known to have occurred, but it may suggest that Mariamne was not always true.

With regard to Sohemus, however, Josephus says there was no infatuation: the man disclosed the king's private command because he conjectured that Herod would not return from Rhodes and that Mariamne and Alexandra would be in power. In other words, he was currying the women's favor in order to rise in the world. This, too, may have been the case. We cannot know what happened at the Alexandrium.

The panel found Mariamne guilty of trying to poison Herod and recommended death. Alexandra, who had been studying the proceedings closely, was not surprised; it looked as if her son-in-law, having murdered her son, would now execute her daughter. But there was still a chance that Herod might not have the sentence carried out, she felt; the ruthless, unspeakable Salome had not triumphed yet.

And as a matter of fact Herod did delay, weakened by his relentless love. He rationalized that perhaps he could imprison Mariamne in one of the fortresses that ringed his kingdom, instead of making her beautiful body a corpse. But while he wavered, Salome came to him and whispered that Mariamne had to die: if she were allowed to live, the grumbling populace would flock to her cause, elevate her as their idol and inspiration, swear to restore her to power and position. It was best to show force at the outset—to kill off this Hasmonaean. Salome told her most influential friends at court to give the king similar advice. Herod ordered the execution to take place.

His sister had won the war of the women; and Alexandra, in the midst of her tears over the daughter soon to die, was afraid that Herod's wrath would descend on herself, especially if he suspected that she had conspired with Mariamne to poison him. Not being sentimentally inclined, she could not forget her own predicament even in her wailing. According to Josephus, our only authority, her conduct on the day of execution was therefore as unmotherly as she could make it. She yelled insults and reproaches at the daughter who was walking to death; screamed that Mariamne had shown vile ingratitude to the kind and generous king, her husband; shouted that Mariamne had been a wicked girl—a whore and almost a poisoner. The queen walked proudly to execution, paying no attention to the accusations. Alexandra jumped on her and pulled her hair. The queen walked on in quiet scorn.

The only partial excuse for Alexandra's conduct (assuming that Josephus' account is true) is that she believed one or two of the accusations she was hurling at her daughter—for instance, she may have thought or known that Mariamne was a whore. Although the grim onlookers had seen too much of her to put any faith in her transparent performance, and although Salome must have been laughing at the comedy all the while, Alexandra did escape Herod's wrath. He was too debilitated by the death of his wife to do anything. In fact, for the time being he was crazy.

He cried; he looked for her—and saw her; he rushed around the palace in a frenzy of grief. He held parties that were supposed to be gay, hoping that the wine and the silly hubbub would distract him from what he could not forget. Sometimes he ordered his servants to summon Mariamne, since he wanted to talk with her. They said they would bring her and went away shaking their heads, and he threw

himself on his lonely bed and sobbed because she did not come. He
did not govern the kingdom; the kingdom could rot. He wanted only
the queen who had been unfaithful, the queen who had tried to poison him—the lovely, quiet queen who could not come. She had slept
with his officer Sohemus, and she had brewed poison, and she had deserved to die (even her mother said so); but she had been a beautiful
young girl when he married her at Samaria, and a fond and willing
mother to two daughters and three sons. Even though his successes
had not delighted her in her haughtiness, he had achieved them partly
for her. She had not shared his happiness over them, and now she
could never again share his happiness or his bed.

Finally Herod retired to the land of Samaria: he was going to hunt.
But a plague that was raging through the country seized him, and
then he lay sick and feverish, still calling for Mariamne. At Jerusalem
people said that he would soon be dead, that his sorrow had ener-
vated him and would kill him.

Alexandra listened and revived. The woman was indomitable. With
her father, her son, and now her daughter dead, she was the last true
Hasmonaean. But her grandsons, Mariamne's children, were half
Hasmonaean; although their blood had been contaminated by their
father, at least they had inherited ancestral glory through their
mother. If Herod died of the plague, the kingdom must go to them
rather than to somebody like his foolish Idumaean brother Pheroras;
and she herself could take over as regent during their minority. Perhaps her daughter's death had not been an entirely regrettable thing
if, as the people said, it would combine with the plague to kill Herod.
She must begin her operations immediately, so that if he died she
would be ready to take over; and if he did not die, she would be
ready to combat him as soon as he got well.

Alexandra's intention was to gain possession of the fortresses in Jerusalem—both the military portion of the Antonia, which controlled
not only the Temple but the northeastern part of the city, and another redoubt, which controlled more of the city. With Jerusalem in
her power she might be able to force the people to submit to her will.
The daily sacrifices, then, could not be offered at the Temple unless
she gave her permission; Jews could not come into the city for the religious festivals (as they did several times a year, but especially at
Passover) unless she graciously allowed them entrance. As the daughter of one high priest and the mother of another, she surmised that

the people would rather bow to any ruler than let the sacrifices lapse and be denied access to the holy city for the festivals.

In this respect the plan sounded good. It was also bad, because by taking advantage of religious sanctions she would surely alienate many of the Jews and probably drive a large number to Herod's side. But there was no other recourse—if she wanted immediate action, she had to risk that. There was another reason the plan was bad: it was desperate—the scheme of a woman reduced to flimsy devices after having tried all others.

She told the two commanders that they should surrender their fortresses to her for two reasons. If Herod died she could hold these buildings for his heirs, her own grandsons, so that no usurper would be able to seize them; and even if Herod did not die she could hold them better than anybody else, being his mother-in-law. But the two commanders were not persuaded. They disliked her even more than they distrusted her—and they distrusted everything she said. They realized that since Herod was not yet dead, for their own safety they had better not commit any act that could be construed as treasonable. One of the commanders was Herod's cousin, and both of them ranked among his most devoted subjects; otherwise they would not have been assigned the posts they occupied. Putting Alexandra off, therefore, they sent a messenger to Samaria to tell the sick king what she was trying to do.

Alexandra had made many attempts to acquire power and almost always had failed. She had lost her grandfather and both her children; she had lived for years at the center of sleazy machinations, had fed richly on her Hasmonaean pride, had waited breathlessly for her day of triumph, had wormed and squirmed and scratched her way while waiting, had contorted her soul for unattainable ambition—and had never given up. But now she could do nothing. The sick king ordered her death.

VI

KING FOR ROME

Alexandra's execution apparently revived the languishing Herod. There were things to do, and he had better start doing them. With the court cleared of Hasmonaeans he could reign as a king ought, answerable only to Rome.

He still could not forget Mariamne—but the business of reigning helped a great deal. He realized besides that he must not let maudlin memories sap his strength and make him the slave of a dead woman. Perhaps Mariamne's execution had been inevitable anyway. Like King Antigonus, young Aristobulus, old Hyrcanus, and Alexandra, Mariamne had been after all a Hasmonaean. It seemed that he was death to Hasmonaeans; he came in time almost to accept this impression as a political fact, which meant that it was incontrovertible. Herod's reign constituted a new order, and there was no place in it for any Hasmonaean—even Mariamne.

During these years Rome was stabilized under the firm and wise control of the man whom Herod had so far known as Octavian, but who now was beginning to be called by his new name: Augustus. Herod's role of client king, reigning as Rome's deputy and for Rome's profit, had carried less weight when the Roman government was a shifting, unsure entity—when one did not know from day to day who would be in control. Now, however, the Roman government was Augustus—and looked as if it would remain Augustus for a long time. A client king could finally be certain of the source of his power.

The institution of the client king was a very useful one for the Empire. The principal duty of such a monarch was to maintain peace and order in his dominion, subduing elements resentful of Roman authority (such as the patriot rebels of Galilee). Rome never let a client king forget that he was ruling with her permission and as her administrator. If he displeased her, she could dethrone him and perhaps turn his kingdom into a province. If she was waging war, she could command him to provide troops. He could not, however, declare war against his own enemies without her permission. He had to use her silver and gold coins in his realm, although he could strike his own base metal. He could not name an heir to his throne except with her approval.

It might seem that Herod, with his Eastern conception of a king as a mighty tyrant over quaking subjects, would have chafed under such a system, but he did not. He knew that he could not change Rome or resist her and must therefore resign himself to her. Besides, the system did give him considerable freedom. He could have his own standing army, and Rome could not quarter her armies in his domains unless he said she could. His subjects apparently did not have to pay tribute to Rome—only to him. Provided that he maintained peace and order for Rome, he could be as tyrannical as he wished, centering legislative, judicial, and financial authority in himself, taxing his subjects as he saw fit, lavishing money on whatever projects appealed to him, and killing people who offended him. He was subordinate only to Augustus; as long as he did not displease that man, he could be a despot in the ancient tradition of the East.

Herod's standing army did not contain a preponderance of Jews, and this was perhaps appropriate, since Judaea was not primarily a Jewish kingdom anymore but a piece of the Empire. A large number of his soldiers were foreign mercenaries. There were fierce Ituraeans from the Lebanese valleys, natives of Asia Minor, and even Europeans: adventurers from Greece and Italy, from Thrace, Germany, and other barbaric or semibarbaric lands. Others, however, were converted Arabs from Idumaea like Herod himself, and some were Samaritans—heretical Jews who did not recognize the holy city of Jerusalem as the center of their religion.

It was a motley army but a formidable one, and in spite of its mercenary character it proved reliable. Like Hellenistic monarchs before him, Herod in time established military colonies on his frontiers. Here veterans could farm lands that he had granted them, their only obligation being to return to military service if an emergency arose and, especially, to defend the frontier if enemies crossed it. There were several of these military settlements on the Nabataean frontier east of the Dead Sea.

Herod also made use of the fortresses built by previous rulers of the land to guard its borders, such as Masada and the Alexandrium, and he constructed a couple of new fortresses named after himself: the Herodium, several miles from Jerusalem (built about 23 B.C.), and a second Herodium on the border of Nabataea. All these buildings commanded a wide sweep of country from the crowns of high hills or mountains. Several of them were palaces as well as military structures, with villages at the bases of their mountains. Made of thick stone and topped by towers, the forts had cisterns for the storing of water, and even in some cases aqueducts, so that their inmates could withstand long sieges. A chain of signal stations provided communication between them. With this elaborate system in operation, Herod could rest assured that his realm was as secure from attack by outsiders as he could make it. He could concentrate on improving it internally.

Sometimes the matter of maintaining peace and order could result in profit for a client king. For instance, when Herod by 22 B.C. had proved his ability to keep people under control, Augustus gave him regions north of Galilee, south of Damascus, and east of the Jordan. Their native ruler, a certain Zenodorus, had not tried to curtail the life of plunder that his subjects preferred to farming; instead he encouraged them to pillage the territory of Damascus and share the loot with him. Herod put a stop to that.

There was, Herod knew, little hope of making many of his Jewish subjects love him. The initial resentment that they had felt over his Arab origin had not died down through the years. Even though no pure-blooded Hasmonaeans remained to claim the government, a large number of Jews stayed sentimentally or stubbornly attached to the lost cause. They muttered about the superficiality of Herod's Judaism and wished that they again had a king who could also be high priest. Herod's friendship with the Romans and his subservience to Roman wishes made them want to vomit. When, many years before, the senate at Rome had declared him king of the Jews, he had gone to the Temple of Jupiter for the coronation ceremony. That showed how sincere a Jew he was.

They were especially indignant when (perhaps not until fairly late in his reign) he decreed that thieves be deported and sold into slavery. This decree flagrantly violated Jewish law. According to law a thief was to make heavy financial retribution for what he had stolen, and only if he could not afford this payment was he to be sold as a slave. He was furthermore to be sold only to another Jew, and he was to be released from slavery within seven years. By ordering thieves to be deported, Herod was subjecting them to Gentile masters, who might or might not free them within seven years. Under their foreign owners in foreign lands the robbers would not be able to practice their religion as fully as they could at home; foreign gods might even be forced on some of them.

Herod's intention of course was to make the penalty for thievery so horrible that Jews would be deterred from committing this crime. Robber bands were apparently on the increase in Judaea, and drastic measures were needed if Roman order was to be preserved. The robber bands were perhaps also patriot bands—anti-Roman and generally antigovernment—so that from Herod's standpoint it would be a good idea to send their members out of the country as slaves.

The Pharisees in particular, those guardians of the Law and friends to the common people, protested the decree as cruel and impious, but their protests did no good. In this case Jewish law must give way to Herod and to Rome.

Most of the time the discontent of the Jews did not bother Herod a great deal, since he felt safer if he was feared than if he was loved. As long as his subjects did not break into open rebellion, which would embarrass him in front of Augustus, he seldom cared what they thought of him. Now that he was ruling for Rome, his own thoughts turned more and more toward Graeco-Roman civilization. He would not antagonize his sullen subjects unnecessarily; by no means would he try to force pagan culture on them, as Antiochus the God Manifest had tried to do with the Jews of another era. But if he was to make his name famous he would have to act like a Graeco-Roman monarch. Then people in other parts of the world would appreciate him, even if the Jews did not.

Although the Jews, as heirs of an advanced, humane, and spiritually intense civilization, tended to consider their Asiatic neighbors barbaric, it was plain that the Greeks and Romans considered the Jews themselves uncivilized. Everybody knew that barbarians were converted into civilized men primarily through living in cities, where the manners and customs of sophisticated societies could be imparted and practiced. Jerusalem was a stark, grim religious center sacred to Yahweh—not really a city at all; but perhaps the elements of Graeco-Roman culture could be introduced into it. The Jews could shun them if they wished, but at least the Graeco-Roman elements would be there.

In 23 B.C., Herod began construction of a new royal residence on the western edge of Jerusalem. The Antonia would remain as a fortress, but this new residence would be a palace befitting a Graeco-Roman monarch. Three square towers rose up from it: the Hippicus, named in honor of a friend killed in battle; the Phasael, named in honor of the brother who had split his head against the wall of his Parthian prison; and the Mariamne. (This last tower perhaps commemorated the dead but unforgotten queen—but Herod could claim that it was named after the woman he had recently married: another Mariamne, the aristocratic daughter of a priest.) Inside the enormous palace there were marble walls, ingenious murals, and sculptures done in the Greek style that the Romans knew how to copy. The appointments were of gold and silver; and bedchambers for one hundred guests implied that Herod could be a royal host. Ponds and bronze sculptures decorated the green-lawned courts, which were bordered by pillared walks. The palace would not have looked out of place in any other client kingdom, or even in Italy.

Before building the palace Herod had contributed several other non-Jewish edifices to Jerusalem, among them a Greek theater, an amphitheater, and a hippodrome outside the city. The chariot races that occurred in the hippodrome were not really offensive to his subjects, although the Jews did not have the Romans' fondness for them. The games that went on in the amphitheater were another matter. Staging fights between one beast and another was bad enough, in the view of the Jews; but to let a lion or a tiger kill a man, or to make one man kill another in gladiatorial combat, was sacrilege. Man was the image of God. If the Romans wanted to kill him for sport, let them do so at Rome, not at Jerusalem.

In Graeco-Roman society one way to achieve fame was to patronize games. Herod in 25 B.C. established the Actian Games, which were to take place every five years in celebration of Augustus' victory over Antony in the Battle of Actium. Their first observance was in the brand new amphitheater at Jerusalem, and Herod offered expensive prizes such as gems and gold. The original spirit of the Greek games, when athletes had competed for a wreath of wild olive or bay leaves in their love of sport, glory, and a god, had been forgotten long ago. The king urged Jews as well as Gentiles to participate—and a number of young Jews decided that they would, either because their distaste for Gentile customs had been dulled or because they longed to beat the pagans at the pagans' own activities. So Jewish youths ran and wrestled naked along with Greek youths, as they had done in the gymnasium of a Hellenized Jerusalem more than a century earlier. Untrained in athletics, however, they went down in easy defeat while the pagan spectators laughed at them. They did no better in the musical competitions, having been brought up in a "barbaric" musical tradition. But it made no difference to Herod that the Jews had not distinguished themselves: his Actian Games had caused him to be celebrated widely.

The interior of the amphitheater was embellished with inscriptions honoring Augustus and with gold and silver trophies celebrating his victories. Trophies—consisting of cuirass, helmet, and military equipment such as lances, swords, and shields, all affixed to a tree trunk or perhaps to a stake or peg—were the customary symbols of military victory in the Graeco-Roman world. The Jews, however, seemed not to know this. A body of them (probably including many Pharisees), suspecting that the armor and weapons concealed graven images of gods—that the king had actually introduced idols into the environs of the City of David—clamored until Herod told them to come to the amphitheater. There, before their eyes, he had the trophies disassembled. Only plain wooden pegs stood underneath, and the Jews went away embarrassed if not humiliated.

But even if the trophies were not idols in disguise, the amphitheater remained a vile blot on Judaea, and its perpetrator remained a foul violator of the sacred Law. A group of patriots resolved to make an attempt on his life and, if they could not kill him, at least to kill as many of his followers and hired protectors as they could manage. They would strike when the king, attended by his guards and sycophants, entered the amphitheater. They did not expect to live long afterward—but they would have done something fine before dying.

This forlorn hope consisted of ten men with daggers, one of whom was blind. He could not be of much practical help, but his courage inspired his comrades. If he was willing to be a martyr, so were they.

Herod, however, had organized a very efficient spy system to shield himself against his subjects, and one of the spies discovered the plot and reported it. When the conspirators walked into the amphitheater with their daggers under their robes, they were surrounded by Herod's men. They did not even try to resist. Instead they told Herod's hirelings that their purpose was noble: that they were not base men after money but warriors in a sacred cause, and that the king must be killed for the sake of the Jews. They went so far as to demonstrate the daggers that they had meant to use. Herod's hirelings took these martyrs away so that they could be tormented and put to death.

But in a small way the Jews got revenge. The spy who had reported the conspirators was discovered by enraged nationalists and quickly murdered. Pieces of his body were thrown to the dogs to scrap over.

To many Jews it looked as if God had decided to punish the land for the stain of sacrilege—for the showy, pagan-style buildings, for Greek plays and gladiatorial killings, for flagrant neglect of the Law, for cowering obedience to a king who was not of the house of David or the seed of Jacob. In 25 B.C.—the initial year of the Actian Games —the rain stopped falling. At first people expected the dryness to end after a while; but it did not end, and soon they knew that there would be no harvest. They knew also that they would starve. Some of them had a little grain stored up, but it did not last; some took to eating herbs, but they did not nourish. Sheep and goats strayed over the brown, barren pastures, hungry as the herdsmen, dying in the dryness. Old men and women grew feeble with famine and expired in a querulous craving for food; unreasoning children cried. Since there was no harvest there were no seeds—and therefore there would be no planting, and no harvest the following year. Since the sheep and lambs were dead there was no wool, and the poor faced cold nights as well as starvation. The land had offended Yahweh, and Yahweh was punishing the land.

Then suddenly Herod roused himself to unprecedented munificence. Money could not buy food in neighboring Syria any more than in Judaea, because the drought was parching Syria too; but it could buy food in Egypt, where the generous Nile watered the fields. The trouble was that Herod, having lavished great sums on Graeco-Roman buildings, did not have much money left. He therefore ordered that the gold and silver ornaments in his palace, the elaborate and beautiful bric-a-brac that helped to give splendor to a client king, be melted down. Even his own magnificent tableware was melted down. The splendor was made into money, the money was sent to Egypt, and the Roman prefect at Alexandria, who happened to be a friend of Herod, shipped grain in return. The whole episode had a dramatic quality that was typically Herodian. It may also have constituted an attempt on Herod's part to improve his image with the Jews, if he thought his image was improvable at all; the famine offered an opportunity that one could not hope for every day. But mixed with the personal motive was very likely a sense of kingly duty, and perhaps even a little pity. Herod could not let his subjects die.

The relief of the underfed seems to have been a well-planned, orderly business. Grain was distributed in equal portions to all those people able to take care of themselves. For those who could not care for themselves—the palsied, the armless, the bedridden—bakers were provided, so that these unfortunates would not starve for lack of somebody to turn grain into bread. In addition to the grain intended for immediate consumption, seeds were brought in for planting, and farmers began to say that the following year would be one of abundant harvest. Herod did not forget even to furnish wool to be made into clothes.

So the Jews ate until they were full, enjoyed warm garments, planted their seeds, and hoped; and rain finally fell, and the next year the harvest was good. Many in the land praised Herod; for the moment he was almost loved. Outside Judaea he was praised even more, as people heard about his liberality and marveled that a monarch could be so selfless. No doubt even the government at Rome was impressed. But in his own land the admiration could not last long. His favorite projects continued to work against it.

A couple of years before the famine, for example, Herod had begun the renovation of the old city of Samaria. He devoted men and money to this project for the next few years. The land that surrounded the city, and that was known by the same name, lay north of Judaea proper but south of Galilee. Superficially it looked like just another part of Judaea—hilly in many sections, adequately supplied with fields of grain and fruit trees. The people of Judaea, however, hated the Samaritans, and the Samaritans reciprocated with enthusiasm.

The hatred dated back almost to the late tenth century B.C., when the resplendent kingdom of David and Solomon had split into two separate nations—the northern one called Israel, the southern one called Judah. Jerusalem, which had been David's capital, became the capital of Judah, and in time the city of Samaria became the capital of Israel. It was at Samaria that the infamous Ahab reigned in his ivory palace. Relations between the two cities were at best unfriendly. The southern Jews, for instance, realized with pious horror that Ahab favored the old Canaanitish gods, and that his wife Jezebel promoted the worship of the Baal of Tyre by killing the prophets of Yahweh. The fact that many of the subjects of Ahab remained true to God did not impress the inhabitants of Judah.

The dislike of the southern Jews for the city of Samaria included also the land around it. When the Assyrians conquered the kingdom of Israel late in the eighth century B.C., they sent other subjugated peoples into the area as colonists. It seems that a number of these colonists—Arab tribesmen, Babylonian farmers, other pagans groveling before profane gods—intermarried with the Jewish population. The result was, according to the purer Jews of Judah, a mongrel breed: the unspeakable Samaritans. When the southern Jews came back from their exile in Babylonia and started to rebuild the Temple at Jerusalem, which the Babylonians had destroyed, the Samaritans offered to help. Their offer was indignantly rejected; the citizens of Jerusalem could not think of accepting assistance from an ethnic and religious hodgepodge. The Samaritans in retaliation refused to recognize the Temple as the center of Judaism. Instead they built their own temple on Mount Gerizim in their own land. That made them schis-matics, heretics, even though their rites resembled those of the south-ern Jews. The break was now unmendable—and it remained so for centuries.

As for the city of Samaria, it became one of the Hellenistic towns that threatened the integrity of the Jews. Finally John Hyrcanus the Hasmonaean had unleashed against it the Jewish loathing for Greek things: in 108 B.C. he reduced it to a ruin and sold its population into slavery. It revived afterward but as a relatively unimportant place, still Greek-oriented. Herod married Mariamne here in this foreign town rather than in the Jewish land that he had not yet quite won from Aristobulus. When Herod visited Octavian (Augustus) in Egypt in 30 B.C., the Roman presented him with Samaria along with the Jericho balsam groves and many other places.

The king refounded this object of Jewish hatred on an elaborate scale. Temples, a palace, a theater, a hippodrome, and pillared promenades soon graced it in Greek fashion. While the farmers in Ju-daea died of famine, he lavished love on the enemy city. He renamed it Sebaste in honor of Augustus, who was called Sebastos in Greek. On the acropolis Herod built an ornate Corinthian temple to Augus-tus, so that the populace could indulge in the cult of emperor worship that so appalled the Jews. He imported six thousand colonists of Graeco-Roman sympathies to get the revived city off to a good start.

More than that, he designed the place as a military stronghold, in which he could take refuge from the wrath of his Jewish subjects if the need ever arose. Encircling Sebaste was a great wall from which round towers rose. The king could sit behind the wall among the pleasures of his Hellenistic creation and feel safe from his fellow Jews.

On the Samaritan coast lay the town of Strato's Tower. Although it was a seaside city, it had no harbor, since its coast for many miles both north and south was rocky and unindented. The town had once possessed a little importance, but did not amount to much in 22 B.C., when Herod commenced its renovation.

Herod had shown vision in the transformation of the city of Sa-maria into Sebaste; he showed even more in the transformation of Strato's Tower. He was determined to make the town a great port, a grand entrance into his kingdom, a Graeco-Roman metropolis of beauty and dignity. He would call it Caesaraea, after Caesar Augustus. It would not be designed as a Jewish city, but perhaps even Jews would learn to be proud of it.

Herod spent twelve years on the Caesaraea project, and enormous sums of money. The new city was built of white limestone, which gleamed in a great semicircle as the traveler approached from the sea. Its vast circular harbor was a triumph of engineering worthy of a Roman province, not to speak of a client kingdom. A breakwater constructed of enormous limestone blocks reduced the violence of the Mediterranean. A turreted mole protected the harbor against the strong winds from the southwest. To the left of a voyager sailing into the harbor rose a tower topped by three colossal statues; to the right rose two gigantic blocks set erect against each other and topped by three more colossal statues. As in any Graeco-Roman community of importance, there were a theater, an amphitheater, and a hippodrome at Caesaraea, as well as temples to an assortment of gods. The most magnificent temple, dominating the port from the eminence on which it stood, was dedicated to Caesar Augustus and Rome. Inside it were two huge statues: one of the goddess Roma, the other of Augustus himself, enthroned and looking like Jupiter.

For the Jews no city could equal Jerusalem, because Jerusalem was the center of religion, the holy city. As they watched this new, white port rise, however, many probably thought that their ancient inland capital, with its dark, dirty alleys and its jammed slums, was a less attractive place. Some Jews even moved to Caesaraea to mix with the Greeks who worshiped at the graceful temples to the Olympian gods and at the solid abomination raised to Rome and Augustus.

Meanwhile, and on into the latter portion of his reign, Herod built or embellished other cities. In the border region between the land of the Samaritans and Judaea proper, for instance, he founded a city which he named Antipatris (after Antipater his father) and which would become the principal stopping place for traders between Caesaraea and Jerusalem. North of Jericho, in the lush valley of the Jordan, he founded a city that he named Phasaelis after the brother who had died a prisoner of the Parthians. He even built a new Jericho, a couple of miles south of the old one. Old Jericho was one of the most ancient of cities, already aged when it had fallen to Joshua and the Israelite invaders of Canaan; beneath it lay the bones of people buried when civilization was in infancy. The modern Jericho of Herod had gardens and pools and elegant villas in the contemporary manner; the theater, amphitheater, and hippodrome without which a Graeco-Roman city was scarcely a city at all; and a tremendous royal palace for the use of the king and his court during the winter, when no place in Judaea was more pleasant than this warm, sunny, balsam-scented area close to the tawny wilderness.

South of Jericho, in the wilderness itself, stood the rock-ribbed, almost insurmountable plateau of Masada, where Herod's mother, his sister Salome, and Mariamne his betrothed had been kept safe in 40 B.C. when the king had fled for help to Alexandria and to Rome. The flat top of Masada had already been fortified under the Hasmonaeans. In the years following the defeat of Aristobulus in 37 B.C., Herod fortified it much more, encircling the whole top with a double wall and constructing towers for defense, great buildings for the storage of grain in case of a long siege, cisterns for rainwater, barracks for the quartering of troops, and storehouses for enough weapons to arm ten thousand soldiers. Early in his reign, when he suspected that the insatiable Cleopatra might someday make war on him, he had reasoned that he could retreat to Masada and defy her. After her death he still looked on Masada as a refuge; like Sebaste, it was a place to which he could run in case his own subjects, no longer able to endure his reign, rebelled.

To make his visits to Masada less onerous and to make life bearable if he were ever forced to stay indefinitely atop this isolated plateau, Herod erected two palaces there. The smaller but more spectacular one consisted of three terraces or levels—the uppermost terrace on the surface of the plateau and the other two cut into its steep, rocky northern side. The top terrace, compact and familiar, was nothing but a few rooms and corridors. The middle terrace, however, about sixty feet down the slope of the cliff, had an elaborate circular room with a ring of pillars holding up the roof. Smaller rooms led from the circular area. This level was designed as a place for relaxation from the business of being a client king. The lowest terrace, some forty-five feet below the middle level, was a private Roman-style bath, with pools for cold water, warm water, and hot water, and with elaborate quarters for dining and drinking in the company of supporters, sycophants, and relatives. The plastered walls were meticulously painted to represent veined red and green marble, according to the Roman taste of the period. Beyond the columns one could view, far below, the barren land from which Masada rose and, in the distance, the unruffled glimmer of the Dead Sea and the mountains beyond.

This was a pleasure palace; the other palace, of far more impressive dimensions, could be used for official receptions and the other ceremonial functions of public life. Large as it was, it did not equal the royal residence at Jericho in size; but it was just as ornate, with a profusion of gold and silver objects, colonnades, and mosaic floors and walls. Unlike the mosaics that decorated luxurious dwellings throughout the Roman world, however, Herod's depicted no gods, no human beings, and no animals: at his public palace as elsewhere on Masada, he would not violate the Law against graven images. The scrupulous confinement to geometric and floral motifs was no more than his subjects expected.

VII

KING FOR THE JEWS

In spite of the attention that Herod paid to pleasing Rome, the joy he took in decorating the land of the Jews with Graeco-Roman buildings, and the disregard he manifested toward the feelings of his Jewish subjects, he did make some conscious efforts to benefit those subjects. The relief of the famine in 25 B.C. was not an isolated instance of his concern for the Jews. Even his Graeco-Roman building projects provided construction jobs for poor men, as long as their religious scruples did not deter them from helping to create a city where alien gods would be worshiped. About 20 B.C. he did his subjects another service by remitting one third of their taxes. At this point in his reign, only a few years after his generosity during the famine, he does not seem to have abandoned all hope of winning the Jews over.

It was around the same time that Herod decided to pull down the Temple and erect a new one. The Temple which the Jews had put up after their return from the Babylonian exile, and which was now several centuries old, was impressive—but by no means as grandiose as the fabled Temple of Solomon that the Babylonians had destroyed. Herod would make his new Temple a magnificent dwelling for God, grander than Solomon's, grander by far than pagan places of worship; and he would do it all at his own expense.

If anything could win him popularity among the Jews, it was this. The Temple at Jerusalem was the living heart of Judaism. There were synagogues scattered over the Mediterranean world in places where Jews congregated—at Alexandria in Egypt, at Antioch in Syria, at the trading cities of Asia Minor; but the Temple was the house of God among His people, the only place where the high priest performed his offices. Jewish men everywhere, not just those in Judaea, paid a half shekel every year to the Temple for its maintenance, for the incense and the sacrificial animals and the vestments, or simply for the increase of its heaped-up treasure; rich men donated much more. Jews from foreign cities made pilgrimages to Jerusalem to visit the Temple, especially for religious festivals. The inhabitants of Judaea did not forget that there could be no Temple outside the Promised Land, and the inhabitants of Jerusalem knew that the Temple made their city holy. If Herod provided a finer Temple than ever before—a building to surpass Solomon's—his subjects would marvel at what he had given to the Jews and to Yahweh, and they would praise him more than they had praised the Hasmonaeans. At least he could hope that this would happen.

He probably also hoped that the Temple would constitute an acceptable offering to God. In spite of all his Graeco-Roman sympathies and his tendency to let himself err from the narrow path of his faith, Herod appears to have preserved a rather firm core of piety—a religious sensibility which, although it was not wholly inviolate, was at any rate not pagan. Surely Yahweh would appreciate a glorious Temple and would view Herod more favorably because of it.

There was in addition the desire to be commended by Greeks and Romans. More than the theater and amphitheater at Jerusalem, more than the temple to Rome and Augustus at Sebaste, the new Temple of God would contribute to Herod's renown. It was not every client king that could build so splendid a center for the religion of his people. The old Temple looked old-fashioned anyway, in contrast to the bright modern buildings that Herod had raised in the city and its environs; a Temple more in harmony with these new buildings was almost an esthetic necessity if Jerusalem was to be properly dressed as a client capital. Roman citizens throughout the East would talk of the Temple, and senators would hear of it. Only the Temple of Jupiter on the Capitoline Hill at Rome herself would be more famous—not because it was greater or more splendid but just because it was Roman.

Herod's Temple was to occupy the same site that the old Temple occupied: the finest site in Jerusalem, an eminence from which it would dominate the city. On the west side of the hill lay the Valley of the Cheesemakers, which split Jerusalem into two parts; on the east was the eastern wall of the city itself and, beyond it, the rocky valley of the turbulent Kidron. With the great outer courtyard, where even Gentiles could come to look in wonder, the sacred precincts would cover an area of about thirty-five acres—the whole top of the hill. The Temple itself, like the old one, would be located in the northwest portion very close to the Antonia, the fortress that Herod had built and had named after Antony; and it would spread over a space of approximately five hundred by four hundred feet.

Construction began about 19 B.C. and provided jobs for ten thousand laborers. But these men could work only on the outer portions: the elaborate colonnade surrounding the whole summit of the hill and the least holy parts of the Temple proper. Since no one was allowed in the inner parts of the Temple except priests, no one except priests could build these parts; Herod fully understood that. He therefore had one thousand Levites (members of the priestly caste of Temple assistants) trained in masonry and carpentry. Then he set them to work.

Anxious not to anger his subjects in any way on so important a matter, the king specified that the holy ceremonies were not to be interrupted during the rebuilding; and this command, like his others, was obeyed. The Sanctuary itself took eighteen months to complete; the other portions, being more extensive and elaborate, took another eight years. Except perhaps for minor matters the project was finished about 10 B.C. Herod apparently chose to dedicate it in that year on the anniversary of his ascension to the throne, sacrificing three hundred oxen in the ceremony.

Even for a Gentile, climbing the hill was greatly worth the trouble. The portico that ringed the top was three columns deep on all sides except the south, where it was four columns deep. These pillars were so large that it required three men with their arms stretched out to encircle one of them. Their tops spread out into the stone foliage of Corinthian capitals, supporting ceilings of cedarwood that were paneled and intricately carved. A pagan could stroll down the long, majestic aisles between the rows of pillars and feel very much at home. The whole portico was in the Graeco-Roman tradition; there was nothing Jewish about it.

When a visitor had crossed the preliminary court, which was broad enough so that many thousands of people could assemble in it and still have plenty of room, he came to a flight of steps that led up to a stone balustrade. On the balustrade was carved, in both Latin and Greek, an inscription telling him that non-Jews were not allowed to go any farther and that any non-Jew caught inside would be killed, as he deserved. If the visitor was a Jew, he proceeded inside. If the visitor was a Jewess, she proceeded inside unless she happened to be in a menstrual period, which made her unclean.

Having passed through high double doors, the devotee found himself in a large courtyard called the Women's Court. This was the outermost portion of the Temple proper. Men were allowed in it as well as women; but it was called the Women's Court because women were allowed no farther. The rites that went on in a holier part of the Temple were not for the eyes of Eve's daughters.

A male Jew could mount the semicircular flight of fifteen steps at the western end of the Women's Court and stand in the Court of the Israelites. From here, if he continued looking to the west, he could watch the ceremonies in the next court—that of the Levites or Priests; but unless he was a priest himself he could not enter this court, even if he was Herod.

In front of him he saw the altar, a mass of rough stones that was fifty or sixty feet square. God had said in the Torah: "And if thou wilt make Me an altar of stone, thou shalt not build it of hewn stone: for if thou lift up thy tool upon it, thou hast polluted it." The rudeness of the altar came as a shock after the polished beauty through which the devotee had passed. It reminded him of the primitive days of his people, before there had been Greeks and Romans and pretensions.

On one side of the altar were items necessary to the ritual, such as rings to which the sacrificial animals were fastened, and marble tables for the fat, the flesh, and the entrails. There were sacrifices every day: a lamb before sunrise, a lamb before sunset, various beasts offered during the daylight hours by private citizens for various reasons detailed in the Torah. The priests wore fine linen as they performed the ancient ceremonies. The high priest, who participated only on the Sabbath, at the new moon, and on feast days, wore a blue robe from whose tassels hung gold bells, representing thunder, and pomegranates, representing lightning. On the Day of Atonement he wore an embroidered vest and sash with bands of gold, purple, scarlet, blue, and fine linen, and from his clothes glistened precious and semiprecious stones.

At the far side of the courtyard and on a terrace stood the Sanctuary itself, a flight of steps leading up to it. A man who was not a priest, viewing the building from the Court of the Israelites, saw white marble walls and gold-covered pinnacles gleaming in the sun. A priest could sometimes go into the Holy Place, where the most sacred objects of Judaism were kept.

At the entrance to the Holy Place were enormous doors of gold. Above them hung a gold vine with bunches of great grapes dangling from it. In front hung a Babylonian tapestry of fine linen, which signified the earth. The tapestry was embroidered in red for fire, blue for the air, and purple for the sea, and on it the starry heavens were depicted.

For the dimensions of the Holy Place, Herod had followed the figures recorded in the First Book of Kings for Solomon's Temple. The room was about sixty feet long and about thirty feet wide. Its extraordinary height—at least ninety feet—seems to have been based on a figure in the Second Book of Chronicles that may have been a textual corruption but that Herod and his priests thought accurate. Around this room, on all sides except the side of the golden doors, were three stories of chambers for the safeguarding of the Temple treasures and even of private moneys. Within the Holy Place the seven-branched lampstand burned—each branch representing one of the seven planets. The table of shewbread held its twelve loaves, symbolizing the twelve signs of the Zodiac; and the altar of incense sent up the fragrance of thirteen spices.

Shut off by a veil from the Holy Place was the Holy of Holies: the most awesome spot on earth. No one went into it except the high priest—and he passed the veil only once a year, on the Day of Atonement, when he wore his most glorious garments and his jewels. If he entered it on any other day, or more than one time even on the Day of Atonement, the penalty was death; and from this penalty there was no appeal. During his single annual penetration of the Holy of Holies, he deposited a censer there. Then, surrounded by pure emptiness, he prayed that man would prosper and have peace.

VIII

FATHER OF SONS

About 22 B.C., soon after the city of Samaria had been remade as Sebaste and two or three years before construction work on the Temple began, Herod sent three of his sons to Rome to complete their education. All three had had Mariamne for their mother, and Herod may possibly have found their presence at his court an unpleasant reminder of the woman whose memory he still loved, even though he had believed her a whore. More likely, however, he just wanted to give the boys the best training possible. They were partly Hasmonaean through the blood of their mother, but they were also Herod's own progeny and Herod was fond of them.

At the time they went to Rome, the oldest brother, Alexander, was about thirteen. They were to stay in the capital of the world for the next several years, developing the linguistic and literary fluency that a prince should possess, broadening their knowledge of politics, rubbing off whatever provincialism they might have acquired in Judaea, polishing themselves both socially and intellectually. Their maintenance at Rome was very expensive, but Herod did not care about expense. The youngest boy died before the completion of his education; but Alexander and the middle brother, who bore the stridently Hasmonaean name Aristobulus, learned much.

They lived at the house of Caius Asinius Pollio, a proud patrician of great importance who held Herod in high esteem. In former years Pollio had fought for Caesar, had assisted Antony after Caesar's assassination, had governed part of Gaul, had functioned as consul, had defeated Parthia, and had used the treasure he took from the Parthians to erect the first public library at Rome. As this last act showed, he was a man of literary tastes as well as a man of action. In retirement he read extensively, patronized poets, and wrote tragedies, speeches, and a history of the civil wars through which he had lived. Nothing survives of these works except fragments of the speeches.

Herod thought that under such a man as Pollio—learned, prominent, admired, and acquainted with everybody of significance at Rome—his sons were sure to grow into the cultivated modern princes that he wished them to be: well-mannered, able to converse on the literary works and philosophical questions that were inseparable from Graeco-Roman civilization, schooled in political maneuvering, and known to influential Romans. About 17 B.C., Herod decided that they had had enough education along these lines. He paid a state visit to Rome, in the course of which he was received by Augustus as a scrupulously loyal client king should be received. Augustus, who had watched the boys' progress closely, agreed that they were sufficiently educated to return to Judaea, and Herod took them back with him.

They had been at the Judaean court only a short while when the king found wives for them. To the older brother, Alexander, he gave a princess named Glaphyra, daughter of the client king of Cappadocia in eastern Asia Minor. Glaphyra was in point of birth one of the most desirable young ladies alive at the time. She could trace her ancestry back to Darius, the king of Persia, invader of Greece, and monarch of much of the world many centuries ago; and she could also trace her ancestry back to the Macedonian kings—including the great Alexander, who had put an end to Persia. When she came to the Judaean court she carried a sense of her own illustriousness with her, making her superiority evident among the ladies. Herod might congratulate himself on having obtained so eminent a bride for his son.

Herod's sister Salome had a daughter of marriageable age named Berenice. He gave this girl to Aristobulus, probably for the boy's own protection. Men of much less acute perception than Herod—most of the courtiers in fact—were aware that Salome vigorously resented the presence of Alexander and Aristobulus at court. She despised these part-Hasmonaeans: these sons of the woman who had called her common, of the queen whom she had hated and in whose death she had exulted. Herod must have hoped that if her daughter Berenice's fortunes were tied to Aristobulus' fortunes, Salome would be less eager to destroy the young man.

The match might also serve an admirable political purpose by suggesting that the Hasmonaean-Herodian enmity was finally at an end. Even the most stupid courtiers, however, were not fooled by this suggestion for very long. It seems that Alexander and Aristobulus had derived a high Hasmonaean pride from their mother. They boasted about the Hasmonaean blood in their veins, valued themselves as descendants of the family whose kingly position Herod now held, spoke fondly of their mother, and remarked that perhaps her guilt was not as evident as their father had perceived it to be.

The court at Jerusalem followed the example of the worst Hellenistic courts in being shot through with petty but savage intrigue. People told stories, in whispers if possible, about other people for the purpose of advancing their own cherished interests, or for the delight of pure maleficence, or even for want of something more important to do. The situation was to become worse before the end of Herod's reign, but it was already scarcely bearable. Courtiers went to Herod or to Herod's trusted friends with stories about what Alexander and Aristobulus were saying. They even claimed that Alexander was planning to go to Rome to bring charges against Herod. The king grew more and more disgusted. He hesitated to believe so much ill of his sons; and yet their conduct even to his face supported the stories, and they were after all the faithless Mariamne's children as well as his own.

In the midst of all the courtly hypocrisy, duplicity, and scandalmongering, Alexander and Aristobulus seem to have stayed surprisingly frank and open. Whatever they had learned at Rome, they had not learned much practical dissimulation there. If they disliked something about their father they evidently said so, to Herod himself or to anybody else who happened to be near. In Herod's own opinion the young men had learned little at Rome except arrogance and ingratitude. The courtiers watched, talked, argued, schemed, and counterschemed.

To aggravate the strained relationships at court, an open enmity was developing between the sisters-in-law, Glaphyra and Berenice. Alexander's wife, the Cappadocian princess, descendant of Darius the Great and Alexander the Great, had decided that Berenice was the only object in Jerusalem really worthy of her scorn, and she heaped it on the Herodian girl just as Mariamne had once reviled Salome for not being of royal birth. Berenice of course resorted to her mother. Salome was soon nursing one more grudge; the courtiers had one more interesting item to whisper about or take sides over; and Herod had one more cause of discontent.

The move that he made was not a solution and was perhaps not even wise. It happened that Alexander and Aristobulus were not his only living sons. By Doris, the wife whom he had married before Mariamne, he had a son named Antipater—his firstborn. For many years Doris and Antipater had been living far from the court. Herod had sent the mother and son away when Antipater was a little boy, not for any fault of their own but because the king was preoccupied with Mariamne at the time and their presence might prove inconvenient. Now he decided to summon Antipater to Jerusalem. That would lower the pride of his Hasmonaean sons a little. (Later Doris as well was to be summoned.)

Antipater, named for Herod's own father rather than for a Hasmonaean king, had lain in seclusion a long time. He had probably thought that he would never get out of it, since the obscurity of his education seemed to mean that Herod had destined him for a private life only. Now the attractions of the court, supplemented by the favor of the king, his father, suddenly opened out before him. It would profit him to ingratiate himself as much as possible with Herod and even to help in the proliferation of stories about his half brothers, while keeping Alexander and Aristobulus from suspecting his part in the whole affair. It would profit him to invent, if his inventions were subtle enough and safe enough to hold up under Herod's scrutiny. It would profit him to stay in the good graces of his powerful aunt Salome. It would profit him to use whatever guile came naturally to him—and much came. Alexander and Aristobulus might have had the benefit of watching politics in action at Rome, but Antipater was to be more than their match in the craft of a client court.

The stories therefore continued to circulate, often in whispers, through the Graeco-Roman halls of Herod's palace, and the king discovered that he had intensified his own misery.

For a while, fortunately, Herod found some relief in the coming of Agrippa to the East. Agrippa was Augustus' son-in-law and trusted friend, and the man who had been primarily responsible for the defeat of Antony and Cleopatra at Actium. Now he was in charge of Eastern affairs. In planning his trip to Asia from Italy in 15 B.C. he apparently had not intended to travel in Judaea, but Herod changed his mind for him. The model king could not pass up the chance to impress so significant a Roman—a man who might one day command the whole Empire. Herod hurried to Asia Minor to greet Agrippa, and without much difficulty convinced him to view the exemplary client kingdom of Judaea. The Roman liked the evidences of progress he was shown there—the modern cities, the Temple in process of rebuilding.

After a pleasant visit Agrippa departed to head a military expedition in the Bosporus. Reluctant to see the end of so rewarding a relationship, Herod sailed northwest after him as soon as possible, hoping to rejoin him on the way to the Bosporus. He took Antipater along; a protracted association with the powerful Agrippa might conceivably result in benefit for Antipater. Certainly it could do the young prince no harm, unless he acted like a fool. Alexander and Aristobulus, no doubt to Antipater's joy, were left behind.

A strong wind from the north delayed Herod in the Aegean, and he missed Agrippa at the island of Lesbos. He chased him through the Hellespont and the Propontis but learned at Byzantium that Agrippa had already sailed into the Black Sea with his fleet. Undaunted, Herod chased him in an easterly direction through the Black Sea all the way to Sinope, a city situated more than halfway along the northern coast of what is now Turkey. There he caught up with him at last. Agrippa was pleased to see Herod, whom he had already learned to like in Judaea. In the next few weeks the king made himself both charming and useful—as he had done with Mark Antony many years before—working with Agrippa on political issues and helping him to relax if there was no pressing business to conduct.

When the expedition was over the entourage made the return journey by land rather than sea, through the Graecized provinces of Asia Minor to the great Ionian port of Ephesus on the Aegean. During this progress Herod was bountiful to the populace, providing entertainments, distributing money to those who needed it—working hard on his image, so that the Asiatic Greeks would call him a glorious king no matter what the Jews called him.

But he did not disregard the Jews either. Many Jews lived in the Greek cities of Ionia, and they complained to him that they were being mistreated—that the Roman officials required them to appear in court on holy days and to serve Rome in the army, although such obligations conflicted with the laws and customs which Rome had formerly let the Jews follow. They complained also that the Roman officials were diverting the money that was supposed to be sent as contributions to the Temple, and were using this money for profane purposes. Herod asked Agrippa to hear these complaints, and he employed Nicolaus of Damascus, the brilliant Greek whom he had taken into his service after the overthrow of Antony and Cleopatra, to plead the Jewish cause. Nicolaus must have argued well, though Agrippa's high opinion of Herod was also to the Jews' advantage. The Roman decided that the traditional Jewish exemption from military service should be observed, that Jews need not appear in court on holy days, and that money designated for the Temple must not be tampered with. He and Herod then put their arms around each other in friendly acknowledgment of the fact that a good day's work had been done.

Shortly after this the two men necessarily parted. Herod, sending Antipater on to Rome for a look at the great world that Alexander and Aristobulus had already seen, went back to Jerusalem. There he called the Jews together and delivered a speech in which he told them about his trip. He informed them that Agrippa's decision in Ionia guaranteed the rights of Jews throughout the Empire, made it clear that this decision had been obtained through his own efforts, and hinted that he was an excellent king. He also announced that he would remit one quarter of the taxes that his subjects had paid the preceding year. Herod had seldom been happier with himself.

But with his return to his hate-tortured court the king's happiness vanished almost immediately. His sister Salome had been conducting her machinations against Alexander and Aristobulus with lethal finesse. She had succeeded, for instance, in turning her daughter Berenice, Aristobulus' wife, so violently against Aristobulus that the girl would run to her mother with reports about his activities. Salome could then pervert this information or classify it for future use. She had also enlisted the help of her brother Pheroras—youngest and only surviving brother of Herod, who soon became almost as savage an enemy of Mariamne's sons as Salome was herself. In spite of all this intriguing, however, there was one instance in which the older son, Alexander, received the unexpected support of his father.

Pheroras, a widower, was on bad terms with Herod at the time for refusing to marry two ladies whom the king had suggested, and for marrying instead a woman whose name is unknown but who had recently been a slave. Evidently a person of intelligence and force of character, she fascinated Pheroras, who was already the father of a child by her. Herod disliked her not only for her servile birth but because she favored the Pharisees, the strict religionists who drew most of their backing from the common people and who declared that Herod was detestable.

To compound the trouble between father and son, Pheroras took Alexander aside one day and related a story he said he had heard from Salome: that Herod had fallen in love with his own daughter-in-law, Alexander's wife Glaphyra, the haughty Cappadocian princess. The story was not entirely incredible, since Herod obviously liked Glaphyra, paying her marked attention at court; many observers had already noticed that. According to Pheroras, the liking was passionate.

Even though Alexander had no reason to trust his paternal uncle, he did believe the story. At least he believed it enough to lay it before Herod. Trying hard to hold back his anger and his agony, he accused his father of having become his rival for the love of his wife. Alexander was obviously very much to blame for crediting such slander against his father, but the king's rage turned against Pheroras. Summoning his brother, Herod charged him with spreading vicious lies and with plotting to make Alexander a patricide. But unlike most sons, the king went on, Alexander had shown restraint. He had not hurried to poison his father or stab him to death in a fit of jealousy, but had instead gone to him and confronted him with the ugly, ridiculous tale whispered by an ugly uncle.

Pheroras naturally maintained that he had heard the story from their own beloved sister Salome. The lady herself appears to have been on hand, either because Herod had ordered her to be present or because she thought that she had better see what was going on.

Whether she had really devised the story or not, she denied everything. Her brother Pheroras might be her ally against Alexander and Aristobulus, but she had herself to think of. No one else in fact mattered.

Salome defended herself with her customary agility. Everybody, she said, was against her and was trying to get her into trouble with Herod, whom she had always loved and protected. Pheroras in particular was against her, since she had been trying to persuade him to give up his ex-slave girl. No wonder he had accused his sister—he wanted to get rid of her. But Herod would do her justice. She mounted quickly to a frenzy, tearing her hair and thumping her breast.

Herod's skepticism was not toppled by this display, but in the absence of evidence he decided to let the matter drop. Under the circumstances Alexander had come off very well.

The king's improved attitude toward Alexander, however, was brittle at best, and Salome and Pheroras did all they could to shatter it. The whispers circulated relentlessly: Salome devoted her remarkable energies to hissing insinuations against both Alexander and Aristobulus. Meanwhile Antipater kept writing to Herod from Rome, where he was apparently doing well, having been supplied by his father with letters of introduction to various influential friends at the capital. In his correspondence he sometimes referred to Alexander and Aristobulus, suggesting with a certain amount of delicacy that they needed close surveillance and assuring the king of his own unsurpassed affection. He must have been afraid that Alexander and Aristobulus would use his absence to promote their own interests, and that his father's good opinion of him would diminish if he was not around to strengthen it. But he need not have worried. Alexander and Aristobulus made matters worse for themselves by continuing to boast about their Hasmonaean mother and to act less than civil toward their father. The court of Jerusalem had not yet taught them tact.

Gradually the idea grew in Herod's mind that Alexander and Aristobulus wanted to kill him. Perhaps they planned to seize the throne after he was dead, although he had obtained from Augustus the permission to will the throne to whichever one of his sons seemed to deserve it most. Maybe the throne was a minor consideration; maybe all they really wanted was to see their father put into his tomb. Salome subtly nourished this suspicion. She pointed out instances when (according to her interpretation) the young men's rudeness to their father could only mean pure loathing. She said she had heard things that implicated them in a plot against his life. She objected that he was too kind and generous to see their treachery—that an excess of fatherly affection blinded him to what was plain to everybody else. Herod was now in his sixties. The longer he lived, and the more enemies he acquired, and the more people he caused to die, the more sharply he feared that he himself would die through murder. Salome played cleverly on this fear, which was becoming an obsession.

But he loved his sons—loved them so much that he had sent them to Rome for a princely education and then had brought them back to Judaea so that he could have them around him. It tortured him to think that they longed for his death. How could they possibly requite his love with loathing, and itch to end his life? Sometimes in their features he saw Mariamne, whom he had adored but who had been untrue. They had inherited not only her good looks but her Hasmonaean pride too—and perhaps her disdain for him, and perhaps her faithlessness. Herod could not stand to be taken advantage of: if his own sons were false to him, they would pay. They were the children of his loins, conceived before he had ever suspected Mariamne, and he loved them; but he also abhorred them, and they would pay.

He suppressed the strong inclination to punish or kill them himself, however. Explaining such an extraordinary act to Augustus would prove embarrassing, especially since the emperor had thought highly of Alexander and Aristobulus during the years when they were growing up in Rome. The matter had to be taken care of legally, and in such a way that Augustus would have no basis for criticism. Herod decided to go to Italy with his sons and bring them before the emperor himself for judgment. And the sooner he started out, the better: if he waited very long he might descend to sudden violence in spite of his caution.

In 12 B.C. therefore he sailed with Alexander and Aristobulus to Italy. There is no record of this voyage of hatred—of how the sons acted toward their father and accuser during the long journey, or of what he said to them.

In Italy, in front of Augustus, Herod adopted the role of prosecuting attorney. He described himself as an extremely unfortunate king, a father of ungrateful offspring. These two young men, whom Augustus would remember from several years ago, when they were living at Rome and being educated there at great expense—these two young men despised the father who loved them. They had even conspired to kill him, and their unnatural conduct deserved punishment. He asked for this punishment though he loved them.

Alexander now spoke in defense of Aristobulus and himself—and he spoke disarmingly. Not only was the charge totally false, but he did not think that even Herod believed it. Their father was basically kind. If Herod had really wanted to punish his sons he could have done so in Judaea, where he possessed the authority and power of a king; the fact that he had brought them to Italy showed that he actually wanted to clear their names. And they wished to live—but they would prefer to die if it was considered true that they had wronged their father.

Augustus was not used to the kind of trial in which a father prosecutes his children. Either the whole thing was a farce, or it was a great shame. In any case it impressed the emperor as unnecessary and probably disappointed him in his favorite client king. A man who showed as little good sense as Herod in the governance of his own family might commit costly errors in the governance of a nation. According to the historian Josephus, who described the trial in his *Jewish Antiquities,* the onlookers agreed that Herod had made a grave mistake; and as they looked at the unpaternal king and then at the two handsome young men pleading their innocence, many cried. It did not take Augustus long to reach a decision in favor of the princes. Father and sons were reconciled, onlookers wept tears of happiness, and everybody loved everybody again.

Shortly after the trial Herod presented Augustus with a very large gift of money, and this generosity perhaps did something to revive the emperor's good opinion of him. The money came in very handy, helping to pay for the theatrical spectacles and distributions of grain that Augustus was currently providing for the people. In return Augustus granted Herod the right to half the revenue from the copper mines of Cyprus. Since Cyprus was a very important source of copper (the metal in fact is named after the island), this gift was by far the more valuable of the two. Herod as usual had come out ahead.

He and Alexander and Aristobulus went away; and Antipater accompanied them, as Herod had decided that it was time for his firstborn to return to Jerusalem. Bitterly disappointed in the outcome of the trial, Antipater pretended to be as happy as everybody else.

On the way back to Judaea they stopped in Asia Minor to visit Alexander's father-in-law, King Archelaus of Cappadocia, who was of course happy too: the punishment of Alexander would have put his daughter Glaphyra in a difficult position. Throughout the trip, it would seem, Antipater worked on Herod. He discovered that the king's suspicions were not entirely dead—that they lingered under the surface in spite of all the tears at the trial, in spite of Augustus' view that the charge of conspiracy was ridiculous, in spite of the embraces and the apparent resuscitation of fatherly feelings. Antipater, true to the hypocrisy by which he lived, professed an unwillingness to say anything against his half brothers; but he said a great deal anyway and he was happy to do so.

At Jerusalem once more, Herod summoned the people to the Temple and gave them another speech, reporting those aspects of the trip that he considered suitable for popular ears. He ended by recommending that his sons love one another—and then announcing his decision that when he died the throne would go to Antipater. In the event of Antipater's death Alexander and Aristobulus would inherit the kingdom.

The decision was reasonable, since Antipater was the oldest son. Alexander and Aristobulus in fact should probably have expected it, even though they had formerly been groomed for reigning whereas Antipater had not. But they took it as an insult. Antipater was not entirely satisfied either: much could happen before Herod died, and the mere fact that Alexander and Aristobulus were possible candidates for the throne bothered him.

For this reason and for others, he carried on his campaign of calumny with heightened ardor. Sometimes he himself told stories about Alexander and Aristobulus; sometimes he hired other people to tell stories. Characteristically he dressed his real feelings in a pretense of affection, assuring Herod that it hurt him to discredit his half brothers and never treating Alexander and Aristobulus impolitely. When it was feasible, Antipater went so far as to pose as their defender against slander, even though in actuality the slander might have been his own invention. Even when he reported to Herod (as he often did) that Alexander and Aristobulus were talking sentimentally about

Mariamne and cursing their father for murdering her, he seemed pained by what he had to reveal.

His mother Doris, Herod's first wife, who had been summoned to the palace from seclusion not long after her son, helped a great deal. Doris may have been quiet in retirement, but her return to Herod's court converted her into a woman with much to talk about and most of it bad. She chattered tirelessly against Alexander and Aristobulus, and she slid into Herod's good graces. The king thought so well of her that he valued everything she said. In fact he even took to asking her advice on questions of national policy. Nobody's aspersions against Alexander and Aristobulus made a sharper impression than hers. She was, after all, the first wife Herod had ever chosen.

In the face of all this serpentine activity Mariamne's sons did not change their ways. Too proud to connive, too confident to care about the war of gossip and suggestion being waged against them, they blurted out their opinions just as they had done before, whether or not these opinions were favorable to Herod. They deliberately laid themselves open to informers—who secretly reported their comments to Antipater, who reported them to Herod, often embellished with words that they had never uttered and sometimes twisted unrecognizably. Alexander's wife Glaphyra played into Antipater's hands by being odious. Still insufferably conscious of her pedigree, she said it was a gross insult that her sister-in-law Berenice, daughter of the common Salome, was considered her equal in rank. Glaphyra infuriated Herod's wives and most of his children by remarking that Herod had married his wives not for their high birth but simply because the women happened to attract him sexually.

Even if Alexander and Aristobulus ignored much of the malice that was building up against them, they almost certainly recognized that the rapprochement with their father was over. They must also have noticed that their allies among the courtiers were beginning to treat them coolly. Practiced in interpreting the king's moods and guessing his preferences, the courtiers had already typed Alexander and Aristobulus as a lost cause. Antipater was the rising figure, and Antipater therefore deserved their flattery and service—even their loyalty, insofar as they were capable of loyalty. Besides, when Herod was dead Antipater would be king; and then Alexander and Aristobulus would probably not be around much longer. The courtiers deserted the two brothers quietly but surely, until Alexander and Aristobulus had scarcely anybody left to whisper in their favor. At times Herod himself encouraged people to go over to Antipater. For instance he advised Ptolemy, minister of the royal finances, to make Antipater his friend.

Enraged by the hostility of his sons, caught up in the tangle of malevolence within his family, and greeted by tale-tellers wherever he turned, Herod still had a kingdom to manage. He still had a reputation to uphold as a great client king, and he still had honor to achieve —among the Gentiles if not among the Jews. He therefore contributed money lavishly to revive the languishing Olympic Games, and in 10 or 9 B.C. he held at the newly finished city of Caesaraea the Actian Games, dedicated to Augustus in memory of the defeat of Antony and Cleopatra. Although Augustus provided some money for the games, the emperor's estimate of Herod dropped suddenly about this time. Herod in fact received a letter from Augustus to the effect that whereas he had so far treated the Jewish king as a friend, he intended now to treat him as a servant. Coming as it did after all the attention that Herod over the years had devoted to the cultivation of the great, and coming on top of insistent domestic worries besides, this blow was cruel.

The origin of the breach was something that had happened a couple of years before, when Herod went to Italy for the trial of Alexander and Aristobulus. During his absence the Arabs of Trachonitis, part of the wild territory south of Damascus that Augustus had given to Herod so that he could keep order there, revolted because they were no longer able to lead the life of robbery that they loved. Herod's officers defeated them, but about forty of the chieftains took refuge in the kingdom of Nabataea. Using their Nabataean hiding place as a base, they raided Judaea, plundering and slaughtering in their ancestral fashion.

When Herod got back from Italy he conducted an expedition that succeeded only in killing off the rebels' families. Some time later he demanded that the king of Nabataea, Obodas III, extradite the chieftains so that he could punish them as they deserved, and he also demanded an enormous sum of money which he had formerly loaned to the Nabataean government and whose repayment had now come due. Careful as usual to stay on the good side of Rome, he secured the permission of the Roman governor of Syria before making these demands.

King Obodas III was weak, and most of the power in Nabataea was in the hands of a man named Syllaeus. This Arab some years previously had asked for Salome in marriage. But although Salome was free at the time, Herod had refused to give Syllaeus his sister unless he adopted the Jewish religion—a suggestion that made Syllaeus angry. Now Syllaeus denied that he was harboring any Trachonite chieftains and paid no attention to the demand for repayment of the loan. He also set off for Rome, probably to prejudice Augustus against Herod.

Still with the permission of the governor of Syria, Herod invaded Nabataea. He captured the chieftains, destroyed a fortress, and killed a few Nabataeans in a skirmish. Evidently he did no more than that, although we cannot be sure. When Syllaeus at Rome was apprised of these happenings (perhaps in a somewhat exaggerated form), he decided to make the most of them. Putting on black to signify mourning, he told Augustus that Herod was waging an unjust war against Nabataea, and that he had killed twenty-five hundred leading Nabataeans and done much damage to the country.

In Augustus' view Herod had wantonly broken the Roman Peace. The very idea of one client kingdom attacking another client kingdom was disgraceful. The whole incident confirmed the impression that Augustus had received at the trial of Alexander and Aristobulus: Herod was not so capable a client king as he had once been. It is possible that Augustus also felt that in many ways Herod was arrogating too much authority to himself. The Temple that he had raised to his exclusive Jewish God was another example of his overweening independence; in a sense it constituted an insult to the Roman deities. Convinced that Herod needed a severe reminder of the force of Rome, Augustus sent the letter.

The upset king dispatched two embassies to Rome, but Augustus declined to give them audience. Meanwhile the Trachonite Arabs, realizing that Herod was not to be feared right now, pillaged at their pleasure. A new king came to the throne in Nabataea in 9 B.C.; he immediately wrote Augustus a letter denouncing Syllaeus as a man of ungoverned ambition and no principles, who had poisoned the preceding ruler. He sent this letter by way of envoys who also bore many gifts for Augustus, including a crown of gold. But Augustus, still believing that Syllaeus was in the right, told the embassy to go back to Nabataea and to take the gifts with them. Herod continued to sweat.

At court meanwhile the domestic tension heightened. The rumors focused more and more on the older brother, Alexander, although Aristobulus was by no means forgotten. Herod's paranoiac tendency, which years before had made him think that Mariamne wished to poison him, now made him institute a reign of terror. Trusting none of his associates, imagining cabals in all the recesses of his court, putting faith in nobody except Doris and Antipater, he had his nobles tailed by spies. Despite his efforts to be secretive about all this, it soon became obvious what he was doing. The courtiers then began accusing one another of disloyalty, fabricating tales about one another, telling lies about those whom they hated. Masters and slaves alike were taken to the torture chamber, and many died there in agony. Antipater had a pleasant time as he fed his father's doubts, pointed out particularly questionable persons, and encouraged the king in his course of persecution and death.

Under torture, people told Herod that Alexander had called him an old fool who dyed his hair black to look young; that Alexander had said Antipater would never be king, had conspired with Aristobulus to have his father assassinated on a hunt, and had commissioned a poison to be given to his father. Herod ordered Alexander arrested and thrown into prison.

During his confinement, according to Josephus, Alexander did an almost incredible thing. He wrote a long "confession," elaborately describing plots against Herod and claiming that he himself was involved in them. He named other people who supposedly were involved too: in particular his uncle Pheroras and his aunt Salome. If this "confession" contained all that Josephus says it contained, it sounds like the product of an inventive but slightly disordered brain. At least Alexander does not seem to have inherited enough of the Herodian deviousness to have schemed in secret against his father. Perhaps he felt that this time Herod was really going to kill him, and perhaps he derived a perverse pleasure out of creating one last grand piece of foolish fiction for his father to swallow. Very likely he also got pleasure out of the thought that he could drag Pheroras and Salome down with himself. He even stated that his aunt, still sexually passionate despite her many years, had made him go to bed with her one night.

But King Archelaus of Cappadocia heard that his son-in-law was in prison and rushed down to Judaea like a *deus ex machina* to extricate him. He was not of course heartbroken about Alexander, but he wanted to make sure that Glaphyra would not be subjected to the embarrassment of having her husband executed for treason. According to Josephus (who may not be strictly reliable, but who is our only source), Archelaus used the psychological device of maligning Alexander so that Herod, who after all had a strong sense of family, would be forced to defend him. Archelaus evidently stormed into the palace shouting words that went something like this: "Where is my villainous son-in-law? I'll tear him apart with my own hands!" He also appears to have announced that if the accusations against Alexander were true, his daughter must divorce that scoundrel. Herod, yearning to love his son, afraid of betrayal by his own flesh and blood, torn and sick, remembering Mariamne, finally took the position that Alexander was not so bad as people painted him. He showed Archelaus the "confession," and they studied it together. The outcome was a new interpretation of the document: Alexander was not the plotter but the victim of a plot by the false-tongued Pheroras. Herod no doubt recalled that his brother had proven untrustworthy on other occasions. Once again Alexander was exonerated. As for Pheroras, Herod pardoned him.

With his daughter saved from possible disgrace and the domestic affairs of Herod's family settled for the time being, King Archelaus took his leave. Herod, who accompanied him as far as Antioch, expressed his thanks by means of valuable presents: a great deal of money, a throne of gold set with jewels, several choice eunuchs, and an attractive concubine.

The next distinguished visitor at Herod's court did Alexander more harm than Archelaus had done him good—opened in fact the last act of the tragicomedy. This man was Eurycles, an aristocratic Greek, citizen of a degenerate Sparta that no longer liked simplicity and no longer bred heroes. Already rich, Eurycles had decided that at the court of a rich king he could get richer, and that taking advantage of Alexander and Aristobulus was the best way to do so. He gradually ingratiated himself into Alexander's confidence—mentioning, for instance, that the prince's father-in-law, King Archelaus of Cappadocia, was one of his dearest friends. Alexander in return let loose his grievances: that Herod hated him, that Herod loved only Antipater and had named Antipater heir to the kingdom, that Herod had killed Mariamne, that Herod was a stupid, stubborn, cruel, blind old man. Eurycles then retailed these remarks to Antipater, who paid him handsomely for them. Later on, Antipater paid him to go to the king in person with his reports. Eurycles posed before Herod as a real hero, claiming to have deterred Alexander from executing his long-planned patricidal designs. He played up Alexander's envy of Antipater; he emphasized the prince's ambition to rule Judaea and avenge the death of Mariamne; and he said that after killing his father, Alexander intended to take refuge with Archelaus or with Augustus himself, to whom he would reveal how Herod had been oppressing the Jews.

Very grateful, Herod gave Eurycles an immense sum. The enriched Spartan left in a hurry, before people could compare notes. Proceeding to Asia Minor, he informed King Archelaus that Alexander was a very nice person, and he modestly took credit for cementing the improved relationship between Alexander and Herod. Archelaus gave him money too.

Eurycles had brought Herod's suspicions to an almost unbearable intensity. The agonized old monarch, smelling murder everywhere, afraid of his own sons, moody and ferocious and often screaming like a savage, was not far from insanity.

Antipater chose this time to send more informers to him. In the course of the tortures and testimonies it appeared that Alexander had written a letter to the commander of one of Herod's fortresses, the Alexandrium in Samaria, asking him to receive Aristobulus and himself after they fled from their father's court. Herod naturally assumed that they planned to take refuge in the fortress after killing him. He suspected among other things that they were in league with King Archelaus of Cappadocia, whom he now considered his enemy. He had both of them chained.

In a final effort to ferret out the truth, he summoned Alexander from prison one day and brought him face to face with Glaphyra. The Cappadocian princess hammered at her head with her hands and wept loudly to see her husband in chains. From devotion to his wife or from the depths of self-pity, Alexander cried too.

Ptolemy, head of the royal finances, was present as examiner. He had once been Alexander's friend; now he was the friend of Antipater. He asked Alexander how much Glaphyra knew about his activities.

Alexander replied that he had no secrets from his dear wife—the woman who had borne his children.

Glaphyra exclaimed that she knew of no outrageous acts ever committed by her husband.

Alexander said it was true that Aristobulus and he had decided to visit his father-in-law, King Archelaus of Cappadocia, and then go on to Rome; but he added that the truth did not extend beyond this. In other words, he and his brother were not conspiring with Archelaus against Herod. Glaphyra, as might have been expected, supported the claim.

The examination was over; the chained Alexander was taken back to his cell.

Herod, instead of being convinced of Alexander's innocence, now felt sure that the two brothers and King Archelaus were involved in a plot against him: that his sons were traitors and almost certainly wanted to be murderers. To his mind their intention of visiting King Archelaus and then proceeding to Rome proved their disloyalty.

At this period—about 7 B.C.—Herod had fairly good ground for hoping that Augustus' opinion of him had altered for the better. He had sent to Rome as his spokesman the great orator and counselor Nicolaus, the man who had so successfully pleaded the Jewish cause before Agrippa in Ionia a number of years before. Nicolaus, supplied with evidence and legal genius, was supposed to show Augustus that Herod had been right all along in the Nabataean affair and that Syllaeus was a lying scoundrel.

After the scene with Alexander and Glaphyra, Herod dispatched envoys to Augustus. On the way to Rome they were to stop in Asia Minor to deliver an official reprimand to King Archelaus. At Rome, if they discovered that Augustus was once more ready to treat Herod as a friend rather than a servant, they were to give the emperor a letter written by Herod, accusing Archelaus of collusion with Alexander and Aristobulus, together with documents implicating the brothers in treason.

Meanwhile Nicolaus, helped immeasurably by Nabataean Arabs who had deserted Syllaeus, had won Augustus over to Herod's side.

The time was therefore auspicious for Herod. From a psychological standpoint, however, it probably was not wise of the king to bother Augustus with this family matter so soon after their reconciliation, especially since the emperor liked Alexander and Aristobulus and had found them to be unjustly accused by their father several years earlier.

But Augustus could not disregard this client king who had been close to him and who had now been exonerated in the Nabataean affair. With reluctance and much misgiving, he wrote Herod a letter granting him the ancient Roman power of life and death over his sons. He added, however, that Herod should be very careful about using this power and should hold a public trial of his sons—not in his own kingdom of Judaea but at the old Phoenician city of Berytus (the modern Beirut) on the coast of the province of Syria. It must be a fair, open, and unprejudiced examination of the evidence against the brothers. Those hearing the evidence should include not only Herod's relatives and friends but also the top Roman magistrates in Syria (who would presumably be impartial) and King Archelaus too, since he was so closely associated with Alexander and Aristobulus. If the two princes were proved guilty of trying to murder their father, they could be punished with death; but if it was established that they were only planning to flee from Judaea, either to Archelaus or to some other well-wisher, they should be given no more than a warning.

Herod followed most of Augustus' instructions, but he did not invite King Archelaus to the trial. His anger against the Cappadocian monarch had not burned out. Archelaus had already stated that although he had agreed to receive the princes on their flight from Judaea, he was not involved with them in any kind of scheme against Herod. But Herod considered this statement an egregious lie and was afraid that at the trial Archelaus, whom he knew to be a good arguer, would plausibly pronounce more lies, prejudicing the court in the princes' favor.

Some of the most important individuals in the Roman East converged on Berytus for the trial. They included Herod himself—impatient now to kill his sons, thinking of little except their vileness and how he would requite it; his brother Pheroras and his sister Salome —almost tasting their triumph against these children of the long-dead Hasmonaean queen; Saturninus, the distinguished governor of Syria, with his distinguished sons; Pedanius, a high official directly under Saturninus; Volumnius, head of the province's finances; plus other eminent persons from various Eastern cities. In all, about one hundred fifty people gathered to hear the king of the Jews accuse the princes.

Alexander and Aristobulus themselves were not there. Herod had quartered them in a little town between Berytus and Sidon, where they would be conveniently out of the way yet close enough to appear in court if summoned.

It must have been embarrassing to many of the auditors when Herod rose and launched into his speech. According to Josephus, he screamed and ranted, making a great deal out of his sons' insolence toward him—which, he exclaimed, showed that they hated him and wanted to kill him. He read out loud from letters written by Alexander and Aristobulus, in which their intention to flee from Judaea was mentioned. Unfortunately for Herod's purpose these letters were not incriminating: they did not say anything about a scheme to assassinate Herod or even to betray him. But they said a great deal about how obnoxious a father he was; and the king capitalized on these remarks, building them up into evidence of disloyalty and of a patricidal plot. Close to tears, he mounted to his peroration. Augustus, he said, had given him the right to punish his children. The Law of the Jews, besides, stipulated that if a father possessed "a stubborn and rebellious son," he should bring the son before "the elders of the city" and accuse him of disobedience. "And all the men of his city shall stone him with stones, that he die." But although Herod might follow the Law in his own land, here in Syria he would ask the court to decide about the base princes.

Saturninus the governor spoke first. In his opinion Alexander and Aristobulus were guilty of flagrant offenses, but the auditors had no right to condemn them to death. Clemency, he implied, was the humane and civilized approach. His own three sons were present in the room; it would not be proper for him to recommend the execution of another man's sons, no matter how much Herod had suffered. Several other persons, including Saturninus' sons, also came out for moderation.

But then Volumnius, the financial agent, voted for death. He explained that anybody as savage toward his father as Alexander and Aristobulus certainly deserved to die. Most of the people who spoke after Volumnius also favored death. Some wanted to please Herod; some, hating Herod, wanted to make him commit the gross offense of killing his own children; a few perhaps felt that death was the only just sentence. The votes of Salome and Pheroras are not recorded.

A wait of many days followed, while Syrians and Jews wondered whether Herod would inflict on his sons the ultimate penalty. He went south along the Phoenician coast to Tyre, taking Alexander and Aristobulus with him. At Tyre he was soon greeted by Nicolaus, who had sailed from Italy to join him there. He told his faithful counselor the outcome of the trial and asked how men in Rome felt about his sons. Nicolaus replied that men in Rome felt Herod should not kill the princes no matter what they had done; it would be enough to put them in chains.

Perhaps the king, having won at Berytus, was finally wavering now that irrevocability faced him. It is unlikely that a flood of affection for his sons overwhelmed him so belatedly. He still must have wanted the princes to die; but a fear of public reaction throughout the rest of the world, and particularly at Rome, may have caused him to hesitate. His reputation could be seriously injured.

He brought his sons into Judaea, to the glistening port whose completion he had celebrated with splendid games three years ago—the Caesaraea of which he was so proud. The city's inhabitants were tense and nervous but too terrified of Herod to express themselves openly. Its population, part Greek and part Jewish, speculated in secret about the king's intention, argued in private about whether death was an equitable punishment, furtively debated the rights and wrongs of the trial itself, asked for news, heard muttered rumors, feared the old king and defended him. But finally a gruff old soldier named Tiro, whose son was a friend of Alexander, went through the streets crying out against Herod. Justice, he shouted, was dead; evil had triumphed; the trial had been a mockery.

This set off another series of examinations and tortures. Tiro stated that Herod's officers sympathized with Alexander and Aristobulus, and the king consequently had about three hundred officers arrested. A barber came forward with the story that Tiro had tried to bribe him to slit Herod's throat while trimming his beard, and that the money for the bribe was to be supplied by Alexander. Tiro and Tiro's son were stretched on the rack; so was the barber. Herod brought these three questionable persons, plus the three hundred disaffected officers, before the most loyal element among Caesaraea's citizens.

The Caesaraeans—taut, highly excited, needing an emotional release, needing victims—pelted them to death with wood and stones.

The king had nearly cleared the land of subversion. Only Alexander and Aristobulus remained to tease his suspicions, and they would not have to wait for death much longer. Herod ordered the princes taken to Sebaste, the Graeco-Roman city that he had fashioned out of the ancient town of Samaria. It was at Samaria, about thirty years before, that Mariamne had become his wife. Now her sons were strangled there.

IX

FATHER AND FIRSTBORN

Antipater was now sure of becoming king after Herod died, but he
still had much to worry about. The news of the strangling had set the
military firmly against him. Within the Judaean populace as a whole,
in fact, he could count few adherents; people were beginning to say
that he had contrived the deaths of his half brothers. Not only the
vulgar but the great, too, spread this rumor. Outside Judaea also,
those in high places thought Antipater contemptible. He did as much
as he could to make himself liked: he sent presents to men of influence in Judaea, in Syria, even at Rome. But this expedient did not
work. The recipients knew why the gifts had been sent and thought
him more contemptible than before.

Herod's conduct toward the fatherless children of Alexander and
Aristobulus was another source of worry. By Glaphyra (whom Herod
now sent back to her father in Cappadocia), Alexander had had two
sons. By Salome's daughter Berenice, Aristobulus had had three sons
and two daughters. All the children were still too little to pose any
immediate threat to Antipater, but Herod's kindness toward them
bothered him extremely. Although they were much too young for
marriage, Herod got them betrothed or promised—and the betrothals that he arranged for them were splendid, assuring them of riches
and high position.

Two of Aristobulus' children, for instance, were to be given to Antipater's own son and daughter. Much as this plan offended Antipater, however, the betrothal of Alexander's older son to a daughter of Pheroras disturbed him more. It meant that this boy would have as his well-wishers not only King Archelaus of Cappadocia, his maternal grandfather, but also rich Pheroras—last surviving brother of Herod himself and already tetrarch of Peraea, the region across the Jordan. With his extensive knowledge of court intrigue Antipater saw that such powerful backers could in time nullify his own claim to the throne.

Therefore he went to his father and, employing a more direct approach than usual, complained. The old king, overwrought and ill—possibly beginning to wonder whether the strangulation of his sons had been fair, and struggling against the horror of the doubt—talked to him testily and put him off. But Antipater was back on other occasions. He shifted to the indirect approach at which he was most competent, and by encomium and cajolery he finally got Herod to modify the betrothal arrangements. Alexander's son would not be betrothed to Pheroras' daughter; Antipater's own son would receive that eligible heiress instead. Since Antipater's son had originally been destined for a daughter of Aristobulus, that left this little girl without a promised husband. But Antipater volunteered to marry the daughter of Aristobulus himself. He probably figured that long before she was old enough for marriage, he could have this part of the bargain dissolved. For the time being, the match was advisable.

The trial and the stranglings insisted on haunting Herod's mind; the doubt as to whether the princes had truly been guilty gnawed at his quiet. Not that he could have enjoyed much quiet anyway, even after the matter of the betrothals was settled. He was constitutionally incapable of tranquillity, and besides, too many other things were harassing him. Much of the time he did not feel well. He was old; in a few years he would have to give up his kingdom and face the God of the Jews. He wanted to put his house in order first. Antipater would reign in his place—that was determined; but did Antipater deserve to reign? If his favorite son had surreptitiously prejudiced him against Alexander and Aristobulus, if his favorite son had in fact deluded him, whom could he trust?

Certainly not his brother Pheroras, still under the influence of his unspeakable wife, the erstwhile slave girl. Their sister Salome, who had split with Pheroras now that Alexander and Aristobulus were dead, told Herod something about the slave girl that helped to make his days unpleasant. Pheroras' wife, she said, was the center of a female cabal directed against him. Another member of the cabal was Antipater's mother, Doris. Antipater himself, she added, associated with these ladies, probably so that with their help he could rob his unsuspecting father of whatever years of life might remain.

Although Herod hoped that his sister in her native malice was exaggerating the situation, he strongly felt that she was telling the truth. Antipater in fact did attend drinking parties with Pheroras' wife and her group. Pheroras himself was an adherent of the group, partly because he followed his wife in everything and partly because he kept dreading that Herod might try again to make him give the woman up. Herod, disillusioned in his son and disgusted with his brother, forbade Antipater to have anything to do with Pheroras' wife and her circle, or with Pheroras either.

Herod's resentment of the woman whom his brother refused to relinquish was so intense that he thought she must be using love potions on Pheroras to retain his violent affection; otherwise Pheroras would have discarded her long ago. But the worst thing about her, in Herod's opinion, was her sympathy with the Pharisees.

The popularly supported Pharisees were at the moment a very powerful force in Judaea. Their stern traditionalism—their minute, uncompromising emphasis on purification through ritual, on the laws put by God into the Torah, and on the interpretations that had grown up around those laws—appealed strongly to the lower classes. So did the Pharisees' beliefs in angels, in a resurrection, in the immortality of the soul, and in an afterlife that would heap retribution on the wicked but reward the long-suffering good and the ceremonially pure (all of which the aristocratic Sadducees denied). So did the old-fashioned simplicity by which the Pharisees tried to live—their rejection of luxury, their deference to elders. So did their hope in a Messiah who would come to rescue the people from misery and pain and bring a new age to the corrupt old world. And so, above all, did their hatred for things foreign.

Their name meant "separatists." Early in their existence the Pharisees had separated themselves from the Hellenism of the later Hasmonaean rulers; and under Herod they were separating themselves from the pernicious Graeco-Roman culture. They were the purists, and the common people consequently looked up to them as qualified leaders. At the beginning of Herod's reign they had supported him, partly because of his evident opposition to the Greek-loving Hasmonaeans whom the aristocratic Sadducees favored; but his enthusiasm for Greek ways and his subservience to Rome soon outraged them. Now they would have liked nothing better than to see him dethroned or dead.

When the Jews were required to swear an oath of loyalty to both Augustus and Herod, six thousand Pharisees flatly refused. The king may have excused them from the oath to himself (the facts are not clear); but he certainly could not excuse them from the oath to Augustus. He fined them instead. Pheroras' wife, rich on her husband's money, paid the fine for them—to Herod's great dismay.

Several of the Pharisees, claiming the power to predict the future, prophesied for Pheroras' wife. They said that Herod would lose his throne; that his descendants would not hold it either, but that it would go to herself and her husband, then to whatever children they might be blessed with. The prophecy sounds like something dictated more by self-interest than by inspiration. At any rate Herod may have thought so when Salome, having ferreted it out, reported it to him. He considered it definitely disloyal, and he had some important Pharisees killed. This action did not improve the relations between Herod and his brother's wife, or between Herod and his brother.

Antipater decided at about the same time that it would be a good idea to get out of Judaea for a while. Strictly speaking, he had not obeyed his father's injunction to stop associating with Pheroras and Pheroras' wife. Although he did not see them anymore in public, he attended the secret meetings they held at night—and Salome might discover this at any moment. His father's distrust of him, besides, threatened his security. If Herod had strangled Alexander and Aristobulus, sooner or later he might not feel averse to killing Antipater too. At least that was a possibility. The old king was almost a madman anyway, in his son's opinion.

Therefore Antipater wrote to his friends at Rome, who then wrote to Herod, suggesting that he be sent to the capital. Herod complied. Once at Rome, Antipater did his father an excellent service by pursuing the charges against Syllaeus. The Nabataean had been ordered by Augustus to give Herod a great deal of money, first, in return for all the trouble he had caused, and second, in repayment of the long-standing Nabataean debt; but he had made no effort to carry out the order.

After Antipater was gone, Herod exiled Pheroras to his own tetrarchy, the land called Peraea on the eastern side of the Jordan. The king had apparently renewed his demand that Pheroras divorce his wife, and Pheroras' unflinching refusal had at last become too much for Herod. Pheroras may have been obstinate not only because he loved the woman but because he believed the prophecy. His wife, it seems, had subtly persuaded him that the Pharisees were true prophets. If the Pharisees said that the throne would not go to Herod's progeny but that descendants of Pheroras would rule in Judaea, it was fact. He looked forward to becoming the father of kings.

The brothers parted on final terms; in fact Pheroras swore solemnly that he would not return to Judaea until Herod had died. Not long after this the pains in Herod's intestines grew worse, and people feared that the king was lying on his deathbed. Since Antipater was far away at Rome, Pheroras was sent for to receive Herod's last instructions as to the government of the realm. But Pheroras kept his oath: he did not come. And Herod, perhaps out of spite, started to feel better.

All of a sudden Pheroras fell sick, and the news was rushed to Herod. Showing more concern than Pheroras deserved, Herod hastened to Peraea to be with his last living brother—even though his last living brother had not asked for him. The king arrived just in time to see Pheroras die. Then the oath was broken: at Herod's command Pheroras returned to Judaea as a corpse, suitably prepared for burial. He was entombed at Jerusalem.

By royal decree the court was thrown into mourning. During this period, while people cultivated the gravity of hypocritic grief—and while Herod perhaps grieved sincerely—the rumor circulated that Pheroras had been poisoned. Two former slaves whom Pheroras had freed went to Herod with a story concerning a woman of Arabia, where the most effective poisons were concocted, and the meal that Pheroras had eaten just before he got sick.

Slave women, freedwomen, and persons of higher rank now screamed on the rack as Herod tried to penetrate the new mystery. The old king's suspicions, never quiet, fed on the agony. It does not seem to have been clearly established whether Pheroras was poisoned or not, or if so, by whom. But in the course of the tortures a great deal of other information came out—information highly prejudicial to the unsuspecting Antipater off in Rome.

People said that Antipater had continued to meet secretly with Pheroras' wife and the members of her cabal after the king had ordered him not to; that he hated his father and thirsted to be king; that he feared that Herod would make Pheroras king instead; and that he wished Herod would hurry up and die. All of this sounded like a prelude to treachery. Then Antipater's agent, a Samaritan, was put on the rack—and this man affirmed that Antipater had procured a poison from Egypt, had arranged to have it conveyed to Pheroras in Peraea, and had wanted Pheroras to kill Herod with it. Since Antipater would be in Rome when the killing occurred, he would escape suspicion. Pheroras, according to the agent, had handed the poison to his wife for safekeeping.

Therefore Pheroras' wife, the new-made widow, was summoned to appear before the king who detested her and whom she had fought tooth and nail while her husband lived. The woman trembled now as she faced Herod. With torture running rampant at the court, she was sure to be subjected to horrible punishment—to be mangled, to have her body ripped apart—and then killed. Herod demanded to know whether Antipater had commissioned the poison. She said he had, and offered to bring it; but instead of coming back she jumped off the roof of the palace.

She was not dead, however—only bruised and unconscious. When she was carried back the king had her tended to, and as soon as she could talk somewhat normally, the grilling resumed.

He asked her why she had thrown herself from the roof, although the answer was obvious. He said that if she revealed everything she knew about the poison and Antipater's treachery, he would excuse her from all punishment. In fact he would not even torture her slaves. But if she persisted in defying him and holding back the truth, as she had been doing for years, he would have her body crushed and torn into many pieces, so that not enough of it would be left to justify a funeral.

This promise got results. She swore that Antipater was the villain who had procured the poison from Egypt and sent it to her husband for use on Herod. Pheroras had planned to administer it somehow, but Herod's surprise visit had changed his mind: he could not kill a brother who, uninvited, had come to see him on his deathbed. She had thrown most of the poison into the fire but kept a little so that if Herod ever started persecuting her, she would have a ready exit.

Again she volunteered to bring the poison to Herod—and this time she came back with it, enclosed in a little box. The king held to his promise: he let her go free. But the mother and brother of the man who had carried the poison from Egypt were put on the rack, and they identified the box. For the king it was conclusive evidence. The son whom he had loved above his other children, the son to whom he had willed the kingdom, the firstborn of all his sons, could not wait for him to die.

But there was still more evidence to come; and Herod, in his masochistic desire to search out the whole truth, heard all of it. One of Antipater's freedmen, named Bathyllus, arrived at court and was promptly tortured. A particularly deadly poison, concocted from the venom of asps and other snakes, was found in his possession. Bathyllus admitted that Antipater, not having heard about Pheroras' death, had sent him from Rome with this mixture, to be delivered to Pheroras for use on Herod in case the Egyptian poison proved too weak to do the job.

Bathyllus also carried letters from Rome designed for Herod's perusal. These letters calumniated two young sons of Herod who, like Alexander and Aristobulus before them, had been sent to Rome for their education. Antipater was evidently jealous of them, thinking that Herod might possibly be preparing them for kingship. Some of the letters had been written by friends whom Antipater had bribed; others were Antipater's own forgeries.

The king might be old, and the pains in his abdomen might be getting worse, but when it came to hypocrisy he was still more than a match for his son. He wrote Antipater an affectionate letter, calling him back to Judaea.

Antipater, however, was already on his way. When he started out from Rome he had much to feel confident about. Augustus had ratified Herod's will leaving him the Judaean throne. His legal triumph over Syllaeus, which resulted in the Nabataean's execution, had disposed of the Nabataean problem for the time being, so that it would not encumber the kingdom he was soon to inherit. This victory had also gone far to prove that he alone was worthy to succeed Herod. His cleverness had inspired the admiration, if not the friendship, of the emperor. The letters denouncing Herod's young sons had presumably done their duty. Perhaps Pheroras had done his duty too, although the man could not be depended on.

But at Tarentum, the port on the heel of Italy, Antipater received the news that Pheroras had died and that Herod still reigned. He could not help feeling extremely disappointed. In Pheroras he had lost a most valuable tool; his father's murder would have to be planned all over again and entrusted to other hands. Very much agitated, he set sail for Asia Minor. When he landed in Cilicia he was given the warm, fatherly letter from Herod. In addition to fondly inviting him back, it alluded to the fact that his mother Doris had been banished from the court. The matter was passed over lightly in the letter, as if Antipater should not worry about it—but it made him apprehensive. If his mother was out of favor, so perhaps was he; and sailing home might mean sailing to torture and death. At the old Cilician port of Celenderis, from which he had planned to embark for Caesaraea, he hesitated. Some of his friends and traveling companions advised him not to sail, stressing Herod's propensity for killing off the members of his family. Others, however, said that failure to return to Judaea would confirm Herod's lowest suspicions about him. Antipater had enough faith in his own adroitness to feel that once he was back at court he could charm his father into gullibility again. Besides, his absence gave his enemies the chance to whisper and rail against him unchecked. So he set sail.

His reception at Caesaraea was ominously silent; it was as if people expected him to die soon rather than to reign as their king. But he showed no surprise or fear. He put on a bold front and, with the magnificent train of followers that had traveled back with him, proceeded to Jerusalem to face Herod.

The guards at the palace doors would not let the magnificent train in. The king had issued orders that only Antipater himself should be allowed inside.

His father, he discovered, was playing host to the governor of Syria —a man named Varus, successor to the Saturninus who had helped to judge Alexander and Aristobulus. Fourteen years later this same Varus would lead Roman legions to one of the most crushing defeats they had ever suffered, when barbarians in the Teutoburg Forest in

Germany massacred them to a man and deeply humiliated the whole Empire. At present, however, there was no ignominy attached to Varus' name—only the majesty of Rome.

Antipater, exchanging a filial front for his previous bold facade, stepped up to Herod to embrace him. He would present to Varus the picture of the dutiful prince back from abroad, glad to be home with his father.

But his father pushed him away and looked in another direction, then launched into a typical Herodian rant—accusing him of attempting murder, calling him a parricide. Tomorrow, Herod shouted, Varus would judge him. He had better go now, because he did not have much time to prepare his defense.

Antipater could do nothing except look injured and leave.

The trial on the following day was a well-attended spectacle. Varus sat in judgment. Herod was present to speak against Antipater as he had spoken against Alexander and Aristobulus. Many relatives of Herod were on hand, including his sister Salome; so were some of Herod's favorite courtiers and some of Antipater's closest sycophants. People who had survived the torture were there also to testify against the prince. Slaves of Antipater's mother Doris were brought in. They had been arrested a few days ago; and a letter of warning from Doris to Antipater, saying that the king knew everything, had been found in their charge. Worst of all from Antipater's standpoint, Nicolaus stood ready to conduct the prosecution—Nicolaus the chief counselor of Herod and the most skillful rhetorician in Judaea, who had won the cause of the Jews before Agrippa in Ionia, who had defeated the sly Syllaeus before Augustus several years ago, and who was apparently invincible.

Antipater may have plotted out a course of action during the night, or he may have decided to rely mainly on his native resourcefulness and craft; we do not know. When the trial began, he fell flat on his face before Herod and implored the king to be fair, to show no prejudice, to let him prove his filial devotion and his unblemished innocence.

The king showed a great deal of prejudice, however, in his speech to Varus. In former years, he said, he had favored Antipater over Alexander and Aristobulus, and he willingly confessed that he had been at fault in this. His partiality toward this wretch of a son in fact had provoked the two brothers to whatever disloyal thoughts they might have been culpable of. It would be impossible to name all the kindnesses he had showered on Antipater. Recently he had let the prince share in the government; he had willed the throne to him, had allotted him a more-than-generous annual income, had supplemented this income with a fantastic travel allowance for the trip to Rome, and had written about him to Augustus in terms of the highest praise. And this son wanted to kill him.

Herod said more. Antipater was a master of duplicity. Varus had better be on his guard against the specious glitter of this devil of a man who had duped his own father. Antipater could speak so easily, argue so deftly, and plead so plausibly that he could win almost anybody over. He must be done away with. Herod called himself a lonely old man; but even so, he said, he would kill all the sons who were left him if they resembled Antipater—if they thirsted for the blood of their father.

The prince, still down on the floor, agreed that Herod had been an extraordinarily kind father. How could any son scheme against so generous a man and expect to get away with it? How could any son hope to hide such glaring ingratitude from God? As a matter of fact, Antipater went on, God knew that he was innocent.

Nicolaus now spoke. In a preamble he marveled at Antipater's remarkable cunning. Then, in a clear and logical manner, he demonstrated that Antipater had defamed the characters of Alexander and Aristobulus and had conspired to poison Herod. Nicolaus maintained convincingly that Antipater should be held more responsible than anybody else for the deaths of his two half brothers, and he described in lucid detail the evidence involving Antipater in the poison plots. After such a masterful presentation, no counterargument seemed possible.

But Antipater after a brief silence had recourse again to God. He swore to God that he was unjustly accused. This was as much as even he could say—but he held to it stubbornly.

Varus had the poison brought in, together with a criminal who was under a death sentence. To test the concoction he ordered the criminal to drink it. The man obeyed and fell dead. Varus rose from his chair, and the onlookers realized that the trial was over.

The next day, when the governor left for the return trip to Syria, people wondered exactly what his decision had been. Herod meanwhile had put Antipater in chains. People said to each other that Varus must have enjoined Herod to do this. The king dispatched a letter to Augustus, telling the emperor about the trial and about Antipater's great guilt. He also sent envoys to Augustus to corroborate the letter. The emperor would decide whether Herod had the right to execute his son.

For the present the prince languished in his chains. Perhaps he would be able to squeeze out of this situation after all, if his sick father died without having carried out the execution. Affairs, however, continued to go against him. Evidence was brought to light that he had even plotted against his aunt Salome. The king wrote a new will, naming another son to the throne and excluding Antipater from any share in his domains.

Herod's intestinal pains were growing worse all the time, and to the courtiers it did not seem likely that he could last much longer. The year was 5 or 4 B.C. As the king's illness was advancing, Christ was born and passed safely through babyhood. (Scholars are now in agreement that postclassical theologians erred by several years regarding the date of Christ's birth, and that Jesus was born in 4 B.C. at the latest—perhaps as much as three or four years earlier.) At this time, says the Gospel according to Saint Matthew, occurred the so-called Massacre of the Innocents, when on Herod's orders all male children of Bethlehem two years old or younger were slaughtered because of a prediction that a boy who had been born in that town would be king of the Jews. Josephus, however, does not mention a massacre at Bethlehem.

Herod was probably suffering from cancer of the bowels, but Josephus' gruesome description of the disease would imply a number of complications. In addition to the sharp abdominal pains, Josephus states, Herod had a ravenous appetite, his feet were swollen with dropsy, he experienced fever and convulsions, he discharged pus, he itched all over, he breathed asthmatically, his breath was nauseating, and he bred worms in his body. Many of the Jews, hearing about Herod's condition, surmised that God was punishing the king for his crimes, especially his offenses against the Law.

But in the opinion of two rabbis there was one offense that needed immediate correction by the people themselves. Some time previously Herod had put up over the great gate of the Temple a massive golden eagle. Fastening a graven image in the holy precincts was in itself an act of outrageous impiety; what made it worse was that this particular image represented Rome. It is surprising that Herod, even though he characteristically pandered to Rome, would contaminate by means of this eagle the structure he was proudest of and had taken so long to build—the one overwhelming testimony to his Judaic faith. Jews entering the Temple looked up and hated the eagle, hated Rome, hated Herod. The two rabbis, revered exponents of the Law, decided that the king's illness should be taken advantage of for the removal of the profane object. There was indeed a rumor that Herod was already dead; and even if it was not true, the government would surely be weaker now than at other times. Even so, however, retribution could almost certainly be expected.

These two rabbis were so renowned that Pharisaic youths would come to them in large crowds to hear them expound the Law. They therefore had a ready-made band of rebels for the accomplishment of the holy work. They told these eager young men that tearing down the eagle would be a dangerous job, that some of them might even die in its fulfillment, but that they would be doing something glorious and their deaths would be beautiful. God besides would reward their immortal souls everlastingly for their noble sacrifice. In a mood similar to that of the men who had tried to assassinate Herod in the amphitheater many years before, these youthful fanatics set out on their pious project.

It was noon, and the Temple precincts were full of people. Suddenly these worshipers were astonished to see agile young men climbing down ropes from the roof above the Temple gate. The climbers carried axes. When they came to the eagle, they chopped away at the hated gold intruder. Ecstatic but terrified of the consequences, the people watched while the bird crashed to the pavement. Some of the young rebels, jubilant and afraid of nothing, mingled with the crowd. But an informer had run to the captain of the Temple guard, which was stationed at the Antonia—the fortress that stood close to the Temple at the highest point on the terraced plateau. The captain, at the head of many soldiers, came in a hurry; there was confusion and the people scattered. So did some of the young fanatics—but about forty of them were caught, together with their two teachers. None of these men had made an effort to escape. Their purpose had been accomplished; martyrdom was now welcome.

The two rabbis and the forty-odd rebels were brought before the ailing monarch, who asked whether it was true that they had dared to throw down the eagle.

It was.

What man had told them to commit this act?

The Law had told them. God, Author of the Law, had singled them out to end the desecration of the Temple. Herod's pronouncements and the decrees of Rome might terrify some people, but in the face of the Law those rules looked pale and puny. The youths and the rabbis rejoiced that God had chosen them and that they had been able to answer His summons.

The king, who could not understand their spiritual satisfaction and who contemplated his own approaching death with horror, expressed surprise that they could be so calm when they knew that they would soon be executed.

They knew also, they responded, that God would give them eternal happiness. They were not calm—they were very eager.

Soon after this the king left for his winter palace at Jericho. He had the rebels brought there also, chained of course. In spite of his sickness he called an assembly of the principal citizens in the amphitheater. Having been carried into the structure, he lay on a couch (since he could not stand) and addressed the crowd with as much force as remained to him. The rebels, he said, had violated the glorious Temple—the building that he, at enormous personal expense, had given to his people. Disguising themselves as champions of the Law, they had committed sacrilege. They must be punished.

Understandably enough the assembly of principal citizens feared that if Herod got started on a series of executions he would not know when to stop, so that justifiable punishment would turn into a bloody fit of torture and killing. The citizens therefore requested him to restrict the punishment to those already caught rather than trying to find, catch, and convict the rebels who had escaped the Temple guard. Herod, too sick to confute his subjects with his usual vehemence, gave his grudging promise. The two rabbis and the youths who had climbed down from the Temple roof were burned alive.

The king's illness was by now almost unbearable to him, and holy men said that God was punishing him for burning the rabbis. Still waiting for word from Augustus about Antipater, he went across the Jordan to a place on the east side of the Dead Sea called Callirrhoë in the desperate, bleak hope that the hot baths at this spot would restore his health. In addition to the baths, the physicians who accompanied him tried another remedy: they lowered him into a tub of tepid oil. He responded to this treatment by collapsing into unconsciousness. Some of the servants, thinking he was dead, set up a howl of lamentation. He revived enough to realize that not many more days were left of his life. In an act of generosity calculated not to injure his kingly image, he specified sums of money to be distributed to the men in his army, to his officers, and to his friends. Then he was taken back to Jericho—where Antipater, still in chains, felt he could not wait much longer for the death that must come soon.

Josephus tells the story that Herod summoned the leading men in the nation to Jericho and locked them all up in the hippodrome. According to this story, the king then asked Salome and her current husband to carry out an ingenious plan he had devised. The Jews, he knew, would not weep with wholehearted grief at his death; in fact, there would probably be a great deal of ill-concealed rejoicing throughout Judaea. He wanted tears instead. Therefore, as soon as he was dead Salome and her husband were to send soldiers to the hippodrome to slaughter the men imprisoned there. The wailing of their relatives would fill the land with sorrow as the king was being laid away in his tomb.

It is difficult, however, to attribute so grisly a plan even to Herod. If he summoned the prominent Jews to Jericho at all, his purpose was perhaps to communicate his final wishes to them, or at most to keep them from causing trouble in the confusion that might follow his death. Although he was not at all averse to making terror a part of his image, surely the inexcusable butchery of many Jewish aristocrats would, even in his own warped opinion, have done his memory more harm than good.

The incessant abdominal pain was alleviated a little by a letter he received from Augustus, giving him permission to do whatever he wanted with Antipater—to banish him, for instance, or execute him. Now Herod could lawfully kill his oldest son, most odious of all his children.

Before he had a chance to carry out this wish, however, the torment in his bowels grew so fierce that he resolved on suicide. He ordered an apple and a knife to peel it with. Grasping the knife in his right hand, he raised it to plunge it into his diseased body. But a cousin rushed up and grabbed the hand, and the king still lived.

Noise and confusion arose in the palace as servants and courtiers bewailed the attempted suicide, talked about it excitedly, and, since they expected Herod's actual death at any time now, perhaps indulged in a little anticipatory mourning. In his cell Antipater heard the commotion and misinterpreted it: he assumed that his father was dead and that the mourning had really begun. The prince calculated that his best chance for release from prison was right now, while the court was in turmoil because the long tyranny had ended. Besides, his impatience had gotten out of control.

In his most winning manner he offered temptation to the commander of the prison guards: a great sum of money for the opportunity to escape. Either the soldier was incorruptibly loyal to Herod, however, or else he thought that Antipater was the wrong man to pin one's hopes on and that he could profit more by exposing the prince. He ran to the king and told him the whole story.

It was the last piece of evidence to be given by anyone against Antipater. The dying, vengeful father sent some soldiers to stab him to death in his cell. The men carried out the order at once.

Herod did not wait long to follow his son; he died within five days. There is no account of his final moments. If he uttered last-breath injunctions or passed away in screams, they are unrecorded. At the king's command Antipater's funeral had been a miserable affair; but Herod's funeral showed all the magnificence that this royal man desired. The king who would be called Herod the Great could not be put away cheaply.

Since he had stipulated that he was to be buried at Herodium, the fort named after himself that stood about twenty miles southwest of Jericho, the funeral cortege had a long walk. It was an impressive cortege, consisting of his remaining sons and a great many other relatives; his bodyguards; his Thracian, German, and Galatian soldiers, and the rest of his army (all the men in battle array as if marching to war rather than to bury a king); and five hundred servants, perfuming the air with costly spices. His solid-gold coffin glistened with precious gems. He lay on a bed of royal purple, and purple cloth covered his corpse. A diadem, signifying royalty, encircled his head; above it he wore a gold crown. His scepter, staff of regal office, lay beside the right hand that could no longer hold it.

Very slowly, accomplishing about a mile a day, the resplendent procession wound through the hot, dry, tawny land south of Jericho and west of the waveless Dead Sea. Finally the mourners saw ahead of them Herodium, the body's destination. Herod had built this fort when he was in his glory, and he had felt highly satisfied with it. Its round towers topped a hill that was shaped like a woman's breast. A flight of two hundred white-marble steps, gleaming in the sunshine, ascended the hill. At the bottom of the rise, where the desert ended, Herod had built palaces to house his guests; and the top too held much palatial architecture as well as the grim fortress. During Herod's visits all Herodium had glowed with color and pulsed with activity, as courtiers and soldiers and servants pursued their pleasures or their duties at this man-made oasis surrounded by waterless wastes.

Up the white-marble steps moved the procession, slow and grand, the soldiers' equipment glittering in the relentless sun, the heavy coffin shining. At the summit, in the citadel that overlooked the sterile land, the bearers left their burden.

X

HEROD'S HEIRS

Herod's death in the spring of 4 B.C. closed a reign of thirty-four years counting from the time he defeated old Hyrcanus' brother Antigonus, or thirty-seven years counting from the time the senate at Rome named him king. Many citizens of Judaea could remember no other master; like the emperor Augustus, Herod had seemed a persisting condition of life. It was therefore almost inevitable that there should be much confusion and conjecture at his death. The citizens felt themselves at a loss in the sudden absence of strong government. The confusion would go on for years—chronically resolved, then breaking out again, and gradually intensifying. Herod's kingdom would be split into three parts. In time much of it would come under the direct control of Rome. But Roman intervention would not settle the disorder, which stemmed as always from Jewish distrust of foreign ways and foreign religions. Religious fanaticism would grow, no matter what was done to quell it.

To complicate matters at the beginning, nobody seemed sure about the succession. The large number of Herod's sons, the execution of sons who were expected to succeed him, the changes he kept making in his will, and the fact that Augustus had to ratify the will in any case all compounded the initial confusion.

In his last days—apparently just after ordering Antipater's death

—the king had altered his will once more. When he died the new will was read aloud by one of his ministers to the soldiers assembled in the amphitheater at Jericho. In this document he gave the kingdom of Judaea proper to Archelaus, his son by a wife named Malthace. To Antipas, another son by Malthace, he gave the fertile land of Galilee and also the district of Peraea on the east side of the Jordan; Antipas, however, was to be called tetrarch rather than king. Archelaus was probably not yet twenty, and Antipas was still younger. To Philip, son by a wife named Cleopatra of Jerusalem, went several largely non-Jewish regions north and east of the Sea of Galilee. Like Antipas, Philip was to rank only as a tetrarch, not as a king.

Although Archelaus was not yet king, he decided to make a speech to his people anyway. After dutifully if not sincerely observing the customary seven days of mourning, he gave the citizens of Jerusalem a costly funeral feast and addressed them from a high platform temporarily set up outside the Temple proper. Robed in white and sitting on a throne of gold, he thanked the crowd for its acclamations and for its enthusiastic approval of him as prospective king. He would not of course call himself king until the will had been ratified by Augustus. But meanwhile it was nice to know that the people did not blame him at all for his father's sins; as king he would rule much more benevolently than his father had done.

Taking him at his word and impatient for the benevolence to start, the people shouted demands at him: that he reduce the annual taxes, that he abolish sales taxes, and that he free the men whom Herod had thrown into prison, some of them a long time ago. Since he considered the people a source of his strength, Archelaus cheerfully gave the impression that he was agreeable to everything.

Later he made sacrifice at the Temple in the prescribed manner and held another feast, this time in company with his closest adherents. Things were not looking bad for Archelaus. If he were careful and congenial he would soon have a kingdom to rule. But he discovered immediately that being careful and congenial was very difficult in a land recovering from tyranny. In particular the Pharisees took advantage of this period of leniency to lead laments for the two rabbis and forty-odd youths executed for tearing down the Roman eagle. Those who had been afraid to weep in public while Herod was alive now set up howls all over the city, and the mourning had strong political overtones. They screamed insults at the memory of Herod, letting out the anger and the Romanophobia that had been so long pent up. In revenge for the execution of the youths and the rabbis, they said, the men who had been Herod's favorites should be punished. Herod had in the course of his wickedness removed the high priest from office for not preventing the destruction of the eagle, and had appointed an inadequate man in his place. This substitute high priest was an offense to Judaism and must be dismissed.

Archelaus planned to travel to Rome at once to make sure that Augustus confirmed the will. But he could not afford to leave an unruly crowd in Jerusalem—a mob of malcontents who might rebel at any moment. In such a situation his father would probably have sent mercenary soldiers to cut the people down, or at least have put their leaders under torture, but Archelaus still hoped to preserve his image as a mild man. Therefore he did not openly object to the people's demands but sent an officer to mollify the crowd. Actually granting the demands would, like rebellion, make him look incompetent at Rome; but if the officer could persuade the people to calm down, everything might turn out all right.

Everything, however, did not. Infuriated by the very sight of the officer, the people yelled and jeered, roared like beasts, created such a clamor that the poor man could not make himself heard. Afraid that if he lingered much longer they would kill him with stones, he reported back to Archelaus, who sent another representative. But this one fared as badly as the first, and so did several more. The mob, growing angrier all the time, shouted out, "Stone them! Stone them to death!" Meanwhile disaffected people kept joining the throng, until the whole thing looked very much like an insurrection. Archelaus thought that perhaps he had better copy his father and use force.

It was the period of Passover, when all Jews were supposed to come to Jerusalem. Many did come—some from towns and farms in Judaea and Galilee, some from Antioch and other cities of Syria, a few from places as far away as Alexandria or Tarsus or Ephesus. Thousands of pilgrims jammed the streets, the press getting thicker all the time. The inns were packed. Those who could find no room in the city itself camped in the fields outside under the April sky. The pilgrims had come to commemorate God's sparing of His chosen people, when He had killed the firstborn of Egypt but not the firstborn of the Jews. Lambs would be sacrificed at the Temple, and everyone would eat unleavened bread in solemn remembrance of God's kindness to Israel. From Archelaus' standpoint it was a dangerous period. These great crowds—their national and religious sensitivities sharpened by Passover, their mood fervent, almost fanatic—might easily be stimulated into rebellion by rabble-rousing Pharisees.

As the multitude of poor people stood in the Temple crying out in protest against the execution of the two rabbis and the rebel youths who had loved God enough to tear down the image, the rabble-rousers provided food for them. The food gave them more strength with which to protest. Archelaus decided that he must abandon clemency immediately, or the whole Temple area would be seething with sedition. He dispatched a cohort of legionaries, under the command of a tribune, to quiet the people, and he instructed them to bring the ringleaders to him for punishment. But even at full strength a cohort consisted of only about five hundred men, an inadequate force for coping with the roaring multitude at the Temple. The frenzied worshipers, armed with stones, mobbed the soldiers. They threw to kill; and although the soldiers succeeded in spearing quite a few, more kept coming. Battered and pounded, their faces smashed and their limbs broken, many of the Romans fell and died. A few, the tribune among them, limped and tottered back to Archelaus.

The worshipers at the Temple turned again to their sacrifices, performing them now with a calm joy. But out in the fields camped thousands of Jews who might feel inspired to revolt any minute. A greater show of force was needed, in Archelaus' opinion. Stung to belated action, he sent the whole army out to the fields. The pilgrims were at sacrifice. Most of them scattered to the hills and safety, but the horsemen slaughtered three thousand. That ended Passover.

Archelaus journeyed from Jerusalem to Caesaraea, from which he would sail to Italy. With him went the great rhetorician Nicolaus; Ptolemy, the head of the royal finances; Salome (who stood to inherit much lucrative property); and a wide assortment of relatives. With all this support it did not seem, on the surface, as if Archelaus should have a hard time winning Augustus' approval, but matters were not that simple. Archelaus' full brother Antipas, unhappy with the prospect of being only a tetrarch and not ruling in Judaea proper, had decided to contest the will. He planned to sail to Italy about the same time Archelaus did. And although their aunt Salome seemed to favor Archelaus' claim to the throne of Judaea, actually she did not. Devious as usual, she worked for Antipas while she traveled with Archelaus. She talked at length with the assortment of relatives, criticizing Archelaus' handling of the Passover crisis and calling him weak and foolish.

Although the emperor was probably tired of dirty squabbles within the Herodian family, he listened patiently to the claims of the rival brothers to the Judaean throne. There was a great deal to be said for Antipas' claim. In his previous will, made before his sanity had been damaged by the approach of death, Herod had designated Antipas as heir to the kingdom. Archelaus besides had not mourned his father's passing with due respect—had in fact feigned sorrow in the daytime but gotten joyously drunk at night—and had started acting like a king almost immediately although he was still not legitimately one. His slaughter of the Jews during Passover had been worse than high-handed, it had been impious: he had killed the pilgrims who had come to worship their God, and he had filled the holy Temple itself with corpses.

In Archelaus' favor, however, as Nicolaus pointed out, were the facts that he was the older brother (though both were still young) and that he had been named king in the will that superseded all Herod's older wills. Besides, the Passover trouble had been caused by men of violence—rebels, destroyers of law and order, menaces to Rome and to Augustus—and Archelaus had been right to kill such people.

At the end of the hearing Augustus made no official pronouncement in favor of either candidate, but his remarks indicated some partiality toward Archelaus.

While matters were in this uncertain condition, the emperor received word from Varus, still governor of Syria, that the contumacious Jews were causing trouble again. A Roman named Sabinus, the imperial financial agent for Syria, was trying to take over Herod's property—ostensibly in the interest of Augustus—until the emperor could confirm the will. He had already threatened Archelaus at Caesaraea before Archelaus and Antipas sailed for Rome; now he proceeded to Jerusalem, where he made Herod's great palace his home. Either through eagerness to show Augustus that he was determined to protect the imperial financial claims or, more likely, from irresistible avarice at the thought of all the gold hidden in Herod's forts, he summoned the commanders of the forts and the treasury officials who had served under Herod, and told them that from now on they would be answerable to him. They disagreed, saying that they were answerable to Archelaus, and soon Sabinus discovered that he had sparked a revolt.

Varus marched from Syria with his soldiers, restored order, and returned to Antioch, leaving one legion at Jerusalem. Sabinus used this legion to harass the Jews; he also armed slaves and used them. He tried to seize Herod's forts and, accompanied by his troops, searched for the hidden treasures, rummaging around where he had no business. He did not understand that the Jews' new sense of freedom could not be easily suppressed and that his terrorist techniques were badly timed. Coming after years of silent, sullen, helpless resentment against a tyrant ruling for Rome, these techniques goaded the people into violence.

Seven weeks after Passover occurred the Feast of Weeks, or Pentecost. It was an agricultural festival, when loaves of leavened bread were offered in thanks to God at Jerusalem; and in 4 B.C., in a land still largely agricultural, it meant a great deal. As at Passover the city was so full that one could hardly move in the streets. Pentecost crowds were usually enormous, but this one was almost unbelievable. Farmers came from the grainfields, vineyards, and olive orchards of Galilee; converted Arabs came from dry Idumaea, Herod's own birthplace; young men came from the fertile oasis of Jericho, less than a day's walk away, and from the arid stretches east of the Jordan. Piety was by no means the only motive. Remembering the Passover riots and reasoning that a religious festival offered the best opportunity for rebellion, thousands were on hand to fight Sabinus and his Roman legionaries. They were well armed and much better organized than the Passover crowds. One group occupied the hated hippodrome that Herod had built to please the Romans; two other groups climbed to the top of the Temple hill and occupied the east and west ends of the plateau. Sabinus in a panic wrote to Varus, asking him for help, asking him to come with his army while there was still a Roman legion left at Jerusalem to rescue. Then he shut himself up in the Tower of Phasael, which adjoined the Herodian palace at the opposite edge of the city from the Temple.

From the comparative quiet of this retreat he ordered the Roman soldiers to attack the Temple hill. Being Roman soldiers, they immediately obeyed; it did not occur to them to ask whether they were serving Sabinus' avarice. In orderly fashion they advanced to the hill, mounted it, and set upon their enemies. They were probably outnumbered, but the Jewish rabble knew little about efficient fighting. Soon the Romans gained the upper hand. The Jews, however, paid very little attention to the fact that the legionaries were defeating them. With fanatical fury they kept fighting anyway, glad to meet their efficient pagan masters face to face, glad to die for Judaism, still stubbornly hoping for victory.

Many of them climbed to the roof of the colonnade surrounding the top of the hill—the elaborate portico, several pillars deep, whose thick and lofty Corinthian columns supported cedarwood ceilings inlaid with gold. From this height they carried on the kind of warfare they knew best, throwing great stones down to crush the Romans more than fifty feet below, sending smaller stones singing from slingshots, firing arrows down with deadly aim. In this situation the Romans were helpless; they could only heave their javelins upward on the chance that a few would sink into flesh before their force was dissipated.

But they had not been trained to suffer defeat at the hands of barbarians. They gathered a great deal of combustible material and started fires that lapped up the lofty columns toward the cedarwood ceiling. The wood blazed; the intricately carved panels and gold embellishments tumbled to the floor still flaming; and the shrieking Jews fell through into the inferno. Most of those who were not burned to death were stabbed to death. Some adroit Jews, whose limbs had not been broken in the fall, managed to escape the Roman weapons and started down the hill; but many of these, before they got to the bottom, met more Romans.

In places where the fire did not burn so fiercely the legionaries charged through. Pushing past the balustrade whose inscription warned pagans to go no farther on pain of death, pushing into the forbidden Temple itself, they ransacked the Holy Place, where the treasure was stored. Much of the money went to Sabinus.

This new desecration of the Temple only aggravated the rebellion. Mobs of maddened Jews besieged the Herodian palace, where Sabinus lay in hiding. Many hoped to drive him away; others hoped irrationally to drive all the Romans away—although these men, if they had taken a moment to think, would probably have realized that the Romans would only come again, chronically and inevitably. Some hoped for nothing except desperate revenge: the chance to kill the followers of the eagle before they themselves were killed. A few may have hoped that this was the time for the coming of the Messiah—the Redeemer whose advent had been prophesied since long ago, the destroyer of evil and harbinger of a new world.

Many soldiers who had served under Herod, and who were of course committed to supporting the Roman government, deserted to the Jews. The noisy, surging mob threatened to burn the palace, in retaliation for the burning of the Temple portico, till the detested building and everyone in it were ashes. Then the mob sent Sabinus the message that if he promised to leave and to take all his Romans with him, he could go in safety. But Sabinus thought the offer a ruse; and besides he expected Varus to arrive from Syria with reinforcements soon.

At Rome, Augustus still delayed a decision about the will. Meanwhile, with Varus' permission a deputation of fifty Jews came to Rome with the request that no king at all be put over Judaea. This deputation had started from Judaea before the revolt against Sabinus began. In a temple that Augustus had raised to Apollo, they laid their request before the emperor. They expanded on Herod's cruelties and enormities, taking perhaps a certain pleasure in describing such monstrous examples of oppression now that the oppressor was dead. Herod, they said, had not only delighted in inflicting torture and death on his subjects, he had also delighted in ornamenting foreign cities at the expense of Jewish cities. And Archelaus showed no promise of being a better monarch, having already slaughtered three thousand innocent subjects gathered for Passover. Perhaps Augustus could join Judaea to the province of Syria. Under the Roman governor of Syria the Jews would certainly be happier than under any Herodian ruler.

The rhetorician Nicolaus, worried that such arguments might prevail, especially since the delegates were backed by thousands of Jews living in Rome, rose to speak against the deputation. The citizens of Judaea, he said, were a characteristically intractable people; they would not be content with the best of kings. But that was no reason why a king should not rule them—Archelaus in particular.

In Palestine certainly, the Jews seemed to be growing more intractable all the time. The revolution spread from Jerusalem to other parts of the land. In Idumaea, for example, two thousand soldiers who had fought for Herod deserted to the rebel cause just as Herod's old soldiers in Jerusalem were doing. A cousin of Herod (the one who had prevented him from killing himself with the fruit knife) led loyalist soldiers against the deserters, and Idumaea became an embattled area.

Adventurers took advantage of the unrest for their own private ends. In Galilee a robber chief named Judas, son of another robber chief whom Herod had had a hard time capturing, seized the royal residence at the city of Sepphoris, confiscated the weapons stored there, armed his men with them, and sallied forth to wreak havoc. His men called him their king, and indeed it was his ambition to reign as an actual king.

In Peraea across the Jordan a certain Simon enjoyed the same ambition. Although Simon had been one of Herod's slaves, at least he looked the part of a king, being tall, strong, handsome, and commanding. His followers, fierce men from the Transjordanian hills, obeyed him as their monarch. He placed a royal diadem on his head, led his force to Jericho, burned Herod's spacious pleasure palace there, plundered the city, and proceeded to riot through the countryside, burning and looting.

West of Jerusalem a lowly shepherd named Athronges claimed to be king. He looked even more regal than Simon, being a man of gigantic stature and corresponding physical prowess, and he had four gigantic brothers who helped him loyally, just as the four brothers of Judas Maccabaeus had helped that great rebel against the Graeco-Syrians a century and three quarters before. Perhaps Athronges even conceived of himself as a latter-day Judas Maccabaeus fighting for Jewish freedom—with Romans instead of Graeco-Syrians for foes, and with Sabinus rather than Antiochus the God Manifest as the prime enemy. In any case Athronges put each of his brothers in command of a troop of men and overran the countryside, killing Romans, killing Roman sympathizers, killing Herodian sympathizers, and sometimes killing inoffensive Jews because one could not always make distinctions. Athronges' greatest victory occurred near Emmaus, a town halfway between Jerusalem and the sea, where his men defeated some Roman soldiers who were bringing grain and weapons to their legion. Forty of the Romans, along with the centurion in charge, lay transfixed with arrows. The rest of the Romans managed to reach safety; but evidently this was only because a Roman officer named

Gratus, in charge of some native troops still loyal to Archelaus and Rome, arrived on the scene and covered the legionaries' escape.

Varus now descended from Syria to put an end to the chaos. He marched along the coast with two legions (a legion numbered somewhat over five thousand men if at full strength), four troops of cavalry, and auxiliaries furnished by native potentates. The port of Berytus, Graeco-Roman in its sympathies, contributed fifteen hundred more auxiliaries. The king of the Nabataean Arabs dispatched a large number of footmen and horsemen to swell the Roman force still further. In the face of such power, rebel resistance suffered. Varus sent part of his army against the Galileans, and this division burned the city of Sepphoris to the ground for having supported the robber chief Judas; it also turned the free inhabitants into slaves. Gratus, having joined Varus' army, went after the slave-king Simon, defeated his fierce Transjordanian followers in a big battle, slaughtered most of them, caught Simon himself in flight through a ravine, and cut off the man's handsome head. Varus with the main part of his army advanced toward Emmaus, and when the terrified citizens had abandoned it he burned the place in requital for Athronges' victory there. Meanwhile the Nabataean Arabs went wild, burning fields, burning villages, robbing helter-skelter, murdering Jews.

From Emmaus, Varus marched to Jerusalem. Embarrassed citizens met him, muttering excuses. They said that they were not responsible for the trouble—that the outsiders who had come to the capital for Pentecost were the guilty ones and had forced the citizens to oppose the Romans. Varus was perhaps amused by the power of a conquering army to make men compromise with truth. But Rome must not look like a lenient victor: he sent part of his force through the country on a search for the leaders of the rebellion, who would be killed if found. Meanwhile Sabinus had slipped away. Though he had been frantic for Varus to come to Jerusalem and save him, he evidently did not think that this was the proper time for a confrontation. He sneaked off toward the coast.

Many rebel leaders were rounded up; two thousand men were left to die on crosses. Order was restored.

Augustus now came to a decision regarding the will. Although he left it essentially as Herod had designed it, he did make certain changes. The greatest of these was that no one was to be king.

Archelaus would bear the title ethnarch ("ruler of the people"), the title that Hyrcanus had held many years before, when Herod's father was alive. Antipas and their half brother Philip would be tetrarchs. Philip was easily satisfied; but young Antipas must have resented the decision, as well as the added proviso that if Archelaus proved to be a good ruler he (and not Antipas) could perhaps be elevated to kingship later on. Archelaus ended up with about half of his father's lands: Judaea proper, Idumaea, and the territory of Samaria. Jerusalem, Sebaste, and the ports of Caesaraea and Joppa would also be subject to him. Antipas ended up with fruitful Galilee and hilly Peraea across the Jordan; these regions would yield him an annual income approximately one third as large as Archelaus'. To Philip went the largely non-Jewish regions north and east of the Sea of Galilee that had been granted to him in the will; they would yield him approximately one sixth as much income as Archelaus'. Salome did not suffer. As Herod had intended, she got the lucrative cities of Jamnia, Azotus, and Phasaelis (named after her long-dead brother Phasael), though they were to be administered by Archelaus. Augustus also gave her a palace at Ascalon.

The Greek-oriented cities of Gadara and Hippos and the ancient town of Gaza near the coast were made directly subject to Syria; this decision probably pleased their anti-Jewish populations. Herod had left Augustus a sizable legacy, but the emperor instead of keeping this money himself distributed it among disgruntled relatives of Herod who had not prospered by the will.

Everything therefore seemed to be settled. A new complication arose immediately—but it proved to be minor. There came to Rome a man who claimed that Alexander and Aristobulus had not been strangled at Herod's command and that he himself was Alexander, to whom the throne by right belonged. Actually he was a low-class impostor from Sidon, but he happened to look somewhat like Alexander and had consequently been put up to the impersonation by a man who hoped to share the profits with him. Many Jews believed him to be their prince; the crowd that followed him was large and enthusiastic. But Augustus saw through him at once. Rather generously the emperor permitted him to live but condemned him to row in the galleys. His promoter was executed.

Pleased or displeased, the litigants returned to the East. As a final inheritance from their father, each of the brothers prefixed the name Herod to his own: from now on, it was officially Herod Archelaus the ethnarch, Herod Antipas the tetrarch, and Herod Philip the tetrarch. Retiring to their assigned territories, they set about their separate tasks.

Of the three sons, Philip was to perform his tasks the best. For thirty-seven years this man reigned quietly over the lands east of the Sea of Galilee and north toward Damascus. His subjects were Arabs, Syrians, Greeks, Idumaeans from the south, and some Jews. He was mild, intelligent, earnest, and unoppressive, dispensing justice from a throne that he carried along when he toured his territories. His greatest project, and his only bid for personal glory, was the peaceful one of building a city. He located it in Ituraea, almost directly east from Tyre, and named it Caesaraea like Herod's great city on the coast; but to distinguish it from that place it was called Caesaraea Philippi—or Philip's Caesaraea.

If more of his subjects had been Jews, however, his reputation might be slightly less high than it is. It seems that he had inherited a little of his father's disrespect for Jewish ways. He erected at Caesaraea Philippi a gleaming temple that delighted the pagan majority of his subjects. It delighted him also—to such an extent that he depicted it on his coins. The Jewish minority must have resented this flagrant pagan boast by a Jewish tetrarch.

Insofar as we can tell, Antipas was much less tyrannical a ruler than his father. That is not saying a great deal; but at least the people in the part of his father's kingdom that was finally allotted to him— the Peraean hills and Galilee with its rich fields and green valleys— felt somewhat less apprehensive than they had felt under Herod. Like his father, however, Antipas reigned for Rome's benefit. Although many of his aristocratic subjects apparently did not mind this, having learned through the years to prefer indirect Roman control to the direct control exercised in a province such as Syria, the poor tended to believe themselves mistreated, especially when they paid their taxes.

Antipas unfortunately shared his family's facility for offending Judaic sensibilities. Like Philip he eventually built a city, which he named Tiberias after Augustus' successor, the emperor Tiberius. Situated on the Sea of Galilee in the midst of lush countryside, it seemed to occupy the choicest spot that the whole tetrarchy could provide. The only difficulty was that under the grandiose new buildings lay ancient tombs; the people who walked the new streets walked over the dead. According to the Law, therefore, the area was unclean, for all its beauty. Many Jews were scandalized that Antipas persisted in building his capital on a place of burial, and they shuddered at the idea of going to live there. In large degree Antipas had to supply a population for the city by forcing subject peoples to move there, welcoming Gentiles, and bribing slaves with the promise of freedom, houses, and lands.

As for the ethnarch Archelaus, winner of the greatest share of Herod's kingdom, he had a very unsuccessful reign. For instance, he fell in love with the proud Cappadocian princess Glaphyra, widow of his strangled half brother Alexander. Worse than that, he married her. According to the Law, Archelaus was not free to take his half brother's former wife as his own—even though she had been married to another man, King Juba of Mauretania in northern Africa, in the meantime. God had laid down this law to His people in the Book of Leviticus: "Thou shalt not uncover the nakedness of thy brother's wife: it is thy brother's nakedness." Archelaus in his selfish passion had ignored God's proscription.

The ethnarch must have done a great many other things to anger his subjects, because in A.D. 6 a delegation of Jews and Samaritans appeared before the aged Augustus to lodge complaints. They declared that the ethnarch's oppression and brutality were unbearable. They had the support of Antipas and perhaps Philip also. It is possible that these men, regarding Archelaus' lands and cities with envy, hoped there would be a new division of them.

Augustus summoned the ethnarch to Rome. When Archelaus arrived, the emperor heard what he had to say for himself, heard the testimony of his accusers, and decided that his own confidence in Archelaus had been grossly misplaced. This son of Herod had proved himself unfit to rule. Augustus exiled him to a city on the Rhone in Gaul—the present-day Vienne. In this place, remote from Rome and yet more remote from warm Judaea, the heir to half of Herod's kingdom finished out his days.

XI

THE IMPERIAL PROVINCE
OF JUDAEA

If Antipas and Philip had hoped that their brother's territory would be divided between them, they were disappointed. Augustus felt that members of the Herodian family had ruled in Judaea long enough. Although he let Antipas and Philip keep their respective tetrarchies, where they were apparently doing a beneficial job from Rome's standpoint, he turned Archelaus' ethnarchy into a Roman province.

There were two kinds of provinces: senatorial and imperial. The senatorial provinces were, by and large, regions accustomed to Roman control and not threatened by either malcontents on the inside or enemies from the non-Roman world beyond the Empire's borders. Their governors, chosen by the senate, were men who had already served as consuls. The imperial provinces were less secure regions—potential trouble spots in fact—and were directly under the control of the emperor, who appointed their governors. It probably did not surprise anybody that Judaea was made an imperial province.

Although most imperial provinces had military governors, or *legati*, Augustus placed Judaea under a *procurator*. Procurators did not rank extremely high in Roman officialdom, being chosen from the equestrian or knightly class rather than from the senatorial order. They were traditionally financial agents, as the infamous Sabinus had

been; but a procurator who was expected to govern an imperial province had to have considerable military powers as well.

The procurator of Judaea was in most respects answerable only to
the emperor, but the governor of Syria possessed the right to intervene in Judaean affairs if some unusually serious matter arose. This
was true even though Galilee, under the control of the client tetrarch
Antipas, lay between Syria and Judaea. The governor of Syria was
also supposed to come to the aid of the procurator of Judaea in cases
of dire military necessity; he had several Roman legions under his
command, whereas the procurator's military force consisted of mercenaries.

Among the procurator's powers was that of appointing or dismissing the high priest, still the spiritual head of Jews not merely in Judaea but everywhere. The procurator could also impose the death
sentence, although Jews who happened to be Roman citizens could
appeal the sentence to the emperor. More important, the collection of
taxes was in the procurator's hands. There were many taxes: on
property, on income, on imports and exports, on the use of public
buildings. As was true throughout the Empire, the job of collecting
them was farmed out to profiteers (called "publicans" in the New
Testament), who paid the procurator a fixed sum and were entitled
to keep whatever they collected in excess of that sum. The publicans
and their underlings, enriching themselves by squeezing payments out
of the helpless poor and out of other men who did not want to pay,
were probably the most hated agents of the Roman administration.

But the Jews, even the poor ones, had certain rights. Their exemption from military service, for example, was maintained. Rome as a
matter of policy allowed subject peoples to practice their native religions undisturbed, and consequently she allowed the Jews to practice
theirs, even though monotheistic Judaism was more anti-Roman than
faiths allowing many gods. The Romans in fact tried conscientiously
to show respect toward the religion of the Jews. For instance, soldiers
were ordered not to march into the holy city of Jerusalem carrying
their military standards, since portraits of the emperor were affixed to
some of the standards and since such portraits violated the law
against graven images. For the same reason bronze coins with the emperor's portrait on the obverse were not struck in Judaea; the bronze
coins minted under the procurators depicted such items as palm trees,
ears of barley, and horns of plenty. But in the case of silver and gold

no exception was made for the Jews: like people in other provinces they had to use the gold and silver coins supplied by Rome, and these bore the imperial face.

Under the Romans the capital was no longer Jerusalem but Caesaraea. Herod's great accomplishment, that magnificent center of commerce and luxury, was a logical choice for the capital. Being a coastal city it was much more easily accessible than landlocked Jerusalem. It was, besides, a sophisticated metropolis with a largely Graeco-Syrian population, where a Roman could feel at ease. In grim old Jerusalem, stiff-necked and parochial and inhabited almost exclusively by Jews who worshiped a solitary God of whom they never made any statues, a Roman could not help feeling out of place. The change of capital also emphasized the fact that there was a new order in the land. The ancient seat of Jewish government was an irrelevancy now that the government was Roman.

Jerusalem's importance as the racial and religious capital of the Jews, however, probably increased as a result of the change. Simply by contrast, the political role of Caesaraea and that city's involvement with Gentile officials rendered the spiritual role of Jerusalem more apparent. Since the pomp of a king or ethnarch had vanished from the ancient city, the dignity of the high priest, the unquestioned head of Jewish life, was all the more obvious. Rome's procurator might have the right to appoint or dismiss a high priest, but the high priest himself was a far more exalted man in the eyes of the Jews.

Rome permitted the Jewish legislative and judicial body, the Sanhedrin, to continue to function at Jerusalem. It had gained power since the death of Herod, who had tried to suppress it as much as he could. Its seventy members, over whom the high priest presided, tried civil and criminal cases and could even send out their own officers to arrest suspects. Rome did not interfere except in the event of capital punishment: the Sanhedrin could sentence a man to death, but the sentence could not be carried out unless the procurator gave his approval. Another Sanhedrin, concerned with religion rather than law, also continued to function under Rome. It controlled the holy ritual in the Temple, considered questions involving the religious calendar, and interpreted and applied the commands in the Torah; and it underlined Jerusalem's position as the spiritual capital.

The mercenary soldiers or auxiliaries who made up the procurator's military force were not Jews any more than the majority of the men in Herod's army had been. Most of them came from Caesaraea or the other principal Gentile city, Sebaste. Their officers were Roman, but the men themselves were, in the main, Syrians who had absorbed much Greek culture. They were not a large army. The whole force was apparently made up of five cohorts, or infantry regiments, totaling about twenty-five hundred men, plus a wing of cavalry comprised of another five hundred men. One of the cohorts (about five hundred soldiers) was normally garrisoned at Jerusalem to keep things under control there. Insofar as we can tell, these foot soldiers occupied the Antonia, the fortress built by Herod on the highest part of the Temple hill but separate from the Temple itself. From this commanding position the men could look down on the suspect city. The procurator usually made the four-day journey from Caesaraea to Jerusalem for Jewish festivals—when, as the Passover and Pentecost disturbances of 4 B.C. had shown, the Jews were most likely to feel rebellious and consequently needed the closest watching. On these occasions he would take along a contingent of perhaps a couple of hundred soldiers from Caesaraea, and they would be quartered in the Herodian palace, where Sabinus had holed up during the Pentecost revolt. The procurator himself stayed at the palace too. It was almost the only place in Jerusalem suitable to Roman official dignity.

In spite of Rome's administrative hierarchy, and the procurator's soldiers, and even the publicans, most Jews believed that Rome did not in any real sense possess Judaea. The land of the Israelites was the Holy Land, promised by God to the seed of Abraham, promised by God to the Jews in exodus from Egyptian bondage, fought for and won by Joshua and his army of heroes, defended by the judges and by David against Philistines, Midianites, and other profane peoples. God had destined it for the Jews, and it would always belong to the Jews. The Law related to it particularly: many injunctions of the Law could best be followed in the Holy Land. The Romans were no more than superficial interlopers, and a time would come—a Messianic time—when they would cease to contaminate the surface.

But meanwhile the interlopers were making their presence felt.

The first procurator, Coponius, assumed office in A.D. 6, and almost immediately there was trouble. When Rome took over a province, she customarily conducted a census to determine who should pay what taxes and to acquaint the imperial government with how much income might be expected from the new territory. Coponius' administration began therefore with a census of the Jews. They naturally objected, looking on it as a tyrannical measure and as a sign of greater tyranny to come. There were claims that things had been much better under the Herodians. But the opposition to the census seems to have been largely a case of crying before being hurt. When the high priest, probably realizing that resistance would be foolhardy, counseled the people to submit, most of them obeyed without further question.

A certain Judas, however, joined forces with a Pharisee named Saddok to foment discontent. Judas and Saddok led a group of adherents in what the historian Josephus calls the "fourth philosophy." The members of this sect accepted the Pharisees' doctrines but believed that politically the Pharisees did not go far enough or move fast enough. They themselves were committed to violence. God, they said, was the only true Master; therefore the Roman mastery was illegitimate. Rabid for freedom, they preached the killing of Romans. It did not matter how many of their own partisans died as long as freedom was finally wrested from the false masters. They would gladly sacrifice their own friends, their own families, for the holy cause.

The Romans managed to do away with Judas, but his death did not put an end to the sect he had founded. It smoldered under the surface. Its fanatical members, dispersed now throughout Judaea, fostered disaffection and sometimes attracted new adherents from the farmers, the shepherds and goatherds, and the village artisans whom they visited in secret. The sect was not strong enough to perpetrate any overt trouble; the killing of Romans and the sacrifice of friends and family were unrealized ideals. But the discontent smoldered on, and the Roman administration through its mere existence provided the fuel.

Superficially these were quiet years, and for many Jews they must have been prosperous ones, since the strong Roman government countenanced the arts, encouraged industry and commerce, let the clever grow rich unmolested, and protected the property of those who already had much wealth. Coponius was succeeded in A.D. 9 by a certain Marcus Ambibulus, who was succeeded in turn by a certain Annius Rufus. The fact that we know scarcely anything about these procurators suggests that their administrations were relatively tranquil ones.

In A.D. 15 or possibly 16, a Valerius Gratus became procurator, and he remained in office for eleven years. Early in his administration there were signs of disturbance. He dismissed the high priest, Ananus ben Seth, who had headed the Jews since A.D. 6, and appointed one Ishmael ben Phabi. Dismissing him after a short time, the procurator appointed Ananus' son Eleazar; dismissed him the next year and appointed one Simon ben Kamith; dismissed him and in A.D. 18 appointed Ananus' son-in-law Joseph, known as Caiaphas. It looks as if he was having a hard time locating a high priest who was sufficiently tractable from the Roman point of view—one who would not be a rallying point for Jewish unrest—although there may have been other reasons, unknown to us, for the rapid changes. At any rate in Caiaphas he seems to have found his man. Caiaphas remained high priest for many years.

Valerius Gratus was followed by Pontius Pilate. Probably in the late fall of A.D. 26—in any case not long after Pilate assumed office —occurred the incident of the military standards. For some reason the cohort that Pilate dispatched from Caesaraea to Jerusalem, evidently as a replacement for the garrison stationed there, was one whose standards would be especially offensive to the Jews. Not all military standards had portraits of the emperor, but one very common type did: this was a spear with a crossbar attached near the top of the shaft and metal disks depicting the emperor affixed below. The standards that the cohort took to Jerusalem on Pilate's orders were apparently of this kind; from the disks gleamed portraits of Augustus' successor, the emperor Tiberius. Why Pilate sent this particular cohort to replace the regular Jerusalem garrison is not clear. Perhaps it was just a mistake: he may not have known much about the people he had been appointed to govern. At any rate the five hundred men entered the holy city at night. The next day the Jews discovered the hateful standards already in place—most likely in the garrison headquarters, the Antonia on the Temple hill.

To a soldier in the Roman army—even to an auxiliary from Caesaraea or Sebaste—military standards were objects of extraordinary importance. Carried proudly in front of the troops on tactical maneuvers, they pointed the way to victory. They symbolized the military profession: its opportunities for personal glory, its sacred tasks of defending Rome against enemies and of extending her dominion over parts of the world previously barbaric. They even had a religious significance. Some of the soldiers thought they were the divine spirits of the cohorts before which they were borne. When an army had won a victory, sacrifices were performed in front of the standards. When the army was in camp, the standards were enshrined in a holy place. The ones that displayed the face of the emperor, commander of all the armies of Rome and the figure for whom all Rome's soldiers must be ready to lay down their lives, were connected with the cult of emperor worship that was growing in the Empire and that Roman policy considered especially desirable for the army.

The Jews must have known some of this, and it must have made the objects all the more execrable. Besides, if the standards had been set up in the Antonia, as they almost certainly were, their nearness to the Temple was in itself an insult to God. Although the Herod-built fortress did not, strictly speaking, belong to the Temple, it stood next to the Temple on still higher ground, from which it overlooked parts of the sacred structure; and stairways connected it with the Temple's outermost court, the colonnaded area where pagans were allowed. Besides, the sacred garments of the high priest were kept in the Antonia. To permit the standards to remain here, and to permit the soldiers to worship these senseless bits of metal in a spot so close to the Holy of Holies, was unthinkable.

A great many Jews set out on foot for Caesaraea, and in that city of aliens they besought Pilate to remove the standards—which would probably mean removing the whole cohort and substituting one whose standards did not include the imperial portrait. If Pilate yielded to the request, he would be weakening Roman authority. The government, he felt, must stand firm; the emperor's representative must not be swayed by a mob of barbarians. But the Jews staged a five-day demonstration. Some of them threw themselves on the ground; many of them howled; none of them left. On the sixth day Pilate had a stand erected in the stadium and addressed the throng from it. Under the seats, according to Josephus, he hid soldiers, so that if the Jews persisted in their protest he could have them massacred in his sight.

They seemed to be asking for massacre, however. Lying on the ground, they pointed to their own throats, inviting the soldiers to slit them. Even a governor with the Roman image strong in his mind could not massacre people who wanted to die. Besides, a slaughter might provoke more trouble in this disorderly land, so that Pilate himself would look like a bad administrator, incurring the emperor's displeasure, and be recalled in disgrace. Pilate therefore yielded: the standards were taken away.

Not much later he angered the people of Jerusalem by appropriating part of the Temple treasury for the reconditioning of an aqueduct. Here again he may have been acting through ignorance. In addition to the water saved in cisterns when it rained, Jerusalem drew its water supply principally from the ancient Pool of Siloam, located within the city but fed by a tunnel that originated at a spring outside the walls; and from two aqueducts that carried water from south of Bethlehem. One of these aqueducts needed major rebuilding.

Included in the Mishnah, the unwritten body of instructions for rabbis, was a tractate called "The Shekels," which stipulated the uses to which the money amassed in the Temple treasury could legitimately be put. Aside from more or less religious purposes, such as payment for offerings and wages for Temple attendants, money from the treasury could be spent for certain more secular purposes, such as the rebuilding of walls and aqueducts. It seemed therefore that Pilate was on safe ground. Water from this particular aqueduct, besides, filled the cisterns at the Temple itself. But he made the mistake of appropriating the wrong Temple fund—one that was reserved for the purchase of animals for sacrifice.

Because of this, and perhaps also because the sullen populace had been waiting for him to do something they could yell at him for, thousands of outraged citizens gathered at Jerusalem. But this time the governor was ready for them. While they were busy screaming at him not to rob the sacred treasury—while they were intent on showering him with whatever colorful obscenities came to mind—they did not notice that he had scattered his soldiers among them. The soldiers wore ordinary Jewish clothing over their armor and carried clubs under the clothing. They gradually worked their way to the outside until they surrounded the crowd. Then they swung into action, striking in all directions with the clubs, hitting the harmless as well as the most vociferous, giving joyous expression to their resentment of the Jews. Several Jews were clubbed to death; others were seriously injured. Pilate had probably not intended the chastisement to proceed so far, or he would have had his men use swords rather than clubs.

But the riot was definitely over. The money was used for the aqueduct.

In these years of Roman domination, when discontent festered among the Jews of the middle and lower classes, when there seemed to be no one to go to for help and when even the high priest Caiaphas was unsympathetic, the thoughts of the people turned with greater and greater yearning to the promise of a Messiah. It was a promise that had been uttered for many centuries, a promise that glowed in the prophetic books. The term Messiah meant "an Anointed One"—as the Greeks said, a Christ. Originally it had been applied to a high priest or king; but it took on the connotation of a Savior—someone who, as God's agent, would redeem the bewildered people and bring about a glorious time for the whole world.

Sometimes the Messiah was said to be a lowly, abused figure: "despised and rejected of men," as the author of the fifty-third chapter of the Book of Isaiah described him—"a man of sorrows." The sins of the world would be laid on his shoulders; he would be "brought as a lamb to the slaughter" and his soul would be "an offering for sin," and only after he had "made intercession for the transgressors" would the glory come.

But this picture of the Messiah as a meek sufferer in atonement for the sins of others did not appeal to the Jews nearly so much as another picture: one that emphasized his regal, triumphant aspect. According to the author of the ninth chapter in Isaiah, "Of the increase of his government and peace there shall be no end, upon the throne of David, and upon his kingdom, to order it, and to establish it with judgment and with justice from henceforth even forever." The Book of Daniel contained a vision of the regal Messiah: "And there was given him dominion, and glory, and a kingdom, that all people, nations, and languages should serve him; his dominion is an everlasting dominion, which shall not pass away, and his kingdom that which shall not be destroyed."

It was this kind of vision that drew the Pharisees, the rabbis, the common folk of Judaea, and even the heretical Samaritans—though not the aristocratic priestly caste of the Sadducees, who rejected Messianism just as they rejected the concept of eternal life. Among the folk, various ideas concerning the Messiah gained popularity, but the persuasion that he would conquer misery, wickedness, and injustice underlay them all. Some said that after he had annihilated evil he would reign on earth in peace and happiness for a thousand years; and then the Resurrection and Last Judgment would take place, and the good would enter God's eternal kingdom. Others thought that the Resurrection would take place as soon as the Messiah had killed evil —that there would be no thousand-year interval of earthly content. Many people looked forward to two Messiahs: one, of the seed of Joseph, would die in battle against the army of evil, but the other, of the seed of David, would rally the army of good and overwhelm the enemy. The Pharisees stressed the conception of the Messiah as the descendant of David, and humble folk no doubt came to identify the army of evil with the army of Rome.

Among those who preached the coming of the Messiah was John the Baptist. He had probably been educated by the Essenes, the nearly monastic sect living in an isolated community in the dry Dead Sea region. With the Essenes, Messianism was an extremely important point of faith. In the leafless wilderness around the Dead Sea, in A.D. 27 or 28, John talked about the Messiah, drawing tremendous crowds—people from Jerusalem, at times even soldiers and publicans; and in the Jordan, the green-banked, tree-shaded river that wound through the dust and rocks, he baptized people in the name of the coming Christ.

Antipas the tetrarch, who still ruled Galilee many days' journey to the north, had also been permitted, in Augustus' final decision about the will, to rule Peraea—the land east of the Jordan. He spent some time in this region, coming with his court to the fortress palace of Machaerus, which had been built by his father Herod on a lonely hill overlooking the Dead Sea. While the tetrarch and his courtiers inhabited this grim splendor in the midst of desolation, he naturally heard a great deal about John. In a way he may even have been intrigued by John's teachings. But with his wife it was a different matter.

Antipas had married Herodias, formerly the wife of his half brother Herod Philip—a son of Herod who was apparently a nonentity. (In the New Testament, Herodias is mistakenly said to have been the former wife of Philip the tetrarch, the half brother who had received the largely non-Jewish part of Herod's kingdom and who ruled it well.) Antipas erred in making Herodias his wife. His marriage to a sister-in-law was as much a breach of the Law as Archelaus' marriage to his sister-in-law Glaphyra. In fact it was worse—because Glaphyra was already a widow, whereas Herodias' husband Herod Philip was still alive.

Herodias and Herod Philip had probably never found each other very congenial. She was the daughter of the strangled Aristobulus, and her marriage to Herod Philip was one of the matches that Herod had arranged to smooth matters over after the strangulation. She had been a child at the time; the intervening years had evidently not increased her regard for Herod Philip. When Antipas fell in love with her, there was no course but to marry him, even though this meant divorcing Herod Philip and violating the Law. Antipas, uncontrollably eager for her, felt the same way: the Law was irrelevant to their passion.

It happened that he, like Herodias, was already married—to a daughter of the king of the Nabataean Arabs. This lady, incensed when she discovered that she was to be supplanted, rushed home to her father, who declared war on Antipas. The emperor quickly stopped the war, but the affair did not bode well for the newlyweds. In the succeeding years John made himself more troublesome than the Nabataean king had been. When he was not preaching the advent of the Messiah, he was usually preaching against this illegitimate marriage. According to Saint Mark, he told Antipas flatly, "It is not lawful for thee to have thy brother's wife."

Because of the great crowds that he drew, John was a figure of political importance; his attacks on the tetrarch and the tetrarch's wife were therefore potentially dangerous. Antipas might have let things ride even so, but Herodias was compounded of sterner material. Her grandfather was, after all, her husband's father, Herod himself; and she seems to have inherited his force of character along with his cruelty. Her grandmother was Mariamne, so that the proud blood of the Hasmonaeans flowed in Herodias' veins. No ragged, honey-eating baptist was going to call her marriage illegitimate. She spoke with Antipas, who admitted the political peril of letting this wild man continue to rave. He threw the preacher into prison.

We can only speculate on whether Antipas at first intended to have John killed. The execution of so popular a figure might set off an uprising; and if sedition spread through the land, Rome might remove the tetrarch from his office and add Antipas' territories to the imperial province of Judaea. It is possible, besides, that Antipas held John in superstitious awe as a man who could work wonders and who was closer to God than most men. On the other hand John's death would remove a very annoying sore and would satisfy the insistent Herodias. After keeping John in chains for a year or more, Antipas finally decided to have him killed.

According to the accounts in the New Testament, he was forced into this decision by an oath he had given his stepdaughter, who danced at a feast and pleased him greatly. A strong tradition says that her dance took place at the fortress palace of Machaerus; another tradition says that Antipas was more attracted toward her than a man should be toward his stepdaughter. The New Testament, which calls Antipas by his assumed name of Herod, calls the stepdaughter only a "damsel"; but she was Salome, Herodias' daughter by her first husband. Herodias had probably named her after the indefatigable Salome who was Herod's sister. The story of how she danced, and of how Herodias prompted her to ask for John's head, and of how the detached object was brought in on a platter and presented by her to Herodias, has probably received as much fond elaboration as any story in the New Testament; and it continues to fascinate.

We do not hear much more about the damsel Salome, except that she like her mother became a tetrarch's lady. She married her uncle Philip, half brother to Antipas, and presumably went to live with him at the newly built capital, Caesaraea Philippi—from which he ruled his Graeco-Arab dominions better than Antipas ruled his own lands.

While John was lying in prison, Jesus Christ was preaching in Galilee; it was about the year 28, the time of the Sermon on the Mount. According to Saint Matthew, John's followers went to Jesus after the execution and told him that John was dead. "When Jesus heard of it, he departed . . . into a desert place apart." Inevitably word of Christ's teachings came to Antipas. Matthew claims that Antipas identified Jesus with the beheaded preacher: "And said unto his servants, this is John the Baptist; he is risen from the dead, and therefore mighty works do show forth themselves in him."

Later, at a time when Christ had become still more famous, Antipas proceeded to Jerusalem for Passover. Attended by the pomp of his court, he stayed at the Hasmonaean palace—the old building where the Jewish royal family had lived before the days of Herod. Pilate was in Jerusalem too, and as usual during his visits to this inimical city, he stayed at the Herodian palace. The tetrarch of Galilee and the governor of Judaea did not like each other. Perhaps this was because they were the two most important political figures in the area. Pilate besides may have felt a certain Roman scorn toward this petty native prince, this celebrant of barbarian festivals such as Passover, and Antipas may have suspected the scorn. It is also probable that Antipas had been trying to curry favor with Augustus' successor, the emperor Tiberius, by reporting instances of Pilate's maladministration, and that Pilate was aware of the tetrarch's tale-telling.

The responsibility for keeping Roman order during this annoying Passover festival, when almost anything could happen, was a grave and disagreeable one for Pilate. When the city, swelled with pilgrims from all over, became excited about Jesus, Pilate knew that he could expect added unpleasantness. Jesus was brought to the procurator after the Sanhedrin had finished with him, and he presented problems. The Sanhedrin had condemned him to death; Pilate could either nullify the sentence or approve it and have the man executed.

Since Jesus opposed both the Pharisees and the Sadducees, it was easy to see why the Sanhedrin had considered him guilty of blasphemy. Caiaphas, still high priest after about fifteen years and therefore president of the Sanhedrin, had been particularly set against him, and Caiaphas possessed enormous influence even if some of the Jews did suspect him of catering to Rome. The trial seems not to have been strictly legal in some respects: it took place at night rather than in the day; the judge, Caiaphas, was anything but impartial; no formal accusation was entered against Jesus; and the required space of a day did not intervene between the end of the trial and the delivery of the verdict. Jesus was, however, convicted of blasphemy for claiming to be the true Messiah, the Son of God, and for declaring that the Sanhedrin would "see the Son of Man sitting on the right hand of power, and coming in the clouds of heaven." At this assertion Caiaphas evidently tore his own clothes in dramatic distress.

Pilate was inclined to disallow the sentence of death. When he questioned Jesus, he could not see that the prisoner had committed any capital crime. Certainly Jesus had not been disloyal to Rome, and although he called himself a king, he maintained that his kingdom was not an earthly one. The Jews obviously wanted Jesus executed as a false Messiah and an offender against their religion; but

Messianic matters were no concern of Pilate's, and honoring Jewish wishes was distasteful to him. There were thieves, murderers, and rabble-rousers running around loose who had done much more harm than this Jesus. On the other hand a refusal to ratify the sentence might lead to more unrest; the Jews might even appeal to the governor of Syria or to the emperor, and Pilate might find himself dishonored.

While he vacillated between his Roman sense of justice and the feeling that it might be more practical to yield to the Jewish leaders clamoring for death, he suddenly thought he had found a way out of the dilemma. At least Saint Luke says so—although the other three Gospel writers are silent on the point. According to Luke, in the course of the questioning it came out that Jesus was a Galilean: Nazareth, where Jesus had grown up and where Mary and Joseph lived, was not in the province of Judaea but in Antipas' territory. The case should therefore be dealt with by Antipas, and it was convenient that Antipas happened to be in Jerusalem at the time. Pilate, in the belief that he was getting rid of a perplexing question, sent Jesus to the tetrarch. He may even have congratulated himself for tossing such a problem at his hated rival. Or he may have decided that Antipas and he needed a reconciliation and that showing respect for the tetrarch's authority was the best way to please him.

Luke's account of the incident says that Antipas was delighted at the chance to examine this man about whom he had heard so much, and that he hoped to see something sensational—in other words a miracle. But Jesus did not gratify him and, in addition, was taciturn. Antipas' military officers were present, and so were priests and scribes from the Sanhedrin; and Jesus' aloofness proved embarrassing. Antipas, dressing him in a regal robe in travesty of his claim to be a king, sent him back to Pilate, who was not happy to see him.

The Roman spoke to the Jewish leaders and their followers—a sizable and potentially dangerous crowd. Declaring, "I find no fault in this man," he suggested that Jesus be released. It was the custom at Passover to let one prisoner go free; if that prisoner could be Jesus, Pilate would really have found a way out. But his audience demanded that he release Barabbas instead—a notorious thief, killer, and insurrectionist, and one of the disrupters of the Roman Peace whom he would have felt very pleased to execute. Caiaphas' decision had influenced many of the Jews; and even some of those who had at one time believed in Jesus as the Messiah were disappointed when he did not reveal himself in the mode of a conqueror. Every time Pilate proposed Jesus as the man to free, the Jews shouted, "Crucify him!"

Therefore Pilate gave in to these people whom he had resisted on other occasions. But according to Matthew, he washed his hands in front of the crowd, symbolically cleansing them of guilt. "I am innocent," he said, "of the blood of this just person; see ye to it." And Christ suffered the form of execution customarily accorded slaves and other men who were not citizens of Rome.

Philo of Alexandria tells a story about Pilate that Josephus and the New Testament do not mention. There is no way to establish whether the incident actually occurred or, if it did, whether it occurred before or after the execution of Jesus. Philo says that Pilate set up in the Herodian palace at Jerusalem some shields inscribed with a dedication from himself to the emperor. The shields did not depict any animal or person; but the Jews, hating the governor, took exception to them anyway. A delegation of Jewish leaders, headed by Antipas, Philip the tetrarch, Herodias' first husband Herod Philip, and a fourth son of Herod the Great, waited on Pilate to request the removal of the shields. He denied the request, and they threatened to send an embassy to the emperor, exposing him as a robber, a man of cruelty, and a flagrant offender against order and justice. He would not yield. They dispatched letters to the emperor, who ordered him to transfer the shields to Caesaraea immediately.

Pilate eventually did lose his post as a result of a conflict with people under his authority, but those people were not inhabitants of Judaea proper but Samaritans, from the area between Judaea and Galilee. A demagogue, seeking personal profit through religious fraud, had told the Samaritans that if they gathered on Mount Gerizim—which these heretical people held to be holy—he would show them where Moses had buried sacred vessels. The Samaritans revered the first five books of the Bible (the Torah), although they rejected all later books. In the fifth book, Deuteronomy, Moses had written: "The Lord thy God will raise up unto thee a Prophet from the midst of thee, of thy brethren, like unto me; unto him ye shall hearken." The demagogue wished to pass himself off as this prophet.

A group of Samaritans who believed him assembled at a village close to Mount Gerizim, and they were armed. They welcomed other believers until a considerable throng had collected at the village. The people looked forward fanatically to climbing the mountain—and fanaticism was dangerous. Pilate had seen the chaotic effects of fanaticism before; the fact that these enthusiasts were armed made the matter even more serious. He consequently dispatched heavy-armed foot soldiers and horsemen to the area. The Samaritans advanced, and the soldiers massacred some of them, scattered others, and took some prisoner. Pilate executed the most important captives.

The fanatics had been squelched, but the trouble was not over for Pilate. Samaritan leaders complained to Vitellius, governor of Syria. Pilate, they said, had without just cause slaughtered their countrymen. Vitellius seems to have decided that an end must come to Pilate's maladministration. He ordered the procurator to go to Italy and explain his actions to the emperor Tiberius.

The absence was, as Vitellius had probably hoped, permanent. Pilate, who left Judaea late in A.D. 36 or early in 37, did not return to the land of the Jews—even though the emperor was dead by the time he reached Italy. The rest of Pilate's life is only legend. One story says that he was executed immediately, dying a Christian; another, that he committed suicide; another, that he was executed years later under Nero. Nobody knows what happened.

Probably a short while after Pilate's departure from Judaea, Vitellius paid a visit to Jerusalem. He was on the march from Syria against the Nabataean Arabs, who were again menacing Roman security. The king of the Nabataeans, father of Antipas' first wife, still could not reconcile himself to the fact that Antipas had repudiated her and taken Herodias. For the second time therefore the king made war on Antipas, and defeated him. This humiliation of the client tetrarch would have to be avenged, or Roman dignity in the East would suffer. But Vitellius intended to march through Judaea on the way to Nabataea, and this meant carrying military standards through Jewish territory. The Jews naturally sent their leaders to Vitellius to object. Unlike Pilate, whose stubborn asperity he seems to have been trying to undo, he willingly honored the Jews' religious feelings: he sent the Roman army toward Nabataea by another route. He himself, with Antipas, came to Jerusalem for Passover.

His undisclosed object may have been to keep the Jews under close surveillance during the dangerous festival season, as the procurators had done in other years, but the Jews were not rebellious this time. In fact they received Vitellius enthusiastically, glad to welcome a Roman who was different from Pilate. Either on this occasion or on a somewhat earlier visit, he also pleased the Jews by remitting taxes on the sale of produce and by having the high-priestly vestments removed from the hated Antonia, where they were under the custody of the Roman garrison, and placed in the Temple, where they belonged. It seemed to the citizens of Jerusalem that after the oppression a better time had come.

News arrived that the emperor Tiberius was dead. Vitellius, not authorized by the new government to pursue the war against Nabataea, recalled his troops. He also administered the oath in which the Jews promised loyalty to the new emperor: the young Gaius, nicknamed Caligula—"the Little Boot." Actually a much worse time had come.

XII

THE GOD AND HIS FRIEND

Scarcely anything is known about the man called Marullus, who succeeded Pilate as procurator of Judaea; but Caligula, the emperor he served, made himself notorious. Caligula's father, Germanicus, a nephew of the emperor Tiberius, had been a military hero of the Roman people, and Caligula himself during his boyhood in army camps had elicited the devotion of the soldiers. But Rome had grown incalculably rich under the long peace; the aristocracy had been sucked dry by luxury and lechery; many men and women were sated with ordinary pleasures and wild for the sick excrescences of wealth. Caligula became an exponent of all this—a young man-about-town in the most dissolute sense of the term.

He was highly intelligent, even brilliant—a sensitive student of Greek and Latin literature, an orator of considerable power; but he let his intellect be overcome by love of vicious joy and idiosyncrasies approaching madness. When at the age of twenty-five he gained the throne, it did not take him long to fall from the moderation with which he managed to start his reign. Fascinated by refinements of cruelty, he chose the most brutal deaths for his real or imagined enemies, inquiring anxiously whether they were suffering enough. Compared with him, Herod had been benevolent. Since the emperor com-

manded the world and amassed the world's money, he cultivated os-
tentatious forms of extravagance, such as drinking pearls dissolved in
vinegar or serving his guests meat made of gold. Since he stood above
law and morality, he indulged whatever sexual whims came into his
head; he had relations with one of his sisters, if not with all three.
That he supplied his best-loved horse with a house, fine furniture,
and slaves, and that he made the horse a consul, are probably the most
famous among his idiosyncratic gestures. He did these things because
he could do anything, and he could do anything because he was a
god.

In ascribing godship to himself, he is said by Philo of Alexandria
to have reasoned like this: a peasant in charge of goats or cattle is superior to his flock or herd, and therefore the emperor, who is in
charge of men, must be superior to humanity. He started dressing like
various gods—for instance, Bacchus, with a fawnskin as a garment,
an ivy wreath on his head, and a thyrsus, or cone-topped stick, in his
hand. According to the third-century historian Cassius Dio, he also
started dressing like goddesses, such as Diana and Venus. Sometimes
he would adorn himself with the attributes of the great god Apollo,
wearing artificial sun rays on his head, holding a bow and arrows
with one hand and miniatures of the Three Graces with the other,
while myrmidons sang his praise.

But identity through impersonation did not completely satisfy him.
Like Antiochus the God Manifest of Syria, he wanted to be ac-
counted the real thing. So it seems that he had the most admired
Greek statues of gods brought to Rome, had their heads cut off, and
had representations of his own head substituted. At a shrine that he
erected to himself priests offered sacrifices to his golden image. On
the Capitoline Hill at the Temple of Jupiter, king of the gods, he
spoke to the god's statue as if Jupiter were his brother, sometimes
whispering secrets, sometimes yelling threats. When his daughter was
born, according to the historian Suetonius, he took the baby around
to the temples of various goddesses before making up his mind that
only Minerva could supervise the upbringing of so divine a tot. Dio
says that Caligula wished Minerva to suckle the baby; and Philo de-
clares that he placed his daughter on the knees of the statue of the
Capitoline Jupiter as an indication that both Jupiter and he himself
were her fathers. This pageant of divinity was to have serious consequences for the Jews.

There were several million Jews in the Empire, and most of them lived outside Judaea. During the last couple of centuries B.C., the Greek term Diaspora, meaning "dispersion," had come to be applied to the situation of these Jews. The Diaspora had started several centuries before, however, when the Babylonians transported the citizens of Jerusalem into captivity. In later times many of the Jews who grew up in Gentile regions were the descendants of people who had not left Judaea of their own free will. Under the Seleucid kings of Syria, for instance, Jews had been forced to settle in Syria. Jews taken captive in the wars of Judas Maccabaeus and of later Jewish leaders were sent as slaves to various parts of Asia Minor. As a result of involuntary transportation and voluntary migration, Jewish communities flourished not only in Babylonia and Syria and Asia Minor but in Phoenicia, Greece, Cyprus, Crete, Italy, northern Africa, and the islands of the Adriatic—as far west as Spain in fact, and as far east as southern Russia. Early in his reign Tiberius banished about four thousand Jews from Rome to Sardinia. The greatest concentration of Jews outside Judaea was in Egypt at Alexandria, where Jewish craftsmen and laborers made up a considerable proportion of the population.

In the midst of Gentiles the Jews of the Diaspora tried to keep themselves untouched by alien ways. They voluntarily confined themselves to certain districts in the alien cities, where they were governed insofar as possible by their own senate of local leaders and where they worshiped at a synagogue. But they inevitably absorbed a certain amount of Gentile influence, especially from the Greek or Graecized inhabitants of most of the cities where Jews lived. The majority of Jews in the Diaspora spoke Greek as their native language. When they wrote, they wrote Greek. Like the Hellenizing Judaeans under the Seleucid kings, many of them had Greek names. Their houses were Greek in style; they watched Greek or Roman athletic events with interest, and perhaps participated now and then. Even their senates of local leaders were patterned after the city councils of Greek communities.

There was also, however, much resistance to Hellenization and Romanization, just as there was in Judaea itself. Although a few Jews went so far as to apostatize to pagan creeds, most stuck stubbornly to the faith of their ancestors. They paid the annual half shekel to the Temple treasury, made pilgrimages to Jerusalem for Passover or the agricultural festival of Pentecost if they could, and felt guilty about not having moved back to the land that God had given their people. They refused to work on the Sabbath and, for that reason, to serve in the army, which often required physical output on Sabbath days. Sometimes they openly expressed contempt or pity for their Gentile neighbors because the Gentiles were not chosen people.

Since Judaism was not essentially a matter of race and since the concept of Yahweh as much more than a national deity was gaining strength, Jews of the Diaspora engaged in missionary activity among the Gentiles. They invited Gentiles to come to the synagogues or gave them lessons in Jewish beliefs. Certain Gentiles were very much attracted to Judaism. Aristocrats bored with the old religions, idealistic youths eager for a more definite moral code than that offered by the Greek or Roman pantheon, rich Roman ladies intrigued by the exotic mystery cults of the East—these were among the people who flirted with Judaism. Others had more practical motives: a young man, for instance, might wish exemption from military service, or he might have fallen in love with a Jewess, whom he could not marry unless he was a Jew.

By no means all the conversions were serious, however. Some people later repudiated Judaism and returned to the Olympian gods or the Great Mother. And many persons interested in Judaism did not go all the way to conversion. The partly converted were called the "pious" or the "God-fearing." They conformed to some of the requirements of Judaism—perhaps not eating pork or not working on the Sabbath—and they renounced the worship of idols and probably tried to lead chaster lives than their friends did. If a man became a full convert, he of course underwent circumcision, and both male and female converts were spiritually cleansed by means of baptism or immersion and were supposed to go to Jerusalem to present a sacrifice at the Temple. Very likely, if a convert lived at a great distance from Jerusalem—in Spain, for instance, or Mauretania—the necessity of making a sacrifice at the Temple was waived; but otherwise it was expected.

The appeal of Judaism for certain Gentiles, however, did not prove a very effective counter to the anti-Semitism that existed within the Empire. In part this anti-Semitism was an indignant reaction against Jewish criticism of Gentile creeds; in part it arose from the conviction that any non-Greek or non-Roman religion was barbaric, unbeautiful, gross. Some individuals besides were envious of what they considered Jewish privileges, especially the exemption from military service; and a great many felt insulted by the Jews' exclusiveness: the flocking together in certain areas of a city, the unwillingness to modify their monotheistic religion, the flat refusal to marry anybody except Jews.

Anti-Semitism took many forms, some of them predictable ones. As in the time of the Seleucids, Gentiles laughed obscenely at circumcision; and people said that the prohibition of work on the Sabbath was simply a sanction for laziness. Derogatory stories circulated about Jews—for instance, that they were the descendants of lepers, that they worshiped animals, and that every so often they captured a Greek, fattened him up like a goose, sacrificed him to their undepicted God, tasted his flesh and internal organs, and as part of the ritual swore enmity to all Greeks. The Gentile sections of Alexandria in particular relished anti-Jewish tales.

Augustus' kindness to the Jews was not imitated by Tiberius. The reason Tiberius expelled the Jews from Rome in A.D. 19 was probably that he thought they were making too many converts among the Romans, although the more immediate cause was the fleecing of an aristocratic female proselyte by several Jewish opportunists. Tiberius seems to have categorized Judaism with other Oriental religions, such as the Egyptian worship of Isis: they were all non-Roman in spirit and therefore subversive. If Jews at Rome were of an age for military life, he decided, they could serve in the army like other men. Instead of exiling these younger men to Sardinia as he did their relatives, he packed them off as soldiers to the most unhealthful parts of the Empire. And he decreed that Judaic ritual at Rome would cease. For a while perhaps, it did.

Caligula's anti-Semitism was more personal than Tiberius'. Caligula disliked the Jews because in their pious inflexibility they would not recognize him as a god. One of his few close friends, however, was a Jew by religion and one-quarter Jewish by race, his remaining ancestry being Idumaean. This man had been named Agrippa, after Augustus' son-in-law. He was a grandson of Herod, a full brother of Herodias, and consequently an uncle of the Salome who danced. As with Herodias, the Jewish part of his blood was Hasmonaean: his father had been the strangled Aristobulus, and he therefore claimed Mariamne as a grandmother, although she was dead by the time he was born about 10 B.C. Since the Hasmonaean and Herodian lines mingled in him, he was twice royal; but he reigned over nothing.

Agrippa had been brought up at Rome. While his mother Berenice was alive he kept his expensive tastes in check for fear of her disapproval, so that his money continued to pile up temptingly. Berenice had probably learned a great deal about social machination from her mother, the shrewd Salome who was Herod's sister. She exerted herself adroitly on her son's behalf, obtaining for him the favor and protection of the influential Antonia, daughter of Mark Antony and sister-in-law of the emperor Tiberius. After his mother died, Agrippa retained the patronage of Antonia but started spending his money with the instincts of a real prodigal. He joined the loose young aristocracy of the capital and dedicated himself to luxurious living, lavish entertainment of important people, and the gradual accumulation of debts. He also cultivated the friendship of the emperor's son Drusus, who at the time was the likeliest bet as Tiberius' successor on the throne.

This beautiful world crashed around Agrippa when Drusus died of poisoning and the creditors became insistent. There was nothing to do but go away; and he went to Idumaea, where he moped. His wife Cypros, a woman of Herodian lineage, went with him, but instead of moping she wrote to his sister Herodias, requesting help. Although Herodias was not inclined toward benevolence, family feeling prevailed. She apparently spoke to her husband Antipas, and the tetrarch, who as Herod's son was also of course a relative of Agrippa, invited him to come to Galilee. There Antipas made him supervisor of the markets at Tiberias, the capital that had recently been built on an ancient burial place.

Agrippa held his position at Tiberias for seven or eight years, while John the Baptist ranted against Herodias in Peraea and was beheaded, while Jesus preached in Galilee and was crucified at Jerusalem. But the job was demeaning for a man of twice-royal blood, and Antipas made it no better by reminding him chronically that he was a poor relation. Finally Agrippa could not stand it anymore; after a drunken argument with Antipas, he left. With his wife and children he went to the governor of Syria, from whom one of his brothers was already milking money. The brother, however, resented his intrusion and put him in a bad light with the governor, and Agrippa was dismissed. It was A.D. 35 or 36. Agrippa, in his middle forties, had no source of income and was still in debt. The best plan, he figured, was to return to Rome, city of opportunity. His patroness Antonia might be able to do something for him, and so might the emperor Tiberius.

He now embarked on a rapid series of adventures and misadventures, most of them financial. He borrowed a little money from a former slave of his mother and went to the port of Anthedon; was arrested by soldiers sent by an imperial financial agent because of a long-outstanding debt to the imperial treasury; escaped from the soldiers at night; reached Alexandria by ship; borrowed a considerable sum from a prominent Alexandrian Jew, on the condition that three fourths of the money would not be available to him until he landed at the port of Puteoli in Italy; got his hands on this money on arrival at Puteoli; visited the old emperor on the island of Capri; was exposed by a letter sent to the emperor by the imperial financial agent from whose soldiers he had escaped at Anthedon; was told by the angry Tiberius to stay away until the debt to the imperial treasury was paid; borrowed money from his patroness Antonia to take care of the debt; was received back into Tiberius' good graces and made tutor to Tiberius' grandson; borrowed a very large sum from a rich Samaritan in Rome; paid the debt to Antonia with part of it; and spent the rest on Caligula, who was now about twenty-four and who stood the best chance of becoming emperor on Tiberius' death.

Suddenly Agrippa was in glory again—on easy terms with the great, living a life of pleasure and money, keeping Caligula company. Caligula did not like many people (except attractive women), but Agrippa knew how to flatter him and amuse him. He said things that made Caligula laugh. He entertained Caligula with tales of the Oriental courts, anecdotes of Roman society during Caligula's boyhood, stories of his own multifarious experiences. He was intimate yet respectful; companionable yet shrewd. He drank with Caligula, feasted with him, compared notes with him, caused him to feel overwhelmingly important, charmed him absolutely. And once Caligula was emperor, things would be even better. Agrippa went so far as to remark to his young friend that he hoped Tiberius would die soon so that Caligula could take over.

That remark was a bad mistake. It was overheard, and in time it was reported to Tiberius; and Agrippa in his finery was taken off to prison. Once more the beautiful world had crashed around him. Antonia, still the solicitous patroness, saw to it that he had certain amenities. For instance, his guards were less rough than many, he could take a bath every day, and he could receive visitors. But even so, time hung heavy and there was no telling how long Tiberius could hold out.

The incarceration lasted six months before Tiberius finally obliged by dying. One of Caligula's first acts on becoming emperor was to remove Agrippa from prison to his own home. He was still kept under guard, because freeing him right away would look unseemly; but one day the emperor summoned him to the palace for an even nicer surprise than he had been anticipating. Philip the tetrarch had died several years before, and his Graeco-Arab tetrarchy had been annexed to the province of Syria. Caligula now presented this land to Agrippa, together with some other territory in the same area; and he placed a royal diadem on the head of his friend to signify that Agrippa was a king. As an added little token of fondness, the emperor gave him a solid-gold chain weighing as much as the iron chain that he had had to endure in jail.

Agrippa of the twice-royal blood, now royal by right of office, did not leave for his kingdom immediately, although of course he drew revenues from it. In fact he stayed at Rome for about a year more, catering to Caligula's whims, humoring this ruler who thought himself a god. When at last he did decide to sail to the East and look over his kingdom, it was with the intention of coming back to Rome as soon as he could.

Agrippa crossed the Mediterranean to Alexandria, from which he would sail up the Asian coast to some port in Syria. Apparently he did not plan to spend much time at the Egyptian metropolis, where he was not even expected. But sudden trouble for the Jews prevented him from slipping out of the city quite as soon as he had wished.

The Roman governor at Alexandria, a man named Flaccus, was in an opposite position from Agrippa's: he had incurred the emperor's disfavor. A very efficient administrator and a fairer governor than most, Flaccus had done a creditable job at Alexandria for the past several years. Unfortunately, however, he had supported the wrong candidate for the throne, and when Caligula became emperor he felt extremely uncomfortable. It was at this time that several Greek citizens of Alexandria, influential but not high-principled, went to him with the suggestion that the best way for him to win Caligula's approval was to support the city's Gentiles against the Jews. Their suggestion may have been a case of uncomplicated anti-Semitism, or it may have been a means of fighting recent attempts by the Jews to attain full Alexandrian citizenship. At any rate, in view of Caligula's known dislike for Jews it certainly sounded attractive to Flaccus. The Greeks even promised that if Caligula still proved unfriendly, they would back their dear governor against the emperor. Flaccus decided that he had no other recourse than to follow their proposal.

Of all the cities in the Empire, Alexandria was the place where tension between Jews and Gentiles, provoked by countless petty irritants, was most likely to escalate into violence. Although Agrippa had wished to make his short stay there a quiet one, the Jews apparently hailed him with loud enthusiasm. This man of their own religion was a new-made king and someone to be proud of. But the Greeks, remembering Agrippa as a debtor, an adventurer, and an opportunist, angrily resented his having been made a king. When they saw the pomp that invested him now—his bodyguard of spear bearers in armor ornamented with silver and gold—they felt that he was flaunting his undeserved splendor in their faces.

Having been a seat of sophistication for a longer time than Rome, Alexandria was given to sarcasm, satire, and public jokes. The jeering, hooting mob of lower-class Greeks, the citizens most offended by Agrippa's finery, made farcical fun of him for several days at the gymnasium, the center of Greek life in the city. On Alexandria's cluttered streets, where flocks of squawking ibis came to catch the prolific vermin or to eat the refuse from meat shops before it had grown putrid, a naked halfwit named Carabas was a common sight. Harmless and as good-humored as a pet dog, he provided a comic oddity for the ragged boys, who liked to tease him and mimic him. The Greeks used this town character for their masterpiece: a travesty on Agrippa. They swept him into the gymnasium, put him on a platform for everybody to look at, flung a carpet over his nudity instead of royal raiment, placed some papyrus on his addled head in lieu of a royal diadem, stuck a piece of papyrus in his hand for a scepter—and then staged an elaborate parody in which he was the star.

While the audience pointed, giggled, and shouted raw anti-Jewish gibes, youths with rods on their shoulders mounted guard on either side of Carabas in burlesque of Agrippa's resplendent spear bearers. Men drew near him in mock awe, bowed low before this new-made king, asked him solemn questions on national policy, pretended they were criminals and pleaded with him frantically for their lives. Since Agrippa's kingdom had recently been part of Syria, everybody shouted out a Syrian term for "Lord" and laughed and laughed at the great joke. We are not told how Carabas felt about his elevation, but for the mob it was the finest show in a long while.

The governor Flaccus, the man ultimately responsible for public order in Alexandria, should have stopped the proceedings but did nothing. Even though he had committed himself to an anti-Semitic policy, his inaction is difficult to understand. He must have realized that he could not gain the imperial favor by countenancing this satire of the emperor's dear friend Agrippa. Possibly he was depending on the promise of the Greek leaders to support him no matter what happened, or perhaps he was afraid to contravene the will of so unruly and uproarious a mass of people.

It is not known just when Agrippa left Alexandria—only that before his departure he promised to perform a valuable service for the city's Jewish population. Not long after Caligula's accession the Alexandrian Jews had composed a complimentary address assuring the new emperor of their loyalty. They had given this document to Flaccus in the expectation that although he would not allow them to send it to Caligula in the hands of a Jewish delegation, he would arrange to have it transmitted in some other way. Flaccus, however, had merely retained it; so that at a time when other people were presenting the emperor with congratulations and professions of fervent devotion, the Alexandrian Jews looked remiss. Before Agrippa left the city, they went to him for help. He took what must have been a copy of the document and told the Jews that he would see that it got to the emperor; and he kept his word.

The trouble at Alexandria had only begun; it soon grew much worse. For example, the Gentiles demanded that the Jews set up statues of Caligula in their synagogues. Philo, the learned and aristocratic Jew who lived through the affair and left two accounts of it, implies in his diatribe *On Flaccus* that this demand was made soon after the Carabas farce. If it was, the Greek mob, or at any rate the mob's leaders, may have feared that in satirizing Agrippa they had seriously offended the emperor and that they had better do something right away to prove their love. The demand, which suggested righteous indignation on the part of the Greeks, would admirably serve this purpose. Besides, it would divert the emperor's attention from themselves to the Jews. They certainly knew that the Jews would refuse to pollute their synagogues with images of Caligula, and that the refusal would be a gross insult to the imperial god.

Even if Flaccus had not already adopted an anti-Jewish policy, he would naturally have had to oppose the Jews on this issue. He evidently seized the synagogues, closed them, and issued some sort of proclamation calling the Jews foreigners and declaring that they did not have the right to plead for their position. Some of the synagogues may actually have been desecrated by statues of the emperor. Philo's other account of these disturbances, the *Embassy to Gaius*, says that synagogues were also burned.

The anti-Semitic movement kept gaining momentum. The Gentiles invaded the Jewish quarters of the city, drove the screaming, unarmed Jews out of their houses, appropriated the furniture and costly objects if there were any, and displayed the choicest items exultantly in the streets or fought over them. It was June, and shops were closed throughout the city in token of mourning for Caligula's favorite sister—the one whom he had treated as his wife. The emperor himself in his sorrow had decreed mourning all over the Empire and had announced that a man who laughed or took a bath during this sad period would be executed. But the mobs broke into the closed shops of Jewish tradesmen and artisans and cleaned them of their wares. Thousands of Jews were herded into a camp outside the city proper and confined there, almost on top of one another. There were so many that they fouled the air.

In the days that followed, some Jews ventured into the city, perhaps to find work, more likely to buy or beg for food—since they and their families were starving, although the wheatfields of the Nile Delta stood rich with grain. If these Jews were caught in the city, they were snarled at, screamed at, stoned, clubbed, stabbed, or reserved for burning. Even with the demolition of Jewish houses and shops, which provided much firewood, some parts of the city could not always furnish enough wood for a good blaze. In such cases green brushwood was gathered and set on fire; since it smoldered rather than flamed, the Jew tied in its midst, coughing and gasping and choking, would gradually smoke to death. The city was all of a sudden savage, crazy for Jewish blood. Men who had caught a Jew would tie a strap to one of his ankles and drag him through the markets; and other men, needing some physical outlet for their abhorrence, would jump on him to hear him squeal. They would jump on him until he was dead, and then they would jump on his corpse.

It was probably late in August that Flaccus arrested the members of the council, or senate, that governed the city's Jewish population —all of them prominent Jews, many of them very old. Philo does not mention why Flaccus ordered the arrest; possibly the refusal to let Caligula's statues into the synagogues was involved. The eminent, aged men were paraded through the streets, some in thongs and some in iron chains. At the theater they were stripped and whipped. To add to the indignity they were scourged with lashes—not with the flat blades of swords, as their station required. This seems to have bothered Philo very much, as it implied that they possessed no citizenship in Alexandria. After the whipping some were carried out on stretchers, already dead; others were marched out to die. The show was very likely staged in celebration of Caligula's twenty-sixth birthday, on August 31. More cheerful performances, better suited to a theater, followed the anti-Jewish display: there were dances, pantomimes, and the playing of flutes.

It was enough. The leading Jews decided to send a delegation to Caligula to lay their sufferings before him and, incidentally, claim full Alexandrian citizenship. The embassy consisted of five persons, of whom Philo himself was the head. But the Greeks sent a counterdelegation, led by a self-confident, rhetorically accomplished scholar.

When Caligula first saw the Jews at Rome, he waved to them pleasantly and sent them a message that he would hear their case as soon as he had a chance. The chance, however, was not forthcoming, and Philo's party followed him south to the port of Puteoli, near Naples and Pompeii. Caligula had several villas in this area—elaborate, pseudorural pleasure palaces, pleasure gardens, and watering places —and he relaxed from his imperial chores by staying at them in turn. He still could not find time to listen to the Jews (or, apparently, to the Greeks). But while Philo's party was waiting at Puteoli, a messenger arrived with news from Judaea that staggered the delegation. Caligula had ordered a great, gold-plated statue, portraying himself as a god, to be set up in the Temple at Jerusalem.

The emperor's order was the outcome of an incident that had taken place in the city of Jamnia, located not far from the Palestinian coast.

Herod had willed Jamnia to his sister Salome, and Augustus had ratified the lucrative bequest in the hearings about the will that had involved Archelaus and Antipas. But Salome had died some time ago, and on her death Jamnia with the land surrounding it had become the emperor's property. Although it was therefore not a part of Judaea, it contained many Jewish inhabitants. It also had a sizable Gentile population, however; and one night a group of Gentiles sneaked into a synagogue and built a makeshift brick altar there to the god Caligula. The Jews promptly committed the disloyal act of tearing the altar down. The Roman official who represented the emperor's financial interests at Jamnia was, incidentally, the same person who had had Agrippa arrested for a debt to the imperial treasury several years before, when Agrippa was a poor man trying to get to Rome. This official dispatched a letter to Caligula describing the incident of the altar and playing up the Jews' disloyalty, and the emperor had the expected reaction: the fury of a crazed man. These Jews, not only in Jamnia but all over, had rejected his divinity long enough. Now he would force it down their throats. He issued the order about the gold-plated statue.

The order was not sent to Marullus, still procurator of Judaea, but to the governor of Syria, a certain Petronius. Caligula anticipated trouble from the Jews, and Petronius had the necessary troops under his command. He was to withdraw half the soldiers stationed in Syria, so that they could guard the statue on its journey through Judaea to Jerusalem. If any Jews tried to prevent the statue's progress or its installation at the Temple, they would be run through.

In their horror the Jews could think only, It must not happen. It must not happen. Stories were told about the terrible times of Antiochus the God Manifest, when the statue of Zeus, the Abomination of Desolation, had been set up in the Temple and the followers of Yahweh made to eat pig. Caligula's statue, according to the rumor, was to be put in the Holy of Holies itself: the indefinable, ineffable place that no ordinary Jew could enter, that not even ordinary priests could enter, that the high priest himself could enter only once a year without incurring death—the blank, inmost chamber of the Temple, the room reserved for God. First, the Jews decided, they would go to Petronius and plead for the inviolability of God's house; and then if necessary they would die.

Petronius understood their position as well as a Roman could. Although he marched toward Judaea with a couple of legions of Roman soldiers plus Syrian auxiliaries, he did not like to draw closer. As yet the soldiers had no statue to convey—but there must be one soon, and he hated the prospect. After all, these provincials were entitled to their religion, and perhaps it deserved respect. Petronius had evidently acquired a little knowledge of Judaism, either because he was intellectually curious or because as governor in Syria and, before that, in Asia Minor, he had come into frequent contact with Jews of the Diaspora. The worship of Yahweh was largely an exotic secret to him, but he perhaps knew enough to appreciate the Jewish stand and even to sympathize with it.

He realized besides that since the inhabitants of Judaea felt so strongly on the matter of the statue, there was no predicting what crimes against Rome they would commit. And unfortunately Jews throughout the Diaspora—in Syria, in Alexandria, in Rome—felt the same. If they were all to rise in rebellion (this was conceivable though not probable), the distress and death would amount to much more than one statue of the emperor was worth. Even if only the Jews in Judaea rebelled, the results would still be tragic; and no doubt their insidious rabble-rousers were already busy in the Judaean towns, whispering violence.

However, the emperor had given the order, and the governor of Syria was his servant. Whether or not the Little Boot was a god on earth, he must be obeyed.

Caligula had not stipulated that a statue be sent from Rome or that one already standing somewhere in the East be used. Petronius therefore commissioned one to be made—not in Judaea itself, however, but at Sidon on the Phoenician coast. At least there would be no riots at Sidon, where the Gentile population far outnumbered the Jews.

The governor marched to Ptolemais, also on the Phoenician coast but very close to Judaea. Here he intended to put up his army while the object was being made. If insurrection arose anywhere in Judaea during the construction, he could march to the trouble spot in short order. Meanwhile Jews from the cities and villages of Judaea, Galilee, and Syria kept arriving at Ptolemais—thousand after thousand of them, the doddering as well as the young. They gathered in the plain outside the city, where they abandoned themselves to ritualistic expressions of a real grief, moaning and crying and beating their chests. If we are to believe Philo, they were not a chaotic mass but were organized into six groups: old men, young men, boys, old women, young women, girls. When Petronius went out from the city to appear before them, they further dramatized their sorrow by falling on their faces in the dust and wailing. At last they rose, and as they came close to crowd around him they held their hands clasped behind their backs (the traditional pose of disarmed captives) to suggest that they were at Petronius' mercy or at the mercy of Rome. All of this indicates that the demonstration must have been carefully planned and directed by their leaders.

Petronius explained what his audience already knew: that the power of Rome was too great to be resisted, that the emperor's will could not be ignored, that an army waited nearby to enforce the imperial wish. The Jews' most eloquent elders explained what Petronius already knew: that men of their religion could not go against the Law even for an emperor, that although to disobey the emperor's command was unwise, to disobey the command of Yahweh was impossible. They had no choice; even the Romans could not prevent them from dying for the Law.

In addition to Philo, Josephus has left accounts of these troubles —one in his *Jewish War* and a longer one in his *Jewish Antiquities*. His versions differ from Philo's narrative in several respects. For instance, he says that the demonstrations occurred in the season of sowing (which in Judaea was in the autumn), whereas Philo says they occurred when it was time to gather the ripe grain (that is, in spring). Josephus also says that Petronius proceeded to Antipas' capital, Tiberias in Galilee, for another confrontation with the Jews, whereas Philo does not mention a confrontation at Tiberias. The rightness or wrongness of either author will probably never be proved; but most scholars consider Philo's account more trustworthy because he was a contemporary (Josephus wrote half a century later) and because his narrative contains fewer details that strain credulity. At Tiberias, according to Josephus, or at Ptolemais, according to Philo, the Jewish elders requested permission to communicate with the emperor in the hope that he would relent (even though most of them, like many other inhabitants of the Empire, probably believed by this time that Caligula was insane).

Philo says that Petronius, after discussing the request with his advisers, decided not to let the Jews send an embassy to Rome—which was what the elders had asked for—but to slow down the work on the statue and to dispatch a letter to the emperor on his own. In this

letter he argued that a first-rate statue, one worthy of Caligula's godship, would require a long time to complete, and that if an attempt
was made to install the statue at present, the desperate Jews would
probably react by setting fire to the fields of grain ready for harvest.

Caligula apparently had two reactions to this letter. He burned
with fury; but at the same time he remembered that Petronius, with
four legions under his command, was too powerful a man to be repri-
manded savagely—the result might be a military revolt. He therefore
wrote Petronius a politic letter praising him for the exercise of due
caution but urging him to hurry anyway. The situation had not improved very much. The Jews waited, tense, grimly fanatic, for the
completion of the hated thing. At this point—or even earlier, according to Josephus' account—King Agrippa entered the picture as the
hero.

From Alexandria, Agrippa had proceeded to his gift kingdom
south of Syria to take care of matters there, as planned. The main
problem posed by the kingdom was a family one: his sister Herodias
and her husband Antipas, who still reigned as tetrarch in nearby Galilee, were jealous of him for having it. The poor relation who had
worked for them as supervisor of the markets at Tiberias, who had
provided a butt for their barbed humor and had finally, inexcusably,
gotten so angry that he quit their service, was now back as a king and
an uncomfortably close neighbor; and Antipas, who had been ruling
for over forty years, was still just a tetrarch. It was too much to endure—it was too insolent. The comments that John the Baptist had
screeched ten or fifteen years before were a minor insult compared
with Agrippa's kingship. Herodias felt the injury even more strongly
than Antipas did; after all, Agrippa was her brother. She convinced
her husband that the two of them should sail to Italy and talk with
the emperor—tell him how wonderful they were, tell him how unde-
serving Agrippa was, persuade him to make Antipas a king too. That
would show Agrippa.

But when Agrippa heard about their plans he rushed his own messenger to the emperor, along with letters accusing Antipas of treason.
The emperor was at Baiae, close to Puteoli, in a pleasureland of palatial villas and gardens and baths and beaches edging the blue bay.
Here he read the letters, in which his friend Agrippa said that Antipas had entered into a conspiracy with the king of Parthia against

Rome. According to Agrippa, Antipas had enough military supplies stored away in Galilee to equip a force of seventy thousand heavy-armed foot soldiers, and this military power was intended to help the Parthians defeat the Romans.

Antipas and Herodias now arrived at Baiae. Caligula asked Antipas whether all this equipment was really stashed away in the Galilean armories; and Antipas had to admit that it was, although of course he denied that it was to be employed against the glorious emperor. Antipas may have been telling the truth (in fact the arms were probably for use against the Nabataeans), but the glorious emperor preferred to believe Agrippa's insinuations. He banished old Antipas to a town in the foothills of the Pyrenees, far from long-established civilization. He also deprived Antipas of personal property. But since Herodias was the sister of his friend Agrippa, Caligula informed her that she could keep her property and need not go to the Pyrenees, as long as she recognized that it was because of her admirable brother that she was granted such favors. This was more than she could stand; she had too much pride to thank the brother who had ruined her husband. She let the emperor know her feelings; and he banished her to the Pyrenees too.

Her possessions, together with Galilee and the other lands over which Antipas had ruled, were given to Agrippa. Possessor of a much-expanded kingdom, companion of the emperor and gatherer of great revenues, he was now a most fortunate man. He used his eminence for the cause of the Jews.

We do not know when Agrippa arrived back in Italy. He may have followed as closely behind his own letter as he could, or he may not have come until Antipas had been safely exiled. Possibly he was early enough to accompany the emperor on an abortive military expedition to Gaul and Germany between September of 39 and May of 40—and of course to mitigate the rigors of the expedition by his entertaining presence; or perhaps he reached Rome and Caligula in the summer of 40. In any case he was on hand when needed most. Again the stories told by Philo and Josephus differ; but both of them portray Agrippa as having a stronger sense of responsibility toward the Jews than the self-indulgence of his previous life might lead one to expect.

Josephus says that when Agrippa heard about the statue, he held a fantastically elaborate and expensive banquet for the emperor. Caligula assumed that Agrippa was looking for some personal reward in return. Very much impressed by the party, he promised to give Agrippa anything he asked. The king, however, nobly replied that he had not gone to all this prodigality to obtain any benefit for himself but instead to gain help for the Jews. Would the emperor please rescind the order to have the statue set up in the Temple?

The lavish banquet is certainly a method Agrippa would have liked to use; but in other respects Josephus' story sounds too contrived to be anything but fiction. Philo's story does not ring entirely true either, but on the whole it is perhaps more credible. Philo states that Agrippa had not heard about Caligula's order but noticed that the emperor seemed disturbed about something, and that he seemed particularly disturbed—in fact enraged—whenever he looked at Agrippa. The friend and favorite had too much tact to ask Caligula, "Are you angry at me?" But his perplexity showed in his face; and Caligula, noticing it, finally offered an explanation. He was angry at the Jews for appealing to Petronius not to erect the imperial statue in the Temple, and since Agrippa was a Jew by religion and partly by race, his friendly feelings toward Agrippa had suddenly gone sour. The least credible part of the story is what happened next: Agrippa fainted and was carried off on a stretcher.

Philo does not indicate whether Agrippa fainted because he feared that the Jews could look forward to a rough time or because he feared that his own pleasant and lucrative relationship with the emperor was over, but the end of the story suggests that he was more worried about the fate of the Jews than about his own fate. After recuperating at his Roman home for three days, he sent Caligula a letter which, although it was diplomatically phrased, amounted to a plea for the Jewish cause. He wrote as a descendant of Herod, as a descendant of the Hasmonaean high priests and kings, as a spokesman for the Jews not only of Judaea but of the whole Diaspora, and (he hoped) as the emperor's cherished friend. The Roman government had been kind toward the Jews in the past, and the Jews had in consequence been loyal to Rome. For example, he himself provided funds for the daily sacrifice of a bull and two lambs at the Temple for the emperor's health and happiness. Jews were not different from other people: they hankered after their own beliefs like everybody else —and they could not stand to see the heart of their religion violated. It would be a terrible thing if the emperor tried to have a statue placed in the Temple.

The capricious Caligula does not seem to have stayed angry at Agrippa for long, and the letter perhaps even mollified his anger at the Jews. At least he wrote to Petronius that unless the statue was already set up, it should not be installed—for a while at any rate. But he added that Petronius must immediately punish, or send to Italy for punishment, anybody who interfered with the setting up of statues to the emperor outside Jerusalem. This was probably not an outrageous stipulation, although Philo feels it could easily have fostered civil conflict. Caligula may have envisioned the Jews as preventing statues from being erected to himself in Syria or in predominantly Gentile cities of Judaea, such as Caesaraea and Sebaste. The Jews, however, were quiet, perhaps from emotional exhaustion as much as from the belief that the menace of the statue was definitely over. It was over for the time being; but the egomaniacal emperor could revive it at any moment.

In Italy the Jewish delegates from Alexandria finally got a chance to speak with Caligula. No one knows how long they had waited. It may have been months, it may have been more than a year. They were back in Rome from Puteoli at the time. Flaccus, the governor in Egypt, had already been arrested at Alexandria, perhaps on charges contributed by Agrippa. He had been brought to Rome for trial, and, with a poetic justice that he surely did not appreciate, had been accused of gross maladministration by two eminent Alexandrian Greeks, formerly his fellow conspirators against the Jews. He had been exiled to the stony little island of Andros in the Aegean Sea. Not much later he was murdered there on Caligula's orders. All of this in fact may have happened before Philo's delegation ever reached Italy; it certainly happened before the interview with the emperor took place. But the matter of the synagogues remained to be discussed, and so did the question of the rights and privileges of Alexandrian Jews, and the matter of their loyalty or disloyalty.

The emperor had been relaxing for several days in some villas on the Esqueline Hill near Rome. It was to these villas and their vast and elaborate gardens that the Jews were summoned. The deputation of Alexandrian Greeks was on hand too, so that the emperor, like his brother the great god Jupiter, could hear both sides and deliver an impartial verdict.

The Jews bowed respectfully. Much as they despised this young madman, they had better show him high regard if they wished to come off with their lives. In the light of all that had happened, they did not hope optimistically to achieve their purpose, but they would try.

Caligula inquired sarcastically, as if asking for enlightenment, whether these were the people who hated gods and who denied his own godship, in contrast to all other nations.

The charge was unanswerable.

Caligula reached his hands toward the sky that he believed to be partly his own possession, and invoked its powers. The Alexandrian Greeks snickered, thinking their cause already won. In the enthusiasm of evident triumph they called down on Caligula the blessings of all the gods they could think of.

They were in one of the villas, which Caligula, with the eye of an interior decorator, was surveying with a view to possible changes. Some of the rooms were not sufficiently magnificent to suit him. It did not always look as if he were paying much attention to the embassies. One of the Greeks, speaking sweetly, claimed that the Jews, unlike other men, refused to offer sacrifices in thanksgiving for the preservation of the emperor's life.

This was an accusation that the Jews could refute. They told the emperor indignantly that they had sacrificed hundreds of animals when he came to the throne, when he recovered from a plague that had overrun the Empire, and most recently when he went to Gaul and Germany on his expedition.

Caligula commented that the Jews had offered these sacrifices to their own God rather than to Caligula, and that ended the discussion. He went on with his survey of the villa apartments. The Jews, too frightened now to say a great deal, followed along behind, and the Greeks accompanied him—conversational, humorous, full of jokes about Jews. The emperor, occupied with giving orders for the refurbishment of the villa, did not seem to be listening closely to the comedy; but he suddenly turned on the Jews and asked why they did not eat pork.

The Greeks giggled and tittered at this instance of the imperial wit, and the Jews explained that not everybody followed the same customs. Various pleasures, they said, were forbidden to various peoples: pork was forbidden to Jews.

One of the Greeks remarked jauntily that for some people lamb was taboo; Caligula just as jauntily called this a wise restriction, since lamb tasted awful anyway. Everybody laughed except the Jews.

Finally Caligula introduced the topic that Philo's delegation had been waiting for but had not had the temerity to introduce on their own: why did the Jews think they deserved the rights of citizens at Alexandria?

They proceeded to give him reasons; but manifesting a passionate interest in the villa, he hurried into its largest room and issued enthusiastic instructions as to what was to be done with the windows. Instead of being fitted with translucent white glass, they should be fitted with translucent stones of various colors, which would create a more splendid effect and yet let the light in. It would be an excellent room —good enough for a god.

Calm again, he reminded the Jews that they had been speaking to him. They hazarded another explanation of why the Jews of Alexandria should possess the rights enjoyed by citizens of the great metropolis; but they only wasted their breath.

The emperor was very fond of Alexandria, and he had already made plans for visiting it within the next few months and receiving its adulation. Perhaps he felt that the monotheistic, inflexible Jews would spoil the beautiful, witty city by the mere fact of sharing in citizens' rights, or that the Greek population would not receive him well if he had just favored the Jewish population. At any rate he surrendered to another flash of enthusiasm on hurrying into another room: it must have lifelike murals on its walls, depicting this and that. The Jews decided they had said all they could say.

But suddenly Caligula softened. He declared that the Jews were not really evil—only despicable. They were in fact a ridiculous people, and their pigheaded denial of his godhood was the proof of their ridiculousness. The audience was over.

The Jews, however, did not have to wait much longer for redress. One day late in January in the year 41, as Caligula was proceeding through a passageway that led from the imperial theater, an officer in the Praetorian Guard sank a dagger in his throat. The god died.

Agrippa was still at Rome on that day of confusion, luxuriating in the income from his kingdom. According to Josephus, he played an instrumental part in getting his friend Claudius, Caligula's uncle, made the next emperor. Claudius was the grandson of Mark Antony and the son of the Antonia who had patronized Agrippa so devotedly during the lean years. A fifty-year-old man now—intelligent without flamboyance and earnest without noise—he contrasted sharply with his assassinated nephew. His attainments were not social but scholarly: he had composed in Greek a history of Carthage in eight books and a history of the Etruscans in twenty. Conversationally maladroit and seemingly slow in the fast-moving capital of the sophisticated world, he had impressed many people as an unlikely candidate for imperial honors. Perhaps Agrippa recognized the capacity for government that underlay his evident bookishness, or perhaps Agrippa just wanted Caligula's successor to be somebody he knew well. Of course he was not as close to Claudius as he had been to Caligula; he did not respond as easily to scholarly thoroughness as to social grace and cruel young wit. But no better candidate offered.

Caligula had been especially hard on aristocrats, and many members of the aristocratic senate—relatives perhaps of patricians whom Caligula had picturesquely executed—felt that an emperor was potentially too dangerous to their class and therefore wished the republic to be restored. Most of the soldiers, however, wanted the continuation of imperial rule. They considered it simpler and more efficient than rule by a large and often disunited aristocratic body. Besides, whoever was made emperor would no doubt distribute an emolument to the soldiers.

In the chaos following the assassination some members of the palace guard kidnaped Claudius, with the intention of persuading him to become emperor. He was taken to the Praetorian camp, where he would be safe from the possibility of murder by some overenthusiastic republican. The senate was holding an emergency meeting, and Agrippa acted as a messenger between the senate and Claudius. In the *Jewish Antiquities* Josephus says that Agrippa urged a diffident Claudius to take advantage of the moment, push his claim to the throne, and not be deterred by the senate's opposition. But in the *Jewish War* Josephus says that Claudius himself, apparently eager to be emperor, took the initiative and that Agrippa merely delivered to the senate the responses that Claudius had thought of. In either case, Agrippa made sure that Claudius noticed his devotion. While most people were running around in frantic disorder, reliable Agrippa was on hand to see the thing through.

He had gambled well, and the reward was handsome. Claudius, in gratitude for his loyal service, gave him the whole province of Judaea as an addition to the lands over which he already ruled. The procuratorship was abolished; the grimness of strict Roman suzerainty was mitigated; Agrippa would reign in Judaea as a client king.

Agrippa had now reached the apogee of his ambitions. King in the Arab regions south of Syria, in Transjordanian Peraea, in the fruitful Galilean valleys, in the territory of Abilene northwest of Damascus, in heretical Samaria, in the Jewish homeland and in holy Jerusalem itself, as well as in foreign Caesaraea and Sebaste, he commanded an area as large as the one over which his grandfather Herod had reigned. The senate added consular honors to the eminence he already enjoyed. He who had once been a debtor was incalculably rich; he who had lain in prison five years ago was a great man.

When the Jews in Alexandria heard that Caligula was dead, they rioted gleefully against the Greeks. After their revenge had been quashed, Claudius issued an edict warning both the Jews and the Greeks against creating further disturbance in the second city of the Empire. But in the same edict he criticized Caligula for oppressing the Jews, and confirmed the rights that they had held at Alexandria under the Ptolemies and the privileges that Augustus had guaranteed them. Claudius then issued another edict, in which he confirmed those same privileges for Jews throughout the Empire. He also praised the Jews for loyalty to Rome and encouraged them to keep their own religion.

Behind the second edict—perhaps behind both—was Agrippa. As he had done with Caligula, he adroitly used his friendship with the new emperor for the benefit of his people as well as for his personal benefit. The word went out that he was the main reason for Claudius' graciousness toward the Jews. Consequently, when he arrived in Judaea he was welcomed almost as a savior. Here was the man who had risked his own security to help the Jews on vital occasions, the man without whom they would be suffering. His grandfather might have been a hated tyrant, but Agrippa himself was the brave champion of Jewish ideals. After the Roman insults, after the Roman soldiers and the threat of the statue, he looked superb. Besides he was Hasmonaean as well as Herodian. His grandmother had been Mariamne; in him the Hasmonaeans were restored. Since he governed only as a client king, the Jews were not really free, but under this friendly and beneficent man they could feel freer than they had felt for generations.

His sense of the appropriate did not fail him in this period of popularity. On reaching Jerusalem he performed at the Temple the sacrifices of thanksgiving, carefully following the specifications of the Law in all details. His sense of the histrionic did not fail him either: in the sacred precincts he hung the chain of gold that Caligula had given him.

Caesaraea, that interloping city of Greek ways, was no longer the capital; Agrippa ruled from Jerusalem like the kings of old. He did not grow lax about the Law, as long as he was among people who prized it above life. When one of his daughters became engaged to marry the prince of Commagene, he required that the prince adopt Judaism before the marriage could take place; and since the young man was slow, there was no wedding. When mischievous youths in the Syrian city of Dora set up a statue of Claudius in the Jewish synagogue, he complained to the governor of Syria, who was still Petronius. Ever since the emperor's edict guaranteeing Jews throughout the Empire their privileges, it had been illegal to interfere with their mode of worship. Petronius, glad that he was finally at liberty to aid the Jews on the matter of an imperial statue, wrote an angry letter to the chief citizens of Dora, accusing them of countenancing sacrilege. The statue was removed.

Most of Agrippa's subjects continued to regard him as a godsend, and he continued to make plays for their affection. For instance, he remitted the household tax. He even demonstrated his firm Judaism by persecuting heretics who followed the crucified Jesus. One of them, a Galilean named James, he succeeded in executing. He had a certain Peter arrested too—another Galilean, formerly a fisherman but now, it seemed, a self-appointed authority on religious matters. Peter escaped, but even so Agrippa had convincingly illustrated his own strict orthodoxy.

And yet he had, after all, been brought up in the great world, and the most pleasant parts of his life had been passed outside Judaea. Although he was intensely proud of being one of the chosen, the amenities of Graeco-Roman civilization proved too attractive for him to give up. Exclusive Judaism appeared austere and unsociable. He was devoted to it, but he felt the need to allay its grimness. And so he became a paradox, drawn toward two cultures. His sincere religious faith, for which he had hazarded so much, satisfied only part of him. In a gracious pagan environment he could easily forget the rigorous injunctions of his religion.

He ruled from Jerusalem but almost preferred Caesaraea, and his Caesaraean palace contained statues of his three daughters—graven images that Jerusalem would not have stood for. Ironically most of the Caesaraean Greeks rejected him, hating him for his strong support of Jewish principles and his important achievements on behalf of Judaism. They said that although his grandfather Herod had unfortunately subscribed to Judaism too, his grandfather had been much less offensive about it.

Nevertheless, when he had a chance Agrippa took Herod for his model. He placed beautiful, airy, elegantly proportioned Graeco-Roman buildings wherever circumspection permitted. Toward Berytus on the Phoenician coast of Syria, the city where his uncle Alexander and his father Aristobulus had been prosecuted for treason by his grandfather, he was munificent in the Herodian manner. A costly theater, an amphitheater for Greek athletic contests, Roman-style baths, and the marshaled columns of long porticoes all testified to the hope that his name would be celebrated among the Greeks and Romans long after he was dead. At the dedication of the Berytus amphitheater he furnished fourteen hundred men to fight in pairs and annihilate one another with the arts of war in front of appreciative Gentile spectators. The men were condemned criminals anyway, so that from a Roman point of view their deaths made little difference; but the citizens of Jerusalem would not have understood.

Even on Jewish soil—at Caesaraea at any rate—he patronized the theater. In spite of his careful conformity to the religious observances of Judaism, some of his subjects inevitably began to suspect that his tastes were divided. One time while he was enjoying himself at Caesaraea, there was a show of disloyalty at Jerusalem, though it probably did not involve many people. A certain Simon, a man with a fierce scrupulosity about religion, gathered an audience in the holy city and in a violent, denunciatory speech said that Agrippa was unclean. We do not know what specific support he gave for the accusation; perhaps he had heard that Agrippa had ignored the ritualistic precautions he should have taken before entering places of contamination, such as theaters. Simon went on to declare that since the king was ritually dirty, he should no longer be allowed inside the Temple.

Agrippa's commanding officer at Jerusalem dashed off a letter describing the speech, and the king ordered Simon to come to Caesaraea. Herod would probably have had the insolent man executed, but here Agrippa differed from his grandfather. He interviewed Simon at the theater, telling him to sit down and then asking whether anything he saw in front of him constituted a breach of the Law. The strict Jew, overwhelmed by the graciousness of royalty, could do nothing except ask for pardon; and the king granted it.

On that occasion as on many others, Agrippa's talent for saying and doing the right thing served him well; but in an entirely different matter it did him no good. At Tiberias, formerly the capital of Antipas' tetrarchy of Galilee, Agrippa wanted to hold a conference of kings. This, he anticipated, would be a truly splendid affair, not liable to adverse criticism by either Jews or Gentiles, reflecting glory on himself throughout the East and probably even at Rome. Five rulers came to Tiberias on his invitation: Antiochus, the king of Commagene, north of Syria; Polemo, the king of Pontus in northern Asia Minor; Cotys, the king of Lesser Armenia; Sampsigeramus, the priest king of the city of Emesa in Syria; and Agrippa's own brother Herod, king in the Ituraean city of Chalcis. For once, however, Agrippa had miscalculated. Marsus, Petronius' replacement as governor of Syria, came down toward Tiberias—and the glory crumbled.

Agrippa went out of the city politely to meet the governor, taking along the five kings. But Marsus, when he saw this array of royalty, somewhat stupidly suspected that the conference was a conspiracy against Rome. He told the kings to go home. Agrippa, wildly indignant, could say or do nothing to save the shattered conference. For once he had not made a good impression.

In the spring of A.D. 44, when Agrippa had been king of Judaea for about three years, spectacles were held at Caesaraea to honor the emperor. They were probably in celebration of his safe return to Rome from Britain, which he had just added to the Empire. To inhabitants of Judaea the island of Britain, somewhere way off to the north far beyond the edge of civilization, was inconceivably remote. Nevertheless Claudius' successful campaign in that far-off wilderness was no doubt a great thing, and he deserved to be honored for it. More power to Rome.

On the second day of the spectacles, just as dawn was creating a splendor in the East, Agrippa appeared in the theater robed in cloth-of-silver. It was another of his dramatic performances, and his histrionic sense again proved excellent. As the young sunbeams glinted off the shimmering garment, certain people in the audience hailed him as a god. He did not reproach them for this blasphemy: since he was not among Jews, there was no need to discourage the horrifying idea that he might be divine. The whole scene has the appearance of having been staged, as if Agrippa had planted people in the audience to give him divine recognition. Most Caesaraeans abhorred him so intensely for his helpfulness to the Jews that they could hardly have been expected to call him a god of their own accord. Perhaps the king had decided that although he could not be liked by the Caesaraeans, he could be glorified among them.

Not much later he suffered excruciating pains in the intestinal region. The attack sounds like acute appendicitis. Luke, in the Acts of the Apostles, says: "The angel of the Lord smote him, because he gave not God the glory." He was taken to his Caesaraean palace, where within five days he died. According to Acts, "he was eaten of worms, and gave up the ghost."

Although some of the Greeks of Caesaraea had been willing to hail the king as a god, most of them enjoyed his death tremendously. What had started as an official spectacle in honor of Claudius turned into a grotesque spectacle in celebration of Agrippa's demise. The king had not died old—only fifty-four—and the suddenness of the seizure heightened the vengeful delight of the anti-Semitic Caesaraeans. For a few days Caesaraea was almost an Alexandria. It was time to laugh at Jews and to play. While the city's Jewish minority mourned their great leader, the Greeks cheered and shouted in the streets, besmirched his memory with obscenities, stuck wreaths of flowers on their heads, and drank to his death. The soldiers were the worst: they confiscated statues of his three daughters, the oldest of whom was sixteen and already seductive, the youngest of whom was six. They carried these statues to familiar whorehouses, set them up on the flat roofs, and in plain view of the crowds down below pretended to have sex with them. The Jews did not forget the gross comedy.

In addition to his three daughters Agrippa had a son about seventeen years old, also named Agrippa. Many people expected that Claudius would confirm him in succession to the Jewish throne. But Claudius' advisers convinced him that the region must be under tighter control than the young Agrippa could exert. Even though the youth was at Rome and well known to Claudius, he was passed over. The emperor reestablished the procuratorship.

XIII

AGGRAVATIONS

The return of the procuratorship meant more incidents that might in time provoke a full-scale Jewish revolt. Agrippa's reign of three years had been only an interlude. In retrospect it seemed increasingly sweet, especially to Jews of the middle and lower classes. The aristocrats were not so distressed that a procurator governed again; most of them, having done well under Roman rule, thought the *status quo* was good enough. But with the common people it was different. Soon perhaps the long-expected Messiah would come and lead the Jews in glorious battle, until the unspeakable foreigners were driven once and for all from the land.

This hope naturally gave rise to false leaders. One of them, a certain Theudas, flourished under the procurator Cuspius Fadus, who governed Judaea from 44 to 46. Theudas cannot have been intentionally a fraud. He announced to his followers that he would lead them across the river Jordan by making the waters divide—much as the Red Sea had divided for Moses or as the Jordan itself had done for Joshua—and he would not have issued this claim unless he expected to fulfill it. Faithful Jews remembered the words in the Book of Joshua: "And the priests who bore the ark of the covenant of the Lord stood firm on dry ground in the midst of the Jordan, and all the Israelites passed over on dry ground." They gathered on the bank in a fanatic throng, and they brought possessions that they planned to carry with them when they passed over. But it was not the right time for a miracle. The procurator, afraid of their enthusiasm, sent his cavalry. They attacked the assembled Jews, slaughtered many, and took others prisoner. Theudas never had another chance to display his supernatural powers: they cut off his head.

This same procurator, Fadus, also provoked the Jews by trying to take the sacred vestments of the high priest from the Temple. He wanted to put them back into the Antonia, the Roman fort on the Temple hill from which Vitellius, the good governor of Syria, had transferred them only a few years before. The Jews sent a delegation to the emperor. Claudius decided in their favor, but not primarily because the delegation had persuaded him. The young Agrippa was still at Rome. Patterning himself after his father, he championed the Jewish cause; and possessing his father's social skill in dealing with emperors, he succeeded. It looked as if he would go far.

The next procurator, Tiberius Alexander, who governed from 46 to 48, was a Jew—the nephew in fact of the highly respected Philo of Alexandria himself. But his appointment offended the people of Judaea more sharply than the appointment of a Gentile would have done, because he was a fallen-away Jew—an apostate, a Romanizer. Under him conditions grew worse than ever. Taxes were oppressive, famine bit into the land, and patriotic rabble-rousers were executed.

Under Cumanus, procurator from 48 to 52, conditions did not improve and aggravations intensified. As usual Cumanus brought soldiers to stand guard on top of the portico surrounding the Temple area during the celebration of Passover, when trouble was most likely to break out; and these soldiers, anti-Semitic Graeco-Syrians from Caesaraea and Sebaste, viewed the proceedings with scorn and aversion. One time on the fourth day of Passover, a soldier lifted his skirt behind, turned around, and bent over to display his naked buttocks and genitals to the devout Jews crowding the courtyard below. Appalled at the blasphemy, the Jews screamed that Cumanus must punish this filthy man, and some accused the procurator of inciting him to his shameful act. Youths threw stones up at the soldiers. Cumanus responded by ordering his whole army to the Antonia. The Jews thought that if they stayed on the Temple hill they would all be cut down; so they stampeded for the exits and squashed one another to death in trying to get through.

The procurator apparently did not punish the indecent soldier, but he did punish one who committed a much worse offense. At a village not far from Jerusalem, where some soldiers were rounding up Jews who had been remiss about helping to catch a group of robber patriots, this man found a copy of the Torah. Spewing insults against the Jews and their God, he ripped the sacred scroll in half and burned it. To appease the people in some degree, Cumanus had him beheaded.

Although the Galileans were looked down on by other Jews for being lax about religion, they and the other Jews combined to hate the unorthodox Samaritans for rejecting all books of the Bible except the first five, and for refusing to recognize Jerusalem as the center of Judaism. During Cumanus' procuratorship a big battle occurred between Galileans and Samaritans. Many Galileans were killed, and the Galilean leaders appealed to Cumanus to punish the Samaritans. But Cumanus would take no action; he just sat. According to Josephus' *Jewish Antiquities,* he had accepted a Samaritan bribe. Other Jews joined the Galileans in protest against Cumanus' partiality, and he had to massacre some of them. Eventually the whole matter came before Claudius.

The emperor would have decided in favor of the Samaritans, who had influential partisans at Rome, but again the young Agrippa rushed to the defense of the orthodox Jews and again he was successful. Claudius found that the Samaritans had been in the wrong and ordered the execution of their most prominent men. He also ordered a certain army officer in Judaea to undergo punishment. This soldier's crime is not revealed, but he may have been the man who exposed himself at the Temple. He was dragged through the streets of Jerusalem in a public display and then beheaded.

Cumanus' misgovernment had become very evident during the trial; Cumanus was banished.

The next procurator, Antonius Felix, who governed between the years 52 and 60, had been born a slave but had been given his freedom by the emperor's mother. His brother was high at the Roman court, being the empress' lover. Felix himself may already have been in charge of Samaria when Claudius appointed him procurator of all Judaea in 52. At any rate the request that he be named procurator came from the high priest at Jerusalem. Claudius seems to have been delighted to make the appointment; according to the historian Suetonius, the emperor held Felix in high esteem.

This esteem was, insofar as we can tell, richly undeserved. Felix, like his brother the empress' lover, comes down to us as a brilliant but unprincipled opportunist. Connected with the imperial court even while he was a slave, he must have learned at an early age how to put his talents to the best possible use: how to please and how to maneuver, how to rise in the world, get money, and shine. His first wife was a granddaughter of Mark Antony and Cleopatra—in other words one of the most eminent ladies in the Empire. His second wife, whom he married a couple of years after becoming procurator, was one of the three daughters of King Agrippa. She must have found Felix very attractive, since she left her first husband, a king of Emesa, to marry him and since she continued to live with him even though he refused to adopt Judaism.

During Felix' procuratorship the Jewish patriots were more active than ever, stirring up the countryside, murdering Romans and Romanizers whenever they got the chance, retreating into the hills or the desert, carrying on what amounted almost to a guerrilla warfare. They were reminiscent of those inspired warriors of the old days, the followers of Judas Maccabaeus against Antiochus the God Manifest. In Jerusalem arose a variant on the patriots—the Sicarii, or "sickle men," so called because they carried curved, sickle-shaped daggers under their clothes. The Sicarii would whip out their daggers in the anonymity of a crowd, carve up some Roman sympathizer, and put the weapons back under their robes before anybody except the Roman sympathizer was the wiser.

New trouble started at Jerusalem when a Jew from Tarsus in Asia Minor, formerly called Saul but now called Paul, returned to the holy city from abroad. The son of a rich man, Paul differed from almost all other Jews in having been born a Roman citizen. As a fiercely religious Pharisee he had devoted his early manhood to persecuting the adherents of Christ's teachings at Jerusalem—Jews who were not yet called "Christians," since the name was then unknown. These early proselytes to Christ brought sacrificial animals to the Temple, as other Jews did, and piously followed the Law. But their heretical faith in Christ and their belief in the new dispensation made them obnoxious to more orthodox Jews, and Paul had watched with joy while one of them, a certain Stephen, was stoned to death.

Suddenly, however, on a trip to Damascus about A.D. 34, Paul had undergone his famous conversion, after which his fierce religiosity was directed toward converting others to Christ's principles—not only Jews but Gentiles who already knew something about Judaism, and even Gentiles who were total pagans. He had spread the new doctrine as far as Athens and Corinth, passionately preaching it. In Antioch, where he had taught during the early or mid-40's, Roman officials were beginning to call people of his persuasion "Christians"; and by 58, when he came back to Jerusalem, the term "Christian" was perhaps in use there too. Paul entered Jerusalem in the spirit of a son of the younger generation who comes back to his old-fashioned mother.

He was still nominally a Jew; but he realized that in Jerusalem, the seat of the ancient, immutable Law, he would have to prove his Judaism or face violent opposition from Jews unconvinced of Christ. Friends suggested that he sponsor at the Temple four Nazarites—persons consecrating themselves to God according to an ancient prescription in the Torah. He did so, but Jews from Asia Minor raised an outcry, screaming that he had brought Greeks into the holy precincts, that he had sullied the Temple. A mob formed; it was another religious riot. The troublemakers drove Paul out of the holy precincts, shut the doors on him, struck at him, beat him, and threatened to tear him apart.

In the interest of order the Roman garrison stationed at the Antonia on the Temple hill now intervened. The soldiers, not knowing that Paul was a Roman citizen but thinking only that these tiresome Jews were creating another disturbance, chained him, and their tribune ordered that he be taken to the Antonia. People were still yelling and milling around. Paul stood on the staircase leading from the military headquarters to the outer courtyard of the Temple area. With the tribune's permission he delivered a speech to the assembled arm-waving multitude.

To emphasize his Jewishness he addressed them in Hebrew rather than in the Aramaic that was the common language of the streets. But his speech was an explanation of his conversion from a persecutor of believers in Christ to an apostle of Christian principles, and that did not sit very well with his audience. According to Acts, the Jews "cried out, and cast off their clothes, and threw dust into the air"—and also demanded his death. This was the man who spoke against circumcision, the man who drew people away from the Law as given to Moses. But the tribune ordered him to be taken inside the Antonia. To the tribune one Jew was evidently very much like another; he had little sympathy for their incomprehensible religious spats that broke the Roman Peace. So he commanded that scourging be used on Paul. Maybe the truth about this whole mess could be whipped out of him.

Paul then announced his Roman citizenship. It was illegal to scourge a Roman who had not yet been condemned. The tribune as it turned out had entered life as a slave and had had to buy citizenship; Paul, who had been born with it, was in that sense superior. Much impressed, the tribune decided that Paul should appear before the Sanhedrin. That would settle the matter, he hoped.

But it did not. Many of the members of the Sanhedrin were Sadducees of the aristocratic priestly caste, whereas others were Pharisees. Paul cleverly set them to arguing against each other by declaring that he himself was a Pharisee and consequently believed in the existence of angels and the Resurrection of the dead, which the Sadducees denied. The hearing became a squabble. The tribune sent soldiers to rescue Paul before he was ripped to pieces by the angry theological enemies. Paul was taken back to the Antonia and shut up there.

Some of the Jews most opposed to Paul (over forty of them, according to Acts) bound themselves together in a secret brotherhood under oath not to eat or drink until they had killed him. He had to be murdered, they felt, or his doctrines would corrupt ancient Judaism. They devised a plot for assassinating him during his imprisonment. The Sadducean priests, to whom the brotherhood revealed the plot, endorsed it; but Paul's nephew heard about it too, and told the tribune. The Book of Acts does not disclose whether the men under oath ever ate or drank again—but Paul was not assassinated. Instead a strong detachment of soldiers took him to Caesaraea, which since the return of the procuratorship had been again the capital. The tribune wrote an explanatory letter to Felix and dumped the case in Felix' lap.

After several days a delegation from Jerusalem arrived at Caesaraea. One of its members was Tertullus, an advocate versed in the rhetorical skills of the age; it would be his job to present the Jewish claims against Paul. He addressed the "most noble Felix" in terms of practiced flattery, declaring that "by thee we enjoy great quietness" and that the Jews accepted the precious benefits of his procuratorship "with all thankfulness." Having allowed Felix to swallow this adulation, he gracefully and competently stated the Jewish case: that Paul was a dangerous revolutionary, a leader of the heretical sect that believed in Jesus of Nazareth, and a polluter of the Temple. Felix now motioned to Paul to speak. A preacher for many years, Paul was a match for Tertullus. His enemies, he maintained, could not prove their claims. He revered the Law and the prophets; he worshiped the God of his fathers, after his own fashion; like many of his fellow Jews, he held that the dead would be resurrected; and he had been doing nothing reprehensible in the Temple when the Jews seized him.

Through his wife Drusilla, the daughter of Agrippa, Felix probably knew enough about Judaism to realize that the matter could not be easily decided and that perhaps Paul's defense was valid. Deferring judgment, he put Paul under a centurion's charge but allowed the prisoner considerable freedom, such as the right to see whoever came to visit him. He even sent for Paul and in Drusilla's presence had the man expound the new faith, apparently for the purpose of determining whether there was anything wrong with it. According to Acts, after Paul had spoken, "Felix trembled, and answered, Go thy way for this time; when I have a convenient season, I will call for thee." But seasons came and went, and Felix did not find any of them convenient. Paul had been brought to Caesaraea in the year 58; he was kept there until the end of Felix' procuratorship in 60. Among the men that visited him was a disciple named Luke, who listened to him speak of these events and later recorded them in the Book of Acts.

Meanwhile there were other problems at Caesaraea to keep the procurator busy. Antagonism between the city's Jewish minority and Graeco-Syrian majority had broken out. The Jews evidently started it by announcing that since Caesaraea had been founded by Herod, a Jew by religion, the Graeco-Syrians should not have equal civic rights with Jews. The Gentiles of course countered that Herod had intended the city for Gentiles. Riots ensued. Jews and Gentiles tried to crack each other's heads open with stones, Felix let loose his soldiers (many of whom were Greeks for whom Caesaraea was their home town), and Jews were killed. Finally Felix sent representatives from both sides to the emperor—no longer Claudius but Nero. Caesaraea became a running sore.

Felix' successor, Festus, was an earnest man insofar as we can tell. He found Judaea in a near-anarchic condition, with robbers and patriots interfering with travel, Sicarii drawing their daggers in Jerusalem, Jews and Greeks at each other's throats, the Jews themselves split into the Sadducean and Pharisaic factions, sects such as the followers of Jesus compounding the complications, and faithful farmers looking for a Messiah. Into this chaos Festus tried to reintroduce Roman order—but he was too late.

The aristocratic Jews almost immediately reopened the case against Paul; and Festus, new to the situation and not yet knowing what to do, suggested that Paul go to Jerusalem and be tried there, with Festus himself present to see that Roman justice was not violated. Paul turned down this suggestion. Once more exercising his right as a Roman citizen, he appealed his case to the emperor. Festus, probably glad to get rid of him, agreed to let Nero judge him.

Before Paul left Caesaraea for Rome, the younger Agrippa came to the city to congratulate Festus on his appointment. About thirty-three years old at this time, Agrippa had done well for himself. Claudius had allowed him the right to name the high priest, so that he was a power among the Jews. Claudius had also made him, like his father before him, a king, bestowing on him the little domain of Chalcis northwest of Damascus. Later, in the year 53, Claudius took Chalcis from him but gave him in its place a much larger territory including the lands of Batanaea, Trachonitis, Gaulanitis, Auranitis, and Abilene, in all of which the population was not Jewish but Greek or Arab. After Claudius' death, his successor Nero added several lucrative cities to Agrippa's kingdom—the greatest of them being Tiberias on the Sea of Galilee—plus a number of villages and rich farmlands. In A.D. 60 Agrippa was therefore a man of consequence, styling himself (as his father had done) the Great King, the Friend of Caesar, the Pious, the Friend of Rome.

With him to Caesaraea came his sister Berenice, the oldest of the first Agrippa's three daughters. About a year younger than her brother, she had already enjoyed a colorful career. In her girlhood her father gave her in marriage to a rich Alexandrian Jew, a nephew of Philo; when this husband died her father married her to one of her uncles, at that time king of Chalcis, and she produced two children for him before he died. Twice a widow at the age of twenty-two, she went to live with her brother Agrippa—incestuously, according to whispered reports. Agrippa was unmarried and Berenice presided over the social life of his court as if she were his queen. The thought of their marrying each other would not have bothered their Graeco-Asiatic friends, who were used to such unions in royal families, but it probably would have horrified Agrippa and Berenice themselves since the Law forbade brothers and sisters to marry. They may have been in love even so, and the rumors about their sexual life may have been true.

To allay the scandal Berenice sought a new husband, King Polemo of Cilicia—the portion of Asia Minor where Paul's native city of Tarsus was situated—but she required that Polemo become a Jew first. He submitted to circumcision and they were married. Her third husband, however, did not please her, and in a while she was back with Agrippa, who still did not have a wife of his own. A woman of about thirty-two—experienced, regal, and still very attractive—she now walked at the side of her brother in this city of Caesaraea where once, sixteen years ago, gross soldiers on a whorehouse roof had pretended to have sex with her statue.

Festus told Agrippa about Paul, and Agrippa declared that he would like to hear Paul's defense. To the procurator that remark was very welcome. Perhaps this royal Jew, knowledgeable in Jewish legal matters, would be able to make some sense out of the mystifying business, so that Festus would know what to write to Nero about Paul. On the next day, therefore, the apostle appeared before the procurator, the principal Roman army officers at Caesaraea, eminent Caesaraean citizens, and the illustrious brother and sister—great-grandson and great-granddaughter of Herod and Mariamne. Agrippa with kingly beneficence told Paul, "Thou art permitted to speak for thyself." Paul proceeded to do so, describing his Pharisaic upbringing, his persecution of the adherents of Christ, his vision on the way to Damascus, his missionary work for the cause of Christ in obedience to the vision, and his seizure in the Temple.

Festus, impatient with what impressed him as typical Jewish religious fanaticism, said to Paul, "Much learning doth make thee mad."

But Paul turned to Agrippa, speaking earnestly: "Believest thou the prophets? I know that thou believest."

And the worldly-wise monarch, in indulgent amusement at Paul's fervor and perhaps in some seriousness too, gave his famous reply: "Almost thou persuadest me to be a Christian."

The hearing ended soon after this. Agrippa rose, the jeweled Queen Berenice rose, the procurator and the various notables rose. Festus would probably have set Paul free if it had been in his power to do so, but since Paul had appealed to the emperor he must be judged by the emperor. Paul therefore set sail for Italy, where in several years he would meet martyrdom.

Although the second Agrippa may have been esteemed by Roman officials such as Festus, he was disliked by many of the Jews. He reigned after all not in Judaea, as his beloved father had done, but in lands where Greeks and other foreigners lived, remote from Jewish fields and Jewish problems. The story that he was sexually interested in his sister surely did not improve his reputation among the orthodox. His right to appoint the high priest, while it may have gained him respect, did not gain him affection. In the year 59, for instance, while Felix was still procurator, the king had conferred the high priesthood on an aristocrat named Ishmael ben Phabi; and the common people of Jerusalem, apparently led by the Pharisees, had started a brief class war, complete with the throwing of stones, against the aristocratic Sadducean faction.

During Festus' procuratorship, about the year 61, Agrippa angered the priests by building a large dining room in a palace that he owned at Jerusalem. The palace was the old residence of the Hasmonaean kings, directly across the Valley of the Cheesemakers from the Temple itself and on even higher ground than that occupied by the Temple. Agrippa thought with pleasure that while he reclined at ease on his cushions and ate his meals, he could look out over the city, particularly at the performance of sacrifices in the Temple courtyard. The priests were incensed at this invasion of ritual privacy, even though there was nothing in the Law to prohibit what Agrippa had done. They erected a high wall that efficiently blocked the view.

It was perhaps a shame that Agrippa had alienated so many of the Jews, because in a few years he would need all his influence to avert a war against the Romans.

Festus' career as procurator was ended by his death in 62. Albinus, who governed from 62 to 64, was not a good procurator. He may not have contributed a great deal to the seething chaos, but he did nothing to calm it, preferring to suck a profit from his office. One sign of the confusion was the fact that the high priesthood changed hands with demoralizing rapidity. Agrippa II, who still had the power of appointment, seemed unable to make up his mind as to who should hold this post of prime authority among the Jews, and rival claimants mustered bands that battled each other in the holy city. Another sign was the strength of the Sicarii. When they captured Romanizing members of the high-priestly staff, they would make deals with the procurator, refusing to give up these captives unless Albinus gave up Sicarii he had arrested.

As early as the autumn of 62, during the Feast of Tabernacles, a peasant prophet cried doom. In the Temple he reminded the people of the words of Jeremiah: "Then will I cause to cease from the cities of Judah, and the streets of Jerusalem, the voice of mirth, and the voice of gladness, and the voice of the bridegroom, and the voice of the bride: for the land shall be desolate." He walked through the alleys of Jerusalem wailing, foretelling the city's death. This kind of conduct could be harmful to trade, and some of the most prominent citizens had him arrested. But he only kept droning his prophecy. The magistrates handed him over to Albinus, who had him whipped until his flesh was shredded. But he did not scream from the pain; he only kept crying, "Woe to Jerusalem." Albinus asked him who he was, where he came from, what he meant by his lament. He answered, "Woe to Jerusalem." Albinus said he was crazy and released him. But to some of those who heard him in the alleys he was not crazy: he was God's voice, uttering a truth. For the rest of Albinus' procuratorship and into the next few years he wandered through the city intoning his dirge. People brought him food; he took it, did not thank them, just mourned in their faces. "Woe to Jerusalem" was all he said.

Florus, the last procurator of Judaea, did not owe his appointment to his own abilities, which were inconsequential, but to the machinations of his ambitious wife, who happened to be a friend of Nero's wife Poppaea. He seems to have entered Judaea with the intent of getting all he could out of the country—exploiting it extravagantly and almost openly, in the tradition of the worst Roman governors of republican times. Since he came from the Greek coastal region of

Asia Minor, where many Jews of the Diaspora lived, he must already have known a fair amount about Judaism, but this did not predispose him to treat the Jews of Judaea with any understanding. According to Josephus, he descended on them like an executioner on condemned criminals.

Josephus may have been exaggerating, but there is no doubt that Florus' administration, from 64 to 66, convinced even some peaceably inclined Jews that war against Rome was the only answer. It was a time of plunder, rapine, unjust conviction, unmitigated oppression. More and more Jews spoke eagerly of a revolt—spoke of driving the Romans away, killing them in battle, exterminating them with or without the help of a Messiah. Others gave themselves up to weeping; and in Jerusalem the prophet still wailed. When Cestius Gallus, governor of Syria, came to Jerusalem at Passover time, hundreds of thousands of Jews gathered around him and begged for relief from the tyranny of Florus. But Florus himself stood beside Gallus and laughed, and apparently convinced Gallus that these Jews were just being their usual intractable selves. Other subject peoples submitted tranquilly to Roman control; why did the Jews have to be so contumacious?

Among the Jews there were still some, principally aristocrats, who counseled moderation, either because they had fared well under Roman rule or because they dreaded Rome's power. According to his own account in his autobiography, one of these moderates was Josephus, the future historian. At this time he was a man of twenty-eight or twenty-nine and an aristocrat of the first rank: member of the highest grade of the priestly caste, descendant of Aaron the brother of Moses, descendant of the Hasmonaean high priests and kings through his mother. He had not yet adopted the Latinized name Josephus; he was called Yoseph ben Matatyahu. As a youth he had studied the creeds of the Sadducees, the Pharisees, and the rigorous Essenes, and he decided (unlike many of his aristocratic friends) that the Pharisaic doctrine was the best. Recently he had traveled to Rome to obtain the release of some priests unjustly arrested several years before by Felix. He may still have been at Rome in July of 64, when the great fire ate much of the city, and Nero on the roof of his palace poetically fancied that he was watching the burning of Troy.

But whether or not Josephus saw Rome in flames, his visit to the vast, marble-coated heart of the Empire must have impressed him with Rome's insuperable might, so that he viewed the Jewish discontent in a perspective that most of his fellow Jews could not have. Rome, he felt, was too big to combat, too superb to challenge. The Jews might suffer under her rule when men such as Florus were set over them, but they would suffer much more if they called down Rome's wrath on their heads. She would squeeze them, torture them, destroy them. According to the account in his *Life,* when Josephus returned to Judaea he advocated peace. He did not love Rome, though he admired her strength; he loved his fellow Jews, and preached peace from a patriotic motive.

Josephus must have realized, however, that under his countrymen's lust for war lay the consciousness that God had given the land to the Israelites, not to anybody else, and the fact that outsiders had been violating it for generations. The Romans were no more than the immediate cause of what was probably going to happen. The roots went much deeper: through Herodian oppression and Herodian Hellenism and disregard for the Law, past Pompey's desecration of the Holy of Holies, all the way down to the pagan outrages of Antiochus the God Manifest. Most of the Jews were tired of all this; the resentment that had built up for generations was about to explode. Practical, common-sense arguments in favor of peace were useless.

Josephus says that Florus himself tried to provoke a revolt as the only way to cover up his own outrageous acts. This charge is somewhat dubious, but Florus' conduct does not disprove it. For instance, he did not help the Jews of Caesaraea when, on a Sabbath, a Greek turned an earthenware jar upside down in front of a synagogue and sacrificed birds on it. The gesture was satiric: it was meant to suggest that Jews were leprous. The Book of Leviticus contains directions to be followed for the cleansing of lepers, and the directions include the killing of a bird "in an earthen vessel over running water." It was an old tenet of anti-Semitism that Jews were descendants of lepers.

The bird killer had been put up to his pantomime by other Caesaraean Greeks, asking for trouble. A deputation of prominent Caesaraean Jews appealed to Florus, but he threw them into prison on a matter unrelated to the birds. Meanwhile fights kept breaking out between Jews and Greeks. The Jews were enraged not only by the bird incident but by a decision of Nero that Jews should not enjoy the rights of citizens at Caesaraea. The Greeks were enraged because the Jews would not get out of the city. Racial and religious hate tore Caesaraea apart—and it would get worse.

Florus now sent some men to Jerusalem to take money from the holy treasury in the Temple, on the excuse that the emperor needed it. The sum was not very large, but the idea of appropriating any money intended for sacred purposes shocked and infuriated the Jews of A.D. 66, as it had shocked and infuriated their ancestors in the time of Crassus or their fathers in the time of Pilate. They assumed of course that Florus planned to keep the money himself, that the emperor did not want it at all. The more sarcastic Jews walked around with empty baskets, begging money for poor, poverty-stricken Florus. The procurator had had enough of their insolence. He marched to Jerusalem with infantry and cavalry, took up residence at the Herodian palace, sat on his seat of judgment in front of the palace, and told the Jewish leaders to deliver up the demonstrators.

They said that this was impossible—and it probably was, since there had been myriads of demonstrators, and nearly all of them, frightened by Florus' troops, now claimed to be peaceable citizens. Florus replied by ordering his soldiers to plunder the southwest quarter of the city and kill any Jew they met, without bothering to inquire whether he had been a demonstrator. It was an order designed to illustrate the power of Rome and put a lid on Jewish fractiousness. Superbly trained and systematic, the soldiers pillaged and killed. The terrorized Jews jammed the alleys, the women screaming, the children crying; and the short Roman swords stabbed the women and children as well as the men. Some Jews were not killed on the spot but were brought before Florus. He had them whipped savagely, then crucified. Josephus says that about thirty-six hundred people died on that day.

The young Agrippa's sister happened to be in Jerusalem. Berenice, the lady who had required King Polemo to undergo circumcision before she would marry him, was among other things a devoted Jewess. She had come to Jerusalem for the performance of a Nazarite vow, similar to the one for which Paul had sponsored the four men at the Temple—a vow obliging her to practice abstinence and shave her head. The soldiers, aware of her queenly status, teased her by torturing Jews in her presence, then killing them off. Though her own life was in danger, she appeared before the judgment seat of Florus to plead for the Jews. Her head was shaven, her feet were bare, and she was a suppliant, but still she carried herself regally. Florus, however, was unimpressed.

Two cohorts were on the march from Caesaraea to join the soldiers already at Jerusalem. Florus again summoned the leading men of the city. They must instruct the Jews to go out through the gates and greet the cohorts enthusiastically; only that would prove to him that the Jews were penitent. Many of the leading men were aristocratic priests who from the beginning had not been in favor of resistance to the Romans. Only too glad to relay Florus' words to the multitude, they assembled the people in the vast outer courtyard of the Temple and urged them to welcome the troops. But some of the people had been wailing the deaths of those they loved, and others had been cursing Florus. His harshness had not subdued the more militant Jews but had revived their rebelliousness. Now in the Temple courtyard they shouted that they would not greet the cohorts, that Florus must not be obeyed.

It took drama to make them change their minds. The chanters of the sacred songs appeared before the people, and the harpers with their harps, and the priests in their sacred robes, carrying the sacred vessels of silver and gold. They all pleaded with the people to placate Florus, since otherwise he would rob the Temple of its money and despoil it of its holy objects. Priests tore their garments at the thought of such a tragedy, and sprinkled dust on their hair. The people went out to greet the soldiers.

But Florus had contrived a low trick. He had sent messengers to the cohorts to tell them to ignore the Jews' greetings and, if the Jews showed anger at this, to attack them. Josephus uses this duplicity as proof that Florus really wanted to provoke the Jews to war.

When the soldiers did not acknowledge the Jews' greetings, many Jews, as expected, got angry and started yelling uncomplimentary things. The officers gave the order to attack, and the soldiers rammed into the mass of people and struck away at them—not with swords but with clubs. Since clubs were not ordinarily lethal weapons, Florus may not have intended to stage a real massacre. But in trying to avoid the Roman clubs and to squeeze through the gate back into the city, the Jews became entangled and crushed one another. The soldiers besides were largely Greeks from Caesaraea and Sebaste, and once they saw an opportunity to hurt the hated Jews they let themselves go. Those on horseback rode through the crowd, trampling Jews right and left, squashing them, mangling them with the hoofs, enjoying their screams of pain.

The Jews rushed pell-mell through the city, partly in retreat and partly in anxiety. They climbed the Temple hill and occupied both the Temple itself and the Antonia. They wanted to protect the Temple and its holy objects from Florus. He could do what he liked in the city, but he must not touch the house of God.

But Florus did not try to take the Temple hill. He summoned the chief priests and members of the Sanhedrin and announced that he was leaving Jerusalem. After deputing one cohort to keep order in the city (not the cohort that had murdered thirty-six hundred Jews a few days before), he departed for Caesaraea.

Cestius Gallus, governor of Syria, now received many letters— from Florus, complaining about the Jews; from eminent Jews, complaining about Florus; and from Berenice, also complaining about Florus. Cestius Gallus sent a tribune to look into conditions at Jerusalem. At the coastal city of Jamnia the tribune met Agrippa. They went together to Jerusalem, where the Jews convinced the tribune that they were loyal to Rome and that their quarrel was with Florus only.

Agrippa, king of a foreign land and holder of the honorific titles Friend of Caesar and Friend of Rome, now tried to dissuade the Jerusalem Jews from war. He was backed by his sister Berenice and also by the dwindling pro-Roman party among the Jews. In the Xystus, a spacious exercise ground paved with polished flagstones, he addressed the multitude. Up above, on the roof of the Hasmonaean palace, his sister watched and listened. He said he did not believe that all his auditors were for war. Authority must be obeyed. Florus was the man in authority, and although his offenses were flagrant they were not really so terrible. The Romans besides could not be beaten: they owned most of the world and boasted the world's most finely disciplined army. God must like the Romans, or he would not have allowed them to amass so much power. The Jews should pay their tribute, which was overdue, and go in good will.

This speech calmed the people for the time being; but in the next few days the anger rose again. Who was this Agrippa to dictate to the men of Jerusalem? His father, who had reigned in Judaea, might have had the right to tell them what to do, but not this man. He was a Romanizer, and his sister was probably his whore. The most violent rebels threw stones at Agrippa. Accompanied by Berenice, he left Jerusalem and went to his own country, where he would not have to see war-hungry Jews.

A full rupture with the Romans now seemed inevitable. A rebel force under a man named Menahem ben Judas took Masada, the fortified plateau in the dry region west of the Dead Sea, where Herod had put up his betrothed Mariamne for safekeeping when he was trying to become king of the Jews. The rebels massacred the Roman soldiers stationed there and confiscated the weapons stored there by Herod—enough to arm ten thousand men. At Jerusalem, one Eleazar, the seditious son of the conservative high priest Ananias, persuaded the priests at the Temple not to accept animals offered for sacrifice in the name of foreigners. Ever since the reign of Augustus two lambs and a bull had been offered daily at the Temple in the name of the emperor. These sacrifices now ceased.

Many influential Jews at Jerusalem still hoped for peace, when the city rang with cries of war. Not being able to deal with the intractable rebels, they sent to Florus at Caesaraea and to Agrippa in his Graeco-Arab kingdom, asking for military help so that the uprising could be squelched before it grew really serious. Florus did nothing, but Agrippa dispatched three thousand cavalrymen to Jerusalem. With the aid of this force the peace-favoring Jews did battle against the militant Jews. For about a week in the midsummer of 66 they traded stones and darts. The rebels set fire to several buildings, including the old Hasmonaean palace—Agrippa's property, where Berenice had recently lived.

As a foretaste of things to come, the rebels fought not only the peacemakers but each other. Menahem, the conqueror of Masada, returned to Jerusalem, found Eleazar's father the high priest cowering in an aqueduct, and killed him; Eleazar and his men fell on Menahem and his men, captured Menahem, and killed him. The Roman garrison still stationed at Jerusalem was then tricked into laying down its arms and was immediately butchered.

Josephus still probably believed in peace as the only sensible policy. But now that the rebel faction was running wild in the city, peace was no longer a safe thing to advocate, especially for somebody as well known as Josephus. Though not yet thirty, he was already looked up to in Jerusalem as an important political figure because of his extensive learning and great intelligence, his obvious competence, his Hasmonaean ancestry, his family's wealth and connections, and the success of his mission to Rome to get the imprisoned priests released. He was too famous to use the obscurity that might shield lesser men from harm. If we can believe his autobiography, his own recent efforts for peace made him afraid that the rebels would arrest and execute him, so he took to the Temple as a place of holy refuge and ventured out only after Menahem had been killed. Then, according to the *Life,* he pretended to be on the rebels' side. He apparently sounded convincing, even when he said it would be best to wait and let the Romans make the next move. Neither the rebels nor the pacifists thought they would have long to wait: Rome would come down to avenge the insults to her sway.

While Jerusalem sat tense, news reached the city that on the same day on which Eleazar's men had massacred the Roman garrison, and at the same hour of the day, a much larger massacre had occurred at Caesaraea. The brawls beween Jews and Gentiles in that city had come to a sudden head: twenty thousand Jews lay dead at Caesaraea. The whole Jewish minority had been wiped out; only Gentiles remained alive in the capital of Judaea.

Stories of this atrocity spread quickly over the land, and soon the citizens of Jerusalem heard reports that Jews were taking revenge. In maddened bands Jews crossed the borders, sacked Syrian villages, set fire to the houses of Greeks and Arabs, killed in a frenzy of grief and anger. At the cities in the Decapolis, east of Judaea—at Philadelphia, Gerasa, Pella, Gadara, Hippos, Scythopolis, all of them Graeco-Arab communities proud of their acquired Hellenic heritage—the crazed Jews slashed and murdered, looted and burned. They also tore into the old Philistine coastal cities of Gaza and Ascalon, and the port of Ptolemais on the ancient Phoenician coast, and Sebaste, Herod's hated foundation in despised Samaria. The Gentiles fought back if they had a chance, so that in some towns Gentile and Jewish bodies littered the streets together—dead men, dead wives, and dead children rotting in the dust. The inhabitants of Jerusalem felt sure now that the Romans would come soon. The prophet still walked through the alleys, crying, "Woe to Jerusalem."

But for the moment horror did not strike the Jews of the holy city. Instead it struck the Jewish minorities at Syrian cities that the Jews had recently ravaged, and it struck the great Jewish population at Alexandria. That the troubles in Judaea and neighboring regions should touch off the scarcely latent Jewish-Gentile mutual abhorrence in Alexandria was probably to be expected. From riots the thing developed into a terrible slaughter. The governor residing at Alexandria at this time was Tiberius Alexander, the Romanized renegade Jew who had been procurator of Judaea twenty years before. He sent Roman troops against the Jews, and the Greek citizens helped them. Word came to Jerusalem that fifty thousand Jewish corpses clogged Alexandria's streets and filled the air with stench.

Cestius Gallus, governor of Syria, now decided to act. The Syrian cities close to Judaea were in shambles; Judaea itself was in wild disorder; and King Agrippa, his guest at Antioch, had been urging him to make war on the Jews—not because Agrippa had turned against his own people but because he felt that it would be best for the Jews if the insurrection were stopped soon, before Rome became really vindictive. Of the four Roman legions stationed in Syria, Cestius Gallus chose one for the march to Jerusalem: Legion Twelve, called the Thunderbolt. He also drew two thousand men from each of the other legions. The client kings sent soldiers to swell his army: Agrippa himself, for instance, contributed three thousand foot soldiers and one thousand horsemen. Cities in the line of march volunteered auxiliaries, perhaps not as well trained as the legionaries or the kings' troops but eager to battle the Jews. The result was a combined force of about thirty thousand men.

Down the coast this army marched, then eastward toward Jerusalem. But Jerusalem's citizens, tired of sitting in expectation while slaughter was going on everywhere else, were ready and anxious. As soon as news came that the army was approaching, they rushed out of the city to fight—even though it was the Sabbath, when one did not make war. Falling on their enemies like mad dogs from the alleys, they killed several hundred, losing, according to Josephus, only twenty-two of their own number. Agrippa chose this inopportune time to send two messengers to the Jews with the assurance from Cestius Gallus that if they laid down their arms, the Romans would forgive everything. The more militant Jews killed one envoy and tried to kill the other, but he escaped wounded.

Gallus camped on a hill not far from Jerusalem, set his troops to seizing the grain stored in nearby villages, and after several days attacked the city. The Jews—disorganized, accustomed only to riots and guerrilla warfare—fell back from the onslaught of Gallus' war machine, leaving the northern part of the city to the Romans, letting the Romans burn the timber market, letting them get as far as the wall of the palace of Herod. If Gallus had passed this wall, the whole city would have been his. But for some reason he delayed; Josephus, who was probably wishing he would hurry so that the war would be over, says that Florus had bribed several officers to convince Gallus not to try the wall at Herod's palace, since Florus did not want the war to end so quickly. Gallus made an effort to enter the main part of the city by undermining the northeast wall at the Temple, but this did not work: the Jews, desperate to keep the pagans away from the sacred place, drove them off with darts. Then he decided to withdraw from Jerusalem.

The decision was not inexcusable: the cold rains of winter would be coming soon, he did not have enough siege engines for a prolonged assault on Jerusalem, and he ran the risk of being cut off from his home base in Syria by many miles of an inimical Judaea. But tactically the decision was unfortunate for the Romans, since it gave the Jews time to prepare for a formal war; and psychologically it was unfortunate since the withdrawal looked too much like a rout.

The jubilant Jews followed Gallus, nibbling at the rear of his army, shooting their pestilential darts, killing his men. These light-armed Jews were quick on their feet, while the Romans were encumbered by their heavy arms and were afraid to break rank anyway because then the whole line would collapse. After a couple of days Gallus ordered his men to kill their mules, which were slow and retarded the flight. When they camped for the night at Beth-Horon he slipped away in the darkness with most of his men, leaving four hundred brave soldiers to deceive the Jews into thinking that his whole army was still there. The next day the Jews discovered the trick and shot darts into the four hundred, then took off after the main army. But Gallus had gotten too good a head start, and all that the Jews found was pieces of equipment, abandoned on the route by the panicky Romans and their panicky allies.

Jerusalem knew that this was no more than a beginning—that Rome had been insulted, not defeated. Those aristocrats most resolutely against the war left the city, since it was their last chance, and went over to the Romans. Less wealthy Jews of pacific inclinations left also; the Christians went to the Graeco-Arab city of Pella and set up their community there. Meanwhile the moderates took over in Jerusalem and appointed men to serve in the various parts of Judaea.

Josephus did not leave. By choice he was a Pharisee and a moderate himself, rather than a violent friend of Rome like some of the Sadducees. He feared and respected Rome, but he did not particularly like her. The Jews were, after all, his people; he could not desert them for the worshipers of Mars and Minerva. Besides, the moderates who had now formed a provisional government at Jerusalem might still find a way somehow to avert the war. Many of these moderates wished even yet for peace. They might just possibly achieve it at the last moment, although they were making swift preparations for war as they had to do.

It is a sign of the high regard in which the moderates held Josephus that they now sent him to Galilee, the northernmost part of Judaea just south of Syria. Everybody knew that the Roman attack would come from this direction.

Either Josephus was expected to organize Galilean resistance and try to hold off the Romans when they advanced south from Syria, or else he was supposed to persuade the Galileans that peace would be better after all—and then wait and see whether Rome thought so too. In his *Life* he suggests that he was sent to Galilee primarily in the interests of peace, along with two priests who presumably had as much authority as he did. In the *Jewish War*, written much earlier, he says he was made military commander for Galilee. Perhaps the *Life* is right: perhaps the moderates, in the hope that war could be avoided, chose Josephus as one of their three representatives because he was known not to be vehemently anti-Roman. On the other hand the Jewish leaders could hardly have assumed that Rome would decide against war just because the Galileans suddenly wanted peace. The moderates may have instructed Josephus to experiment with pacific measures first, whether or not he was a military commander; or he may have undertaken the duties of a general on his own after he got to Galilee and realized that peace was impossible; or he may have been appointed general for Galilee but decided independently to make a play for peace. We do not know, since we have only Josephus himself to rely on. In the *Jewish War* and the *Life* he created two different images of himself, both of which portray him as a key man but both of which are clouded.

The unlovely Nero, curly-haired and puffy-faced at the age of twenty-nine, was on a musical and dramatic tour of Greece. He had already accomplished a great deal. He had succeeded in having his dangerous mother assassinated (after failing to kill her by means of a collapsible ceiling and a collapsible boat); had murdered his rich aunt by making the doctors give her too strong a cathartic; and had ordered his one-time tutor Seneca to commit suicide. He had held unprecedented sex banquets, had raped girls and boys in public, had enjoyed the fire of Rome if not started it, and had begun construction of the fabulous palace called the Golden House. During a ceremony of triumphal grandeur a few months earlier he had heard the defeated Tiridates, descendant of many kings, call himself Nero's slave; and he had placed a diadem on the head of Tiridates and declared him king of Armenia. Shortly before going on the Greek tour he had closed the two doors of the Temple of Janus to signify that the whole Roman world was at peace, and had struck coins in celebration of that phenomenon.

But all these achievements paled in importance when he made the tour. He traveled as a contestant—competing in the many theaters of Greece against famous performers, trembling before the judges in fear that they would give a prize to somebody else, perhaps trying to bribe a few of them, playing his lyre and singing, starring as a tragic actor, receiving the prizes that he hoped were his due. Nero was an emperor with the temperament of a prima donna. Sometimes he ranted as blind old Oedipus, sometimes as Hercules; sometimes he sang to his lyre. Highly intelligent, extraordinarily sensitive, almost creative, and so egotistical that he permitted no one to leave the theater until he had finished performing, he was at his best on the tour of Greece.

In the course of these activities he received a report of the Jewish revolt. After deputing an officer in his retinue to defeat the Jews, he went on with his singing and acting.

XIV

RUSES IN GALILEE

Josephus took up headquarters in Sepphoris, the capital of Galilee, and got to work. The city was not fully behind the rebels, being traditionally loyal to Rome, but perhaps it feared that the rebels would ransack it unless it went along with them. In Galilee as a whole, Josephus says in the *Jewish War,* the cities contributed fifty percent of their men for military service in the rebel cause, leaving the other fifty percent to work in the fields and to produce the weapons.

Josephus' career in Galilee falls into two parts. In the earlier half of his stay there he was occupied with administrative duties and the business of preparing for war: training the Galilean men as soldiers in the Roman fashion, setting up legal bodies to hear complaints, keeping doubtful cities faithful to the Jewish cause, protecting his office against his enemies, and trying to stifle sources of disunity. In the latter half of his stay he led the Galilean Jews against the power of Rome.

The first half of his job proved difficult and delicate. He had to handle many complex situations and devious people, and his own loyalties were not yet thoroughly settled. The most immediate problem turned out to be a city not strictly under his jurisdiction—Tiberias.

Sepphoris was a new capital. The previous capital of Galilee had been Tiberias, the large city that Antipas had founded on the western shore of the Sea of Galilee; but Nero had given it to Agrippa II as an addition to his kingdom. A great many people in Tiberias, headed by a young aristocratic demagogue called Justus son of Pistus, resented the handing over of their city to King Agrippa. Now that most Galileans were in revolt against Rome, these people felt even more unhappy, since Agrippa was Rome's friend if not Rome's servant. Under Justus' oratorical persuasion they proclaimed that the city of Tiberias should rebel against King Agrippa, rejoin the Galilee to which it logically belonged, and take part in the Galilean revolt from Rome. In other words, they seemed eager to join Josephus' side.

But the Tiberians had not yet advanced far enough in their return to the Jewish cause. At a town nearby, Josephus sent for the principal Tiberians—not only Justus and other members of the war party but also respectable citizens, some of whom were still probably in favor of Rome and Agrippa. He informed these men that the Jerusalem authorities had ordered him to see that the old Tiberian palace, once the residence of Antipas and Herodias and now the property of Agrippa, was burned. It contained graven images—depictions of animals—and was consequently an eyesore to Judaism. The respectable citizens gave their consent grudgingly. The palace had contained these images for many years without anybody's minding very much, but if the leaders at Jerusalem wanted the palace burned it would have to be burned. Josephus, having made the arrangements, left to prosecute other business elsewhere.

But a man named Jesus ben Sapphias, ringleader of the sailors in this busy port and almost as influential a man in the rebellious faction as Justus, got together a mob and burned the palace on his own —not out of piety apparently but because the roof was of gold and there was much treasure inside, such as Corinthian candelabra, costly tables, and large quantities of uncoined silver. Ever since its foundation on an ancient sepulcher, Tiberias had provided a home for Greeks as well as Jews. Jesus ben Sapphias and his mob, in the spirit of racial hate that was sweeping the land, now massacred as many of the Greeks as they could find. When Josephus heard about all this he came rushing back to Tiberias and, according to the *Life,* tried to put things in order by getting Jesus ben Sapphias and his men to turn over the palace loot to himself. He succeeded, and he put the loot in the care of ten prominent Tiberians, to be kept for King Agrippa. In Josephus' view, it seems, carrying out the orders of the Jerusalem authorities was one thing, but wantonly robbing Agrippa was another; it smacked of immorality. Besides, although Agrippa was a Friend of Rome and consequently the enemy of the resistance that Josephus was trying to organize in Galilee, he was also a very powerful man— and that meant a lot to Josephus. It would not hurt to please him.

At least these are possible surmises. Another is that Josephus never had anything to do with the loot—that he invented the story when he wrote the *Life*. He had lived at Rome a long time when the *Life* appeared, and he may not have wanted to indicate that he had been too much a rebel in his young manhood. Although Josephus is usually very reliable about events that do not involve himself, when he becomes autobiographical he becomes untrustworthy, as may already be evident. The accounts of his career in Galilee that he composed for the *Life* and for the much earlier *Jewish War* are irreconcilable. Each account contains incidents not in the other. If an incident occurs in both accounts the two versions differ in details, and the narratives disagree as to chronology. To some extent Josephus must have been writing fiction, even if his autobiographical stories are basically true. The *Jewish War* was apparently intended as an official history of the war from the Roman point of view and for the Roman government; the *Life* was undertaken as a self-defense against Justus of Tiberias—who had published his own report, which said unpleasant things about Josephus. One probably cannot expect strict autobiographical accuracy from either of these situations.

Although Josephus was certainly the leading figure in Galilee at this period, others menaced his position of supremacy. The principal menace was a man called John son of Levi, from the Galilean city of Gischala. John could not claim illustrious descent as Josephus could; no Hasmonaean blood flowed in his veins. But he lifted himself out of his poverty—not by any socially acceptable means, if we can believe Josephus, but by stealing and plundering. A leader, an opportunist, and a shrewd man quick to take advantage of troubled times, he gathered around himself a gang of four hundred followers—vagabonds, outcasts, scum as poor as he had once been; and with this robber band he made a healthy living.

According to the *Life*, he had originally been a Romanizer and in fact tried to restrain his fellow citizens of Gischala when they wanted to break away from Rome. The *Jewish War* does not say that he had ever sympathized with Rome. At any event, by the time Josephus knew him he was very much a rebel. Eager for power, he probably realized that becoming a rebel chief was the surest road to control. He was already the head man in Gischala, and under his supervision a protective wall was being built around the city. But soon he started hoping to become head man in all Galilee, which would mean getting rid of Josephus first. He may not have been bothered by this ambition in the early part of his relationship with Josephus; but it did not take long to appear, and it grew fast.

The two colleagues whom Josephus mentions in the *Life* as having been sent with him from Jerusalem (and who certainly took a less active part than he in the affairs of Galilee, although they supported him when he ordered the burning of the palace at Tiberias) now went back to Jerusalem. Josephus established his headquarters at Cana, a few miles north of Sepphoris, evidently because the citizens of Sepphoris were becoming more and more disenchanted with the revolt and many of them wished restively to return to Roman suzerainty. Cana was a much smaller place than Sepphoris—scarcely more than a village in fact. The Christians sometimes claimed that at a wedding in this town their Jesus had performed his first miracle by turning water into wine.

Not long after Josephus went to Cana, according to the *Life*—a considerable time later, according to the *Jewish War*—John wrote to Josephus for permission to go to Tiberias, which had now definitely separated itself from King Agrippa's realm and was once more a part of Galilee, under Josephus' jurisdiction. John said that he was not feeling well and hoped the hot baths at Tiberias would do him good. In a surprising show of kindness Josephus wrote to the Tiberian authorities, telling them to treat John well and to provide him with a place to stay. But Josephus was being tricked.

John did not feel sick. On reaching Tiberias he immediately set to work to persuade the people that they should revolt against Josephus' government. John planned to seize control of the city for himself as a step toward seizing control of all Galilee. But the man whom Josephus had left in charge at Tiberias sent him a report of what was happening, and Josephus started off at once, dispatching word ahead to the Tiberians that he was on his way. When he arrived at the city a large crowd of people met him, many of them probably confused as to whether they would really be best off under Josephus or John or, after all, King Agrippa. The *Jewish War* says that John was not in the crowd but had sent one of his friends to tell Josephus he was at home sick. The *Life* says that John did greet Josephus, but looked guilty and slunk home shortly.

Josephus went to the stadium and, standing on a high platform, made a speech to the Tiberians, giving them reasons why they should stay loyal to himself rather than going over to this robber from Gischala. Apparently he was a persuasive orator. But while he was speaking several men came up behind him. People in the audience cried out. Josephus realized that the men must have been sent by John to kill him; they had drawn their swords. He jumped down from the platform in the middle of his speech and, along with a loyal Tiberian and perhaps a couple of his own bodyguards, made a quick exit from the stadium. Even a hero cannot stand on a platform and let himself be murdered. At the docks he appropriated a boat, in which he set out over the Sea of Galilee to safety.

Josephus' next job, if we follow the *Life,* was to convince the citizens of Sepphoris that they did not really want to return to the control of Rome. Since his own secret respect for Rome was undiminished, he probably did not find this job an easy one. He went to Sepphoris, however, and made an attempt. The Sepphorites who were most eager to get out from under Josephus' government sent to a brigand named Jesus, who could be hired for any purpose, and asked Jesus to do away with him. Jesus and his band of thieves were at this time in the area of Phoenicia, but he dispatched a letter to Josephus inquiring whether he could come to Sepphoris for a conference. Josephus had evidently not learned from his experiences with John that beyond everything else he should suspect everybody. He said it would be all right for Jesus to come to Sepphoris. Very likely he thought that Jesus wanted to hire himself out in the rebel cause as many other brigands were doing, and that he was coming to discuss terms. But a deserter from the band arrived first and told Josephus that Jesus intended to enter Sepphoris with his whole gang and murder him.

Josephus lost his naïveté. He instructed the sentries at the gates of Sepphoris not to let Jesus' gang into the city but only Jesus himself and perhaps a few of his followers. Meanwhile he collected a large body of his own followers—rebels from the towns of Galilee, rebels from Tiberias—and posted these men out of sight around the edges of the marketplace. It was in the market that Jesus was supposed to meet him. The robber chief came on schedule, was admitted into Sepphoris with a very few followers, and was directed to the market. The large body of Galilean and Tiberian rebels stepped out of hiding, and Jesus and his friends realized that they were surrounded. They were ordered to lay down their weapons, and they obeyed. Josephus remarked magnanimously that he would forgive Jesus if Jesus showed repentance. The robber promised that from now on he would be loyal to Josephus—who at least had accomplished this much even if he had not persuaded all the Sepphorites against rejoining Rome. Waiting outside the walls, the remaining members of the band of thieves heard about what was going on. They wisely left.

About this time occurred an affair that almost proved embarrassing to Josephus. The *Jewish War* places it before Josephus' flight from the would-be assassins in the stadium at Tiberias, whereas the *Life* places it after the Tiberias incident and after the brigand Jesus' capitulation at Sepphoris. Whenever it took place, it shows that Josephus had learned to handle problems of administration with trickery.

Young rebels from a Galilean village had waylaid a cavalcade escorting the wife of King Agrippa's financial overseer across the Galilean plain. The lady escaped, but the treasure traveling with her did not. The enterprising young men plundered the cavalcade, coming away with rich clothes meant to be worn at a court, silver cups and other costly articles, and several hundred gold coins.

Josephus was at Tarichaea, a port on the west coast of the Sea of Galilee not many miles from Tiberias, with which it carried on a chronic commercial feud. It must have been a rich city; it was famous for the pickled fish that it sent in barrels all over the Mediterranean world. It had recently been a possession of Agrippa but now, like Tiberias, had revolted. Josephus was probably surprised on this particular day to see four mules being brought to him, loaded down with the plunder from the cavalcade. The young villagers who had robbed the cavalcade were dutifully delivering the spoil to him because he was supreme in Galilee and would know how to dispose of it.

His reaction was the same as his reaction to the Tiberians who had looted Agrippa's palace. The plunder must be kept for its rightful owner—in other words, King Agrippa himself. But he did not tell this to the young robbers. Instead he said that he would be glad to keep all the plunder so that it could be spent, in time, on repairing the walls of Jerusalem. He confiscated it without further comment.

The youths did not react as well to all this as Josephus had hoped. Frustrated at having relinquished the loot and suspecting what he really intended to do with it, they raged through the villages on the western side of the Sea of Galilee, saying that Josephus was a liar and a traitor, that he favored Rome and was going to give the plunder to King Agrippa the Friend of Rome and to the lecherous Queen Berenice. They did not have a hard time convincing people, since many Galileans already doubted Josephus' loyalty to the cause of Jewish freedom. Word spread quickly and the mood got ugly. Meanwhile Josephus turned the treasure over to two friends of Agrippa, instructing them to deliver it to the king and threatening them with death if they could not keep their mouths shut. This was an extraordinary threat for the chief of the Jewish resistance in Galilee to make.

The next morning knots of angry, vociferous people gathered in the streets of Tarichaea. The Roman army was already on the march toward Galilee, they said, and here was Josephus—their own general, the man who had been sent from Jerusalem as their leader—trying to sneak money to King Agrippa. More and more people kept coming into Tarichaea from nearby villages and from the city of Tiberias, which agreed with its commercial rival on the matter at hand. A huge crowd (one hundred thousand, according to the *Jewish War*) collected in the hippodrome, crying that Josephus should be replaced, that he should be killed, that he should be burned to death. Rabble-rousers kept the mob stirred up, reminding them that the Romans were on the way. One man—Jesus ben Sapphias, who had come from Tiberias with the others—held up a copy of the Torah and shouted that this was what Josephus was really trying to betray. The throng in the hippodrome snarled and screamed louder, demanding Josephus' death.

All this time, if we are to believe his own narrative, Josephus was at home asleep. Jesus ben Sapphias with a group of yelling rebels from the hippodrome proceeded to the house, apparently with the purpose of setting it on fire and letting Josephus roast inside. All Josephus' bodyguards left the house in terror except four (according to the *Jewish War*) or one (according to the *Life*). These four, or this one, woke him up. He must have been a very sound sleeper.

Josephus had no intention of allowing himself to be burned to death or dispatched in any other manner if he could help it. The best plan, he reasoned, was to put on a show. He sneaked out of the house unobserved and made his way toward the hippodrome via back alleys, where he was not likely to meet anybody. He wore black, and his clothes were torn in token of sorrow. His sword hung from his neck, as much as to say that he would offer no resistance. He had sprinkled ashes on his head. In this guise he safely reached the hippodrome, where in front of all the people he fell on his face, squirmed around, rubbed his face into the ground, and wailed pitifully.

He was such an abject spectacle that many people felt sorry for him, as he wanted them to do. Others, not so easily affected, yelled "Traitor!" and shouted questions such as, "What have you done with our treasure? Where is the money you owe us?" He only wept on the ground or stood in shame with his hands behind his back. The thousands of Tiberians in the audience were particularly vociferous; his personification of humility did not move many of them. But then he pleaded for permission to speak: if only they would let him say a few words before they killed him. Jesus ben Sapphias' men, enraged because Josephus had escaped them at his house, now rushed into the hippodrome, more eager for his blood than ever; and it looked as if he would never say anything else except "Help!" But the major part of the crowd roared out that he should speak. This was the chance he had counted on.

He said that they should kill him if he deserved to die, and perhaps he did deserve to die; but he wanted to confess first, to explain. The good people of Tarichaea—his fellow rebels—were dear to him. No matter what they thought, he did not plan to send the treasure to their former master, King Agrippa. He did not plan to keep it for himself either, as some of them might have assumed. He intended to use the money to build a wall around Tarichaea so that the city would be protected from its enemies—Romans, bandits, or perhaps even other Jews. So far he had kept quiet about this intention because he was afraid that the Tiberians would find out about it and seize the money, but now he had been forced to reveal himself.

Cheers came from the Tarichaeans—warm and lusty cheers voicing sudden new love for their leader. Squeals of anger and affront came from the Tiberians. Josephus had succeeded in splitting his audience. Fortunately for him, the Tarichaeans outnumbered the Tiberians. The men of Tarichaea and Tiberias argued with each other in the hippodrome, shot hot insults at each other, let out their civic rivalry. The Tiberians still screamed for Josephus' blood; the Tarichaeans called to him that he did not need to worry, since they would protect him. But he did not like to have anybody angry at him. He therefore made another speech, a short one, promising to build a wall around Tiberias too. Then he went home.

He was not yet entirely out of danger. The most violent troublemakers gathered at his house; some of them may have been the ones that had come there earlier with Jesus ben Sapphias. In the *Jewish War* he says that there were about two thousand of them; in the *Life* he reduces the figure to six hundred. There must have been a large number in any case. He had not yet exhausted his deviousness for the day, however. Going to the top floor, he showed himself to the people and said they were making so much noise that he could not hear them. If they wished to send their leaders inside, he would be glad to confer with them in the quiet of his rooms.

According to the *Jewish War*, the crowd sent in several leaders. Josephus must still have had many servants in the house, and perhaps his runaway bodyguards had returned by this time too. He conducted his enemies to the remotest part of the house and had them whipped unmercifully. When they were striped with blood and could hardly stand, he took them out, dripping red and wobbly, and exhibited them to the crowd. The people, thinking a whole army must be hidden inside, ran away. The version in the *Life* is more conservative: the crowd sent in only one man. But in addition to having him whipped, Josephus had one of the man's hands cut off and hung around the man's neck; as in the other version, the people ran away. Josephus had fooled everybody.

Josephus' self-portrait in both the *Jewish War* and the *Life* draws attention to his role as a peacemaker. In the *Jewish War,* for instance, he says that after the swordsmen of his archenemy John almost killed him in the stadium at Tiberias, the Galilean rebels, indignant at John's attempt on the life of their chief, asked permission to invade John's home town of Gischala; but Josephus, unwilling to let a civil war start in Galilee, nobly said no. One reason Josephus relates this incident (whether or not it occurred) is to point up the undesirability of civil conflict, so that the reader will not later condone the rise of civil conflict in Jerusalem; another reason, certainly, is to paint himself as a patriot, a wise leader who avoided setting Jew against Jew.

Another image he tries to create is that of the successful trickster —the clever liar and perpetrator of outrageous deceptions. Josephus seems to take great pride in his shrewdness. Chicanery is not to his discredit any more than it is to the hero Odysseus' discredit when he dupes the doltish Polyphemus, deludes the crass suitors, or tells tall tales to his faithful swineherd. Josephus does not expect his readers to dislike him for the same sort of duplicity that enabled Jacob, with his mother's help, to cheat his brother Esau out of their father's blessing by fooling the blind old man. Intelligence is essential to leadership, and practical intelligence includes the ability to outwit one's opponents, to extricate oneself adroitly from difficult situations, to overcome odds with invention.

In another incident involving the troublesome Tiberians, Josephus displayed this ability again. The Tiberians, seemingly as whimsical as the wind, had now decided that they wished to return to Agrippa's kingdom, from which they had so recently broken. Perhaps the fact that the formidable Roman army was drawing closer and closer to Galilee had something to do with their change of mind. They may also have been angry at Josephus for not having started the protective wall that he had promised them in the last-minute addition to his speech at the Tarichaean hippodrome. Tarichaea already had its wall; surely, they felt, Josephus favored Tarichaea over Tiberias.

They therefore wrote to King Agrippa, inviting him to resume control of their city; and according to the *Jewish War,* they drove Josephus out. At friendly Tarichaea, Josephus found himself in an awkward position: he had sent his troops to their home towns to gather in the grain. But he contrived to conquer Tiberias without soldiers.

At the Tarichaean waterfront he commandeered all the ships in sight (two hundred thirty of them, the *Jewish War* says). He put a few Tarichaean sailors in each—perhaps the owner and two or three other fishermen, just enough to manipulate a vessel. In his own ship he put his seven bodyguards. With this "fleet" he sailed grandly down the Sea of Galilee to Tiberias. When the Tiberians saw the two hundred thirty ships approaching, they started running around excitedly, crying out in terror, because they naturally assumed that each ship was full of soldiers and that their city was about to be ransacked and raped. Josephus had his vessels stop far enough from shore so that the Tiberians could not look inside them. He himself came closer, in the vessel manned by the seven bodyguards.

The Tiberians threw down their weapons and congregated on the shore—men, women, and children, all afraid. From his ship Josephus delivered a reprimand. They should be ashamed of themselves for defecting from the glorious rebel cause.

They implored him not to invade their city. Ten prominent Tiberians presented themselves before him on the shore; according to the *Life,* he demanded them by name. He put them politely on board a ship, which took off for Tarichaea. He then demanded fifty members of the city council, or senate. These aristocrats presented themselves too. He had them transported to several of his ships, and these ships also set sail for Tarichaea.

In time quite a bit of his fleet was gone, but so were quite a few Tiberians. He had kidnaped the whole Tiberian senate—six hundred men, according to the *Jewish War*—and many hundred Tiberians of lower rank.

About this time, according to the *Life*—somewhat earlier, according to the *Jewish War*—John of Gischala caused trouble again. He sent a request to Jerusalem that Josephus be dismissed (and replaced of course by John himself). This was John's great play for power. Soon four deputies from Jerusalem arrived in Galilee. They had secret instructions to prejudice the Galileans against Josephus and to make Josephus return to Jerusalem, or to kill him if he proved recalcitrant. The necessity to outmaneuver the deputies called forth Josephus' peculiar talents. Among many other things, he managed to get the deputies' messenger drunk and to pump secrets out of the man; to defeat the deputies in bids for popular approval; to dispatch one hundred highly respectable old men to Jerusalem as a counterembassy; to face the deputies publicly in the synagogue at Tiberias and answer their charges of maladministration; to have his command in Galilee confirmed at Jerusalem; and to capture all the deputies and send them back. Meanwhile the Roman army was coming closer.

One impression Josephus creates in both the *Jewish War* and the *Life* is that of an excessively busy, almost frantic leader, rushing around a disordered, hectic Galilee trying to keep the land together while it cracked and split and splintered into factions. The factions included those people who were pro-Roman, those who hungered for war against Rome, those who feared Rome more than they hated her, those who were not quite sure what they wanted, those who liked Josephus, those who liked John or some other demagogue, those who liked King Agrippa, those who detested Agrippa, those who believed the deputies from Jerusalem, and those who were glad to see the deputies return to Jerusalem.

This impression is no doubt accurate. For instance, even after Josephus subdued Tiberias, its leading citizens wrote to Agrippa again, asking him to come and take over the city; and when the anti-Roman Galileans heard about this new defection they wanted to invade Tiberias, plunder it, and kill its inhabitants—and Josephus says he had a hard time persuading them to be quiet. Tiberias was surely the city that caused the most trouble, but Sepphoris, once his headquarters, was unhappy again too. Many of its citizens had been pro-Roman from the beginning, and the nearness of Roman soldiers seems to have made even its moderates fanatically loyal to Rome. The Sepphorites wrote to the Cestius Gallus who had retreated in such ignominy from Jerusalem, asking him to send an army down from Syria or come with one himself and occupy the city. Josephus arrived before the Romans did and took the city, but his troops proceeded to vent their hatred on these Romanizers by looting and destroying the place that had recently been the capital of Galilee. Josephus could not control their vicious plundering, so he thought of a ruse. He instructed some soldiers he could trust to spread the rumor that the Romans were attacking another part of the town; and his troops fled, leaving much of their loot behind.

But soon Gallus' Romans did come, in answer to another desperate request from the Sepphorites, and Josephus' men could do nothing against them. Josephus hurried eastward to fight an army sent by King Agrippa; this force he somewhat equivocally defeated. Whether he was ready or not—whether divided Galilee was ready or not—the Romans were now poised to drive through the land.

The general whom Nero had ordered to defeat the Jews was Vespasian. His father, from the old-fashioned, rural, unflamboyant Sabine country northeast of Rome, had been a tax collector in Asia and had evidently done an unusually honest job there; his mother was the sister of a senator. Although his blood on both sides qualified as genteel, it was by no means of exquisite refinement. He had made his way in the world largely by arms, serving well in Thrace and Germany and distinguishing himself in Britain in 43 and 44, when Claudius was making it a Roman province. The subjugation of the southernmost part of the island was due to his efforts. In 51 he briefly held a consulship; in 63 he was sent to govern Africa. Bluff, sensible, unartificial, and unresponsive to the more delicate amenities of life, he committed the gross error of falling asleep during at least one of Nero's musical performances in Greece. Nero was so offended, according to the historian Suetonius, that Vespasian retired to a little Greek town to wait for the rage to blow over. He was certainly glad to leave the elegant perils of the court for the camp and the battlefield. At the age of fifty-seven, with the face of a bulldog, the neck of a bull, and the body of a sturdy Sabine farmer, he was in prime physical condition to undergo a long march, a rough battle, or a tough siege.

He sent his son Titus, a somewhat more sensitive issue of himself, to Alexandria to fetch a legion. He himself crossed the Hellespont, traveled the length of Asia Minor, came down into Syria, and took up temporary headquarters at Antioch, where he assembled his army. Ignoring the legion that had disgraced itself by retreating from Jerusalem under Cestius Gallus, he mustered two other legions stationed in Syria, plus twenty-three auxiliary cohorts and six wings of mounted soldiers. King Agrippa sent two thousand archers and one thousand cavalrymen; so did the kings of Emesa and Commagene. The Nabataean monarch, more powerful than these other rulers, sent one thousand horsemen and five thousand foot soldiers. From Antioch, Vespasian marched to Tyre, then down the coast to Ptolemais in Phoenician Syria, where Titus joined him with the legion from Alexandria. The complete army, including Titus' legion, must have amounted to at least fifty-eight thousand men. Servants and other camp followers swelled this number.

Many pro-Roman Jews from Sepphoris, who had left their city a while ago to put themselves under the protection of the governor of Syria, welcomed Vespasian to Ptolemais, promising to help him against the rebel Jews. It was the spring of the year 67. Troops sent ahead by Vespasian had already been raiding in Galilee for some time now—taking prisoners and occasionally killing them, terrifying weak souls with anticipations of what was to come, but not succeeding in capturing any of the cities that Josephus had walled. They tried to take a city called Jotapata in particular, and failed: its defenders fought too strongly for their homes.

But now Vespasian marched from Ptolemais eastward into Galilee. The sight was majestic and awesome. First came light-armed auxiliaries, many of them archers, in their Oriental garb; this vanguard had the duties of forestalling a surprise attack from the front and searching areas where enemies might lie in ambush. After the light-armed auxiliaries came heavy-armed Roman soldiers, some on foot and some on horseback—their helmets, cuirasses, spears, scabbards, and big, oblong shields gleaming in the sunshine. Next came a contingent to lay out the camp; and immediately after, engineers, who would level the roads, cut down obstructions in the line of march, remove whatever might impede Roman progress. Vespasian's own belongings and those of his officers followed in carriages guarded by a cavalry escort. Vespasian himself rode after the carriages: square and straight, magnificently armed, with the long red cloak of a general falling over his left shoulder and over the back of his great horse. Foot soldiers and horsemen most famous for their skill in battle had the honor of accompanying him, and so did a special guard carrying lances and round shields.

The cavalry units attached to the three legions rode next—several hundred men in all, each with a long sword hanging at his right side, a long spear or pike in his hand, a quiver beside him containing several long darts, and a shield angled across his horse's flank. Mules pulled engines for hurling stones or javelins into enemy towns. Vespasian's officers followed these—the legates, commanding legions; the tribunes, commanding a thousand men each; and the prefects, commanding auxiliary cohorts—with guards to protect them. The eagle also had its guards: the great, gold, holy imperial image, carried high and proud, that the Jews could not stand. Behind the eagle walked trumpeters; and behind the trumpeters walked the main mass of the three legions—from fifteen to eighteen thousand soldiers marching six abreast, each man in his helmet and cuirass, each man carrying a short sword or dagger at his left side, a long sword at his right side, and a javelin in one hand, with his left arm thrust through the strap on the underside of an oblong shield, and with three days' rations on his back, plus a pick, a chain, an axe, and other pieces of equipment. These were the hard core of the army, the solid, superbly disciplined, stubborn common soldiers who kept Rome in control of the world. After them straggled the servants of the three legions, in perpetual disarray, noisily leading the baggage mules and other pack animals. At the rear, as at the van, were Oriental auxiliaries, with a guard of well-armed infantrymen and cavalrymen for further security.

Josephus was encamped at a village close to Sepphoris. When his soldiers heard that the Romans were coming, most of them deserted: it was better to be home or at a fortified city such as Jotapata when Rome was on the march. Josephus himself took his few remaining soldiers east to Tiberias. He was of course committed to resisting Rome and was determined to do the best he could, but he felt far from sanguine about the whole thing. In fact he thought that the defeat of these craven Galilean rebels was only a matter of time, and so was the defeat of the rest of the Jews. He still wished for the sake of his countrymen and himself that this foolish war had never gotten started.

Vespasian marched to the town of Gabara, a few miles from Jotapata, took it immediately, killed all the young men who had not run away, and burned the place. From Tiberias, Josephus sent a report to the Jerusalem authorities, commenting that unless they wanted to give up right now they had better send him more troops. He turned west again and went to Jotapata. Not far from the Syrian border, in the hills north of Cana and Sepphoris, this city was the key to Galilee; and Vespasian would no doubt besiege it within a very few days.

Jotapata stood on the side of a hill, was protected by a strong, turreted wall, and had a large food supply on hand. Vespasian surrounded it with two rings of foot soldiers and an outer ring of cavalry, efficiently shutting it off from the rest of the world. He attacked it from the north—since only on the north, where the town extended up the slope of the hill toward its summit, was Jotapata approachable for military purposes; on the other three sides steep, ragged precipices fell away into valleys. During the first few days of the siege the Jews ventured outside the wall and fought the Romans in vicious hand-to-hand engagements, trying to drive them away from the northern wall—and succeeding. Then Vespasian resorted to an ancient siege device: he began to build earthworks against the wall. If the sloping earthworks could be brought up to the height of the wall itself, the Romans could mount them and pour into the city, and the wall would be rendered useless.

Under the shelter of movable wooden frames held up by timber posts the Romans labored at the earthworks. From the wall the Jews threw down enormous stones that banged against the wooden frames and sometimes crashed through. To force the Jews from the wall Vespasian brought up his artillery engines—one hundred sixty of them, constructed like gigantic crossbows. Some sent lances zooming up to the top of the wall, and defenders screamed and fell off, squirming like stuck fish. Others sent heavy stone blocks hurtling through the air to squash the Jews; and others rained flaming wood on them, or arrows. The Nabataean auxiliaries filled the air with arrows, javelins, and stones. It was impossible for the Jews to stay on the wall.

Meanwhile construction of the earthworks went on. But if the Jews could not throw things down on the Romans from the wall, they could go outside the city in small bands, descend on one of the wooden shelters under which the Romans were piling up dirt, rip it apart, force the Romans to retreat, and then destroy the earthwork and burn the shelter. In spite of all this harassment, however, the Romans persisted; and the earthworks kept getting higher until they were almost up to the top of the wall. Inside the city the Jews were desperate. They knew they could expect no mercy once the Romans came in.

But Josephus consulted his ingenuity, which proved as always dependable. The wall obviously had to be raised higher, yet no masons would work on it while the Romans were peppering them from below. To protect the masons, Josephus ordered a wooden scaffolding to be affixed to the top of the wall and the hides of freshly killed cattle to be hung on the outer side of the scaffolding. Stones, spears, and arrows fired by the Romans would be caught in the oxhides; even the flaming torches would not burn the hides, which, having only recently belonged to living animals, were not yet dry. The device was not original with Josephus, but it surprised and confounded Vespasian's army. Working in comparative comfort behind the hides, the masons raised the wall by about thirty feet.

It would not have been easy to find two commanders more different from each other in temperament and method than Josephus and Vespasian: Josephus protecting his own people in a frantic situation,

Vespasian carrying out an assignment as well as he knew how; Josephus a volatile, cultivated, and inventive man of thirty, Vespasian a solid and tenacious warrior in his late fifties. Since Josephus had countered the earthworks, Vespasian decided to starve the city out. It would take time, but he could wait.

Actually the Jotapatans were likely to die of thirst long before they starved. Although the city had plenty of grain, it had no source for replenishing the water supply except the sky, and in the hot summer rain did not fall. Josephus was obliged to dole out the little water stored in cisterns. From the heights above the north wall the Romans could watch the demoralized Jotapatans congregating at one spot to receive the water, and they predicted that resistance would soon be over.

Consulting his ingenuity again, Josephus came up with another device; this one was psychological. He had the citizens dip clothes in the little water that was left and hang these clothes, wet and dripping, on the wall for the Romans to see. The Romans looked in consternation at the wall with the water running down it. If the Jotapatans could be that wasteful with their water, they must have more than enough. Josephus' stratagem had succeeded: Vespasian gave up the idea of making the city surrender through hunger and thirst.

But Josephus realized that when the Romans resumed their attacks the city must inevitably fall. It might hold out for quite a while, but it could not resist indefinitely. Together with some of the eminent citizens therefore he made plans for leaving. After all, he could not hope for a very long life if he was on hand when the Romans entered. But the ordinary citizens heard about his intention and urged him to stay. Thinking fast, he said plausibly enough that he could do them more good outside the city, because he could create a diversion that would draw the Roman army away from Jotapata. The argument, however, failed to convince the people. Teary-eyed, thirsty, and ignorant of what to do, the Jotapatans young and old kept beseeching him, saying that if he went they would have no one to lead them.

This was incontrovertible. He stayed, and in the next few days he led savage sallies against the Romans, invading their camp, tearing down their tents, cutting and slashing and setting things on fire in a hopeless burst of patriotism. Vespasian, unwilling to risk his Romans against men who welcomed death as long as they could kill while they died, sent his auxiliaries against them.

Next Vespasian moved up the dreaded battering ram: a great beam of wood rivaling a ship's mast in size. It was suspended by cables from another beam to give the forward thrust increased momentum, and its head was of iron, in the likeness of a ram's head. Under the cover of archers, slingers, and catapults hurling stones and javelins, the Romans drove the ram against the wall—always in the same place, again and again and again. A gasp had risen from the citizens the first time they heard the ominous sound; and now, as they heard it repeated and repeated, they waited in dread for the wall to crumble.

It was time for another stratagem, and Josephus thought of one. He had the Jews lower bags of chaff over the wall to cushion the blows. If the Romans moved the ram to another part of the wall, the Jews just moved their bags of chaff. Finally Vespasian's soldiers attached scythes to long poles and cut the bags down. Then Josephus ordered the Jotapatans to use diversionary tactics. Almost suicidally they rushed out of the city and set the siege engines on fire, as well as the Romans' wooden shelters and anything else that would burn.

Caught up in the frenzy of patriotism, a Jew from a small Galilean town, standing on top of the wall, lifted up a massive stone and slammed it down with such force that it broke the head off the ram. He jumped down from the wall, seized the great iron head, and carried it in triumph back to the wall. As he stood there mocking the Romans, five arrows hit him. With the arrows sticking in his body, he climbed the wall, still clutching his heavy prize, and stood at the top taunting his enemies—then crumpled in death. He and the head fell from the wall together.

His name was Eleazar ben Samaeas, and he might have come out of the Israel of Joshua or the judges rather than out of Josephus' Galilee. But the time of heroes was over, and the practical Romans repaired the ram. Throughout the night it battered the wall, while the arrows and javelins and stones sailed over at the Jews and newly killed men fell on corpses. With the coming of dawn, the wall crumbled.

Vespasian now prepared to enter Jotapata with some of his troops, and he posted horsemen and archers around the city to make sure that nobody escaped. Josephus prepared to receive him in battle, stationing the bravest remnants of his men at the breach in the wall and shutting the women in their houses, so that their terror would not emasculate the men at this hour when courage would be needed. The brassy, profane cry of the Roman trumpets rang through the air; the legionaries gave a tremendous roar; and a cloud of arrows blotted out the sun. The Romans began their assault, rank on rank, in the *testudo* formation, with their oblong shields locked together above their heads for full protection, like the plates in the shell of a tortoise. The Jews desperately drove at them, pressed them back, and killed some, but there were thousands more.

Josephus was not at a loss. He ordered the citizens to boil oil; and pots of the liquid, hissing-hot, were poured down on the Romans. Oozing under their armor, the oil ate through the skin and burned into the flesh, and the Romans lay and writhed and screamed. In addition to oil, the Jews had been boiling fenugreek, or Greek hay, an herb in flower at this time of the year. When boiled, fenugreek acquires the sliminess of okra. The Jews now dumped this stuff onto the wooden gangways on which the legionaries were trying to cross into the city; and the Roman soldiers slipped, staggered, and stumbled like drunkards. Struggling to stay erect, they lost their footing, clung to their companions to keep from falling, and brought their companions down with them in a clattering, twisted, undignified mass of armor and bodies. Vespasian called off his troops; the assault had failed.

In the days that followed, Vespasian had his soldiers raise the earthworks higher and construct three siege towers, each fifty feet tall and sheeted with iron. These were moved up on the earthworks until they stood against the wall, overtopping it and dominating the adjacent part of the city. From the towers the men sent spears, stones, and arrows down at the Jews, skillfully picking them off, gradually reducing the population.

Day after day this happened, but Jotapata still held out. The town of Japha, ten miles away, was moved to heroism by its example and revolted from the Romans. Vespasian had to send a detachment to subdue it; Japha was chastened, but Jotapata still held out. South of Galilee the Samaritans, whose territory was already garrisoned by Rome, assembled on their sacred mountain and talked revolt. Vespasian dispatched a force that (according to Josephus) massacred eleven thousand six hundred of them; but Jotapata still held out. Its citizens suffered—thirsty, exhausted, wounded, in grief for dead husbands or lovers or comrades—and perhaps they surprised themselves by their unyielding heroism. And yet on the forty-seventh morning of the siege they woke to find the Romans inside.

A deserter had suggested that the Romans try to enter just before dawn, when the tired sentries were most likely to be asleep. Vespasian's son Titus stole in with a few men and silently killed the sentries. More legionaries followed. Day dawned slowly through a gray mist while the soldiers roamed in bands through the bleak streets, walked into the houses, and roused the Jews at swordpoint. The time had come to repay these Jotapatans for the cattle hides, the wet clothes, the bags of chaff, the boiling oil, the fenugreek, and all the Roman dead. Some of the citizens were slaughtered in the streets they had defended for so long. Others committed suicide rather than die by unclean hands. Others were thrown over the precipices to their deaths. All day long the Romans killed the Jotapatans. When the number of the victims was added to the number of those who had died during the siege, Josephus says, the total came to about forty thousand. The entire population of Jotapata could not have been much more.

For the next few days there were mopping-up operations. Some of the Jotapatans had taken refuge in underground vaults and caverns; the Romans rooted them out, killed the men, and took the women and children prisoner. Naturally the Romans began to wonder where Josephus was—whether the leader of the Jotapatan resistance lay among the dead. If he did not, the Roman victory was incomplete.

He was still at large, having ducked into a pit off which a capacious cave opened. With him were about forty other Jews. After two or three days a woman who had been hiding with them but who had been captured gave them away. For the events that followed we have only Josephus' own account in the *Jewish War,* and it is open to suspicion.

Josephus states that Vespasian (who must have admired any man that could protract resistance against a Roman army of sixty thousand for forty-seven days) sent two tribunes to the hiding place to promise that if he came out he would not be killed. Well aware of how much damage he had done to the Romans, he distrusted this promise. Vespasian then sent a third tribune, one whom Josephus had known in happier times, and this man convinced him to come out. Josephus also remembered dreams that seemed to imply that he should live and be God's agent, and the dreams helped to convince him. Satisfied, the tribune apparently left. But the other inhabitants of the cave, desperate and thinking of suicide, urged him to kill himself rather than accept life from the Romans. They said that they would kill him if he declined to perform the operation on his own. He delivered a long and eloquent address, arguing that it is impious for a man to deprive himself of his God-given soul through suicide. They were unpersuaded. Suddenly, however, he had an idea: they should all commit suicide, but in turn according to lot. Each man drew a lot; the second man slit the first man's throat, and the third man slit the second man's throat, and so on, until the cave was littered with bleeding bodies. As it happened, the last two lots fell to Josephus and another man. Josephus convinced the other man that the best thing to do would be to give themselves up.

That is the story, for what it is worth. It may be true; it may contain certain deviations from truth; it may omit significant details. Except for one individual, those who could contradict it lay dead in the cave.

When Josephus was brought before Vespasian, the Roman soldiers crowded around to see so famous a commander, to hoot at him, and to demand his death. Titus, touched by the spectacle of a young man fallen from greatness, persuaded his father to keep the promise of life, but Vespasian naturally made Josephus a prisoner and said that he would send him to Rome for Nero's judgment. Although Josephus could congratulate himself on having survived Jotapata, he was still by no means out of danger. Believing himself to be something of a seer, he took Vespasian, Titus, and a couple of other Romans aside and gravely informed them that Nero would not rule much longer— that Vespasian himself would be emperor, and in time so would Titus. God had commissioned him to deliver this message.

At the moment, the sound and solid Vespasian assumed that Josephus had invented the prediction to make a good impression.

XV

VICTORIES

When news of the fall of Jotapata reached Jerusalem, many of the citizens would not believe it. Those who did believe it sorrowed not only for the city but for Josephus, since they assumed that he had lost his life. Word that he was alive and had given himself up to the Romans caused people to call him a coward, a deserter, a renegade. It was rumored that he was well treated by his captors, whereas his countrymen had died. Many Jews learned to hate him.

In the summer and fall of 67, Vespasian proceeded in a slow, deliberate manner. He devoted a great deal of attention to retrieving for that loyal client king, Agrippa, the cities that had revolted from him. Having put Tiberias decisively back under Agrippa's control, he sent his son Titus to Tarichaea, where most of the rebels were hanging out, and later he himself came to Tarichaea. As a result dead bodies cluttered the city and floated putrefying on the Sea of Galilee, where a maritime battle against the rebels had occurred; and the bodies of rebels who had swum to shore only to be killed by Roman soldiers lay decomposing at the edge of the water, so that the Sea of Galilee stank.

Practical as always, Vespasian decided that even loyal Tarichaeans might become discontented in the future. He therefore butchered about twelve hundred old men and other useless people in the stadium, where Josephus had made his speech not many months before. He also sent six thousand young men to Greece to help dig a canal that Nero wanted to cut across the Isthmus of Corinth; sold over thirty thousand others into slavery; and presented still others to King Agrippa, who sold these into slavery too. A war should show some profit.

With Tiberias and Tarichaea secured for Agrippa, Vespasian and Titus turned to Gamala ("the Camel"), which had also been part of Agrippa's kingdom but was now in revolt. It occupied a mountain spur shaped like a camel's hump. Gamala too was subjugated, and many citizens ended by jumping from the fortress to death in a ravine. The only place in the Galilean region that still held out was Gischala, home town of Josephus' old enemy John. Vespasian sent Titus with one thousand cavalrymen to take care of it. John showed willingness to accept Rome's terms but asked for a delay in the negotiations until after the Sabbath. Titus tolerantly granted the delay, and John used it to escape from the city with several thousand followers and some women and children. When Titus learned about the trick he gave chase, killed about six thousand of the followers, and brought almost three thousand women and children back to Gischala, according to Josephus. But John and the rest of his men got to Jerusalem.

Some of the Roman soldiers wondered why Vespasian did not besiege Jerusalem now, especially since civil conflict had broken out in the city. But Vespasian decided to let Jerusalem wait until the bickering Jewish factions had weakened one another. In the meantime he could conquer the other trouble spots, making Jerusalem an isolated center of resistance. Toward the end of March in the year 68 he occupied Gadara, southeast of the Sea of Galilee, and then, retiring to his headquarters at Caesaraea, sent his general Placidus to mop up the rebels in the Jordan region. Placidus, according to Josephus, took two thousand prisoners and killed fifteen thousand people, and others drowned themselves in the Jordan. The decaying flesh fouled the countryside and the river, and many corpses floated all the way down to the Dead Sea and rotted on top of the thick salt water, where no fish swam.

At Caesaraea, Vespasian heard that a revolt against Nero had started up in Gaul, but Vespasian himself continued to serve the emperor strongly and faithfully. With much of his army he ravaged west-central Judaea; took over four thousand prisoners and put over ten thousand Jews to death; occupied Emmaus (fifteen miles north-west of Jerusalem); marched north into Samaria; then turned south-east and went down to Jericho about the middle of June. His general Trajan, having reduced the Transjordan to submission, joined him there. In anticipation of Vespasian's coming, the population of Jeri-cho had fled. At this ancient city, Herod's winter oasis less than ten miles northeast of Jerusalem, Vespasian rested from his labors among the date palms, the cypresses, the balsams that Herod and Cleopatra had valued so highly. Visiting the Dead Sea nearby, he threw some prisoners into the water with their hands tied behind their backs to see if they would float. They floated, and the Dead Sea's reputation was sustained.

His general Cerealis had subdued upper Idumaea. Except for Jeru-salem, the only strongholds still in rebel hands were Herodium (the fortress where Herod lay buried, about three miles west of the Dead Sea), Machaerus (the old castle of Antipas and Herodias, on the eastern side of the Dead Sea), and the great fortified rock of Masada, from which the Sicarii carried on raids along the sea's west coast.

About ten miles south of Jericho stood the complex of buildings known today as the Qumran community. It spread over a terrace or spur jutting from a rugged cliff in a rugged land—the rocky, dusty, buff-and-orange desert region sloping eventually down to the marshy western shore of the Dead Sea. While Vespasian's Tenth Legion took over Jericho, there lived and prayed in this complex a holy brother-hood. As far back as the second century B.C., the founders of the community—apparently in reaction against the gross materialism that they saw in Jerusalem and elsewhere in the land, and probably in re-action against certain aspects of Jewish ritual as well—had taken to these dry and vacant spaces, called in the Bible the Wilderness of Judah. Their spiritual descendants continued to live at Qumran until early in the reign of Herod, when they suddenly abandoned the site. (An earthquake occurring in 31 B.C. may have made them think that God was displeased with them.) About the time of Herod's death in 4 B.C., members of the sect returned to Qumran to resume the life of their ancestors. The brotherhood has recently become famous be-cause of the discovery of its manuscripts, termed the Dead Sea Scrolls. Sectaries had hidden these manuscripts in barely accessible caves that penetrated the rock faces of the desolate land. Their object was probably to keep the documents safe from Vespasian's soldiers.

The discovery of the manuscripts is a rather familiar story by now: in 1947 a Bedouin boy named Muhammad Adh-Dhib, looking for a goat that had strayed from his flock, found the entrance to a cave, tossed a rock into it, heard the sound of a jar shattering, and ran away in fright. Coming back a day or so later to explore the cave with an older companion, he looked into several tall jars with upside-down bowls over their necks—one of which contained three parchment rolls with Hebrew writing on them. The manuscripts, most of them in Hebrew, a few in Aramaic, had evidently been written in the second and first centuries B.C. and the early part of the first century A.D. Some were portions of the Bible—Isaiah, for instance, or sections of Daniel, Ruth, Psalms, Kings, Lamentations, and the Torah. They were approximately a thousand years older than any other extant Hebrew manuscripts of the Bible. Others were Biblical commentaries or apocryphal and pseudepigraphic writings such as the Book of Noah, the Book of Enoch, the Testament of Levi, and the Book of Jubilees. There were hymns of thanksgiving; there was a vision of the New (or Heavenly) Jerusalem. Two scrolls, of copper rather than parchment or papyrus, evidently catalogued and described the locations of about sixty treasure troves throughout Judaea. Another scroll, over twenty-eight feet long, contained stipulations for ritual purity and specifications for the Temple—a building differing in some ways from Herod's. Still another scroll, the so-called *Rule* or *Manual of Discipline,* held regulations governing the daily life of the community. Virtually all the writings were pious; some were apocalyptic or Messianic. The *Rule of War,* or *War of the Sons of Light with the Sons of Darkness,* envisioned a contest to be fought out at the end of time, when right would finally triumph over wrong. It told of the battle standards, the trumpets, the marshaled hosts and military maneuvers of that age of glory.

The community that produced these documents numbered several hundred brothers—a few of them apparently married, since women's skeletons have been dug up in the cemetery. Their buildings were simple rectangular structures of stone and plaster with roofs of reeds and palm branches. A square, squat tower, its walls perhaps four feet thick, could be used for defense. The complex also had courtyards, cattle pens, an assembly hall or refectory about sixty feet long, smaller assembly halls, kitchens, latrines, and the scriptorium, where the scrolls were painstakingly written. The settlement was self-contained, with pottery works, a smithy, a flour mill, and a bakery to help satisfy the limited needs of its inhabitants. They probably herded sheep and goats in the wastelands around Qumran and raised fruits and vegetables on the marshy shore of the sea. Some of them may have lived in caves in the surrounding cliffs.

Their most elaborate piece of engineering involved water. There was no natural source of water on the Qumran terrace or anywhere near. An aqueduct or channel, uncovered for much of its length but cut through solid rock for part of the distance, brought rainwater down from the western highlands to supply a complicated system of plaster-lined cisterns, reservoirs, conduits, tanks, and baths at the settlement itself.

Scholars believe that the Qumran brothers belonged to the sect known as the Essenes, or "Pious Ones," that arose in the second century B.C. and was flourishing in the first century A.D. The Essenes were not ignored by writers of the first century. Pliny the Elder talked about them in Book V of his *Natural History*. Philo of Alexandria described them at greater length in two works, *Every Good Man Is Free* and *Apology for the Jews,* the latter of which was preserved in part by the early church historian Eusebius. Josephus, who had studied the doctrines of the Essenes as a youth, wrote about these people in his *Jewish Antiquities* and, much more fully, in the *Jewish War.*

According to Philo, there were over four thousand Essenes in the first century A.D. Some of them perhaps lived in cities, although most of them must have preferred quiet villages or even lonely places like the site of the Qumran votarists. Pliny says they had no women; Philo says they considered women meretricious beings who enslaved men to lust and to the specious duty of providing for home and family. Josephus, although he remarks that they viewed women as lascivious and faithless, adds that one branch of the Essenes (perhaps the men of Qumran) married—not for sexual pleasure but for procreation, the continuation of human life. To marry for sexual pleasure was to commit oneself to the world's dirt.

Their attitude toward sex suggests their profound spiritual orientation. They despised and perhaps feared the gaily painted world as gross, vicious, worthless, and godless. Subscribing almost to the dualism of the contemporary Gnostics (who believed that all earthly matter is evil and only God is good), they thought that the world had been created by an evil principle—a malign demon, an enemy of God. They valued work and (except on the Sabbath) worked from dawn to sunset if not longer, as planters, reapers, herdsmen, bee-keepers, smiths, potters, scribes. Sweat was estimable to them, since it represented work. For the sweet luxuries that diligence can secure for some people, however, they felt only contempt. Their communal living was an expression of their unworldliness. They owned no slaves; individually they owned no houses, no lands, and no money. When a man became an Essene, he gave his wealth to the order and it was put in the public treasury. If he earned wages as a laborer after joining, his wages went to the treasury. If he grew ill, his medical expenses were paid out of the treasury. The Essenes even possessed their clothes in common, and wore them until they were rags. All those living in the same community ate their meals together and ate the same thing.

Like the Pharisees, they believed that the human soul is immortal, but they went further than the Pharisees in emphasizing the rankness of the body, the soul's temporary prison. Excrement evidently was a sign of this rankness. Just as they did not work on the Sabbath (even preparing its meals the day before), they did not defecate on the Sabbath either. On days when they did excrete, according to Josephus, they walked off to some isolated spot, dug a hole in the earth with a shovel, and squatted over it, covering their vile bodies with their robes so that the divine light would not be offended by what they were doing; and when they had finished they filled up the hole with earth and washed themselves. They were obeying the stipulation in the Torah for keeping clean on military service: "And thou shalt have a paddle upon thy weapon; and it shall be, when thou wilt ease thyself abroad, thou shalt dig therewith, and shalt turn back and cover that which cometh from thee."

Like the Pharisees also, they believed in the existence of angels; but their consciousness of evil angels as well as good angels was so strong as to suggest the Zoroastrianism of ancient Persia. The good and evil angels kept fighting for the souls of men; and not until the holy war at the end of time would the evil angels be overcome.

Although the Essenes were not smiling specialists in public relations, they drew votarists. Pliny implies that men surfeited with the surface splendors and rotten hypocrisies of normal life turned to Essenism; and Philo says that among the Essenes were many mature or elderly men, in whom the strong and fickle passions of the world had already burned out. But the Essenes apparently also trained the young, whether or not the young became brothers. According to Josephus, a candidate for membership underwent a three-year period of probation. In the first year he had to show that he could be continent, resisting the beautiful temptations of evil. In the next two years he had to give further evidence of his austerity, his self-restraint, his ability to practice the Essene ideals; and before becoming a full member, one who shared meals with the brothers, he had to swear most solemn oaths. Philo sets down the three cardinal principles of the Essenes as love of God, love of virtue, and love of man. These principles were fundamental to the oaths described by Josephus, and if a brother offended heinously against the oaths he was cast out. Rather than eat unclean food with unclean men, he resorted to grass and died.

At Qumran the sectaries observed a different calendar of religious festivals from that observed in Jerusalem at the Temple. But this and other differences were not enough to make them heretics, even though such distinctions may have excluded them from the parts of the Temple where other male Jews could go. The Qumran sectaries believed that they were following the Torah more closely than other Jews. They studied the Law with incessant devotion and tried with unflagging ardor to live up to it. They praised God on rising, on beginning a meal, in trouble, in fear, at the start of an enterprise, on retiring, and many other times throughout the day. Their moral code required them to return good for evil, to cheer the downhearted, to keep their speech undefiled, and to stay humble; and it forbade them to envy, covet, or lie. Each Qumran brother had to renew his pledge every year, and if past experience told him that he could not uphold it, he presumably confessed his weakness and suffered expulsion. Ritual purity was extraordinarily important to the sectaries: they evidently underwent baptism once a day if not more often. They had constructed their elaborate water system because the cisterns or baths were used for these ceremonial purifications.

The man whose memory the Qumran brothers most honored was called by them the Righteous Teacher, or Teacher of Righteousness. We do not know his identity, but he seems to have been their leader in the days of their origin and to have suffered under a man called the Wicked Priest, who brought about his overthrow. The Wicked

Priest may have been one of the Hasmonaean high priests or priest kings of the period between Judas Maccabaeus and Pompey—possibly Alexander Jannaeus, who slaughtered or crucified those who opposed his policies. But again we cannot be sure; both the Righteous Teacher and the Wicked Priest are so dimmed by allusion and allegory that we cannot even feel certain that they ever existed as real human beings. In any case the Righteous Teacher was not regarded as a Messiah, or divine savior. He was the preceptor in the ways of purity, and the Qumran sectaries must revere him and never deviate from his discipline. To him it had been granted to know and expound the truth; his exhortations were infallible rules.

And so the brothers sweated in their fields, kept themselves ritually pure, ate their sacred meals together twice a day, were good to one another, praised God, tried hard to triumph over evil, and waited for the war. It would come, the holy war: the War of the Sons of Light with the Sons of Darkness, the glorious final agony talked about in the scroll. The brothers must be ready for it. They would be the Sons of Light and their enemies would be the Sons of Darkness—especially the people called the Kittim, the "Triumphant Empire"—the votarists' name for any great, victorious, evil nation, and at this period probably their name for Rome. The priest-blown trumpets would scream, the hosts would gather, the stallions would charge, the polished bronze shields and gold-inlaid swords would flash in the sun, and the blood would run in that last grand contest, prelude to the end of time. Squadron against squadron, battalion against battalion, hero against hero, truth against falsehood, the war would rage. It would not be a human war only; armies of good angels and armies of bad angels would shake the air with the clangor of their battles. The Prince of Light would lead the good angels; and Belial, Prince of Darkness, would captain the evil demons.

In some of the engagements the Sons of Light would suffer almost unendurably as the power of evil overwhelmed them, but they would ultimately conquer. The two long-expected Messiahs would come at this time: the Messiah of Aaron and the Messiah of Israel, the figures sent by God to preside over a new era. The Messiah of Aaron would be a priest, head of the holy ritual. The Messiah of Israel would be a king of the royal house of David. He would also be a warrior, championing the Sons of Light until the wicked were prostrate forever. Then the good people would worship according to right ritual under the government of God's elect priests, and there would be no more dishonesty, greed, jealousy, lust, or war.

No record exists of what the brothers thought about the Jews' fight against Rome. In their eyes it may have been just another struggle against the unclean, the ungodly, the Sons of Darkness; or it may have signalized the start of the cosmic contest with evil. When Vespasian occupied Jericho, the votarists must have expected his soldiers to come to Qumran soon. They may have trained for battle or made other preparations; presumably this was the period when they hid their scrolls in the caves.

The Sons of Darkness marched out of Jericho through the dry country. Perhaps they slaughtered the Sons of Light in the austere buildings of stone and plaster. More probably the brothers had already escaped to some refuge, such as the fortified rock of Masada. If so, they never returned. In A.D. 68 the holy life was over at Qumran.

XVI

THE CIVIL WARS

From Jericho, Vespasian went back to Caesaraea, where he learned that Nero was dead. Helpless in the face of revolution, the emperor had fled from Rome with a few followers and the Greek boy Sporus, whom he had castrated and married because Sporus looked something like his dear deceased wife Poppaea. At the age of thirty-one, in the darkness of a lonely villa, with horsemen drawing near to take him to execution, he had summoned up enough courage to commit suicide and enough self-esteem to regret that the world was losing so great a performer. Vespasian's command terminated with Nero's death. The siege of Jerusalem was again postponed, and Vespasian waited to have his command confirmed by the new emperor, the elderly general Galba.

At Jerusalem the Jews took advantage of the long moratorium to squabble. The city had already been split by dissension: some people, deciding that they preferred peace, grumbled against the dominant war party or deserted to the Romans, and humble citizens criticized the rich for the conduct of the war. When John of Gischala entered the city toward the end of 67 with his Galilean remnants who had managed to escape Titus' vengeance, the situation became worse. Insofar as we can tell, Josephus was right in characterizing his enemy as a shrewd demagogue. As greedy for power as he had been in Galilee,

John evidently played on the antagonism toward the rich that the Jerusalem mob had inherited from generations of Pharisaic opposition to the well-born Sadducees.

John, however, was more moderate than the bands of robber patriots that now swarmed into Jerusalem because the Romans were driving them out of the rest of Judaea. These extremists, who called themselves the Zealots, tried to take over the city. Hating the upper classes, whom they associated with friendship toward Rome, they loudly blamed the aristocracy for the defeat in Galilee. No doubt they said a great deal against Josephus, although he is silent on the point. They had several of the most conservative aristocrats arrested and then murdered in prison. As a blow at the rich and pedigreed families from which the high priest was traditionally drawn, they chose their own high priest by lot—a village stonemason.

Many of the citizens of Jerusalem, however, were not swayed by the Zealots' tactics, and under the leadership of a former high priest named Ananus son of Ananus, they clashed with the extremists. The Zealots had already seized the Temple, since its commanding position on the hill made it a very desirable stronghold. But Ananus posted six thousand or more guards on the porticoes surrounding the top of the hill, and the Zealots discovered that they were prisoners in the holy precincts.

In this struggle between the Zealots and the moderates John seems to have tried to please both sides, probably watching to see who would win. He told Ananus that he was a moderate, but Ananus suspected that he was actually betraying the moderates' plans to the Zealots and had him swear a loyalty oath. If John did clandestinely help the Zealots, he had chosen the more resourceful side. From their prison in the Temple they managed to get out a message inviting the Idumaeans to come to Jerusalem and help them against the moderates. A short time later the inhabitants of Jerusalem realized that twenty thousand Idumaeans had arrived from the hills and deserts to the south and were sitting outside the walls.

Josephus had little use for these Arabs, these countrymen of Herod who had been Jews now for several generations. He said that they were a wild, unruly lot and that they had come to Jerusalem because they liked to fight. They may also have come because they disliked Jewish aristocrats. At any rate Ananus would not let them in. They would not go home, however, and camped outside the city. That night a terrific storm whirled around Jerusalem, with powerful winds, thunder and lightning, and drenching rain. This did not calm the temper of the Idumaeans, who sat out in it. A few Zealots managed to escape from the Temple during the storm, sneaking past Ananus' guards on the porticoes. They descended into the city, opened a gate, and let the Idumaeans in.

That was the end of moderate control in Jerusalem. As the storm subsided the terror began. The Idumaeans ran through the streets killing everybody they met without bothering to ask whether their victims were friends or enemies. At the Temple they overwhelmed Ananus' men and let the rest of the Zealots out. Morning dawned on eighty-five hundred dead.

In the next few days the Idumaeans and the Zealots carried on their joint reign of terror. Having killed Ananus, they scourged, racked, and executed other aristocrats and robbed at random. But in time many of the Idumaeans grew tired of the sport and disenchanted with their Zealot allies. At least half of them went home again, leaving the Zealots in charge. John was by this time a bona fide Zealot. He now broke away from the other leaders of his party, however, aiming at supreme power for himself in Jerusalem. For a while he came close to achieving his ambition, perhaps because he possessed more qualities of leadership than his colleagues did, perhaps because he was less scrupulous. But a dangerous rival was rising—not in Jerusalem itself but in the country to the south.

This was a young man called Simon bar Giora. He had been in Jerusalem at the time of Cestius Gallus' abortive attack and had distinguished himself as a rebel then. Later he had joined the Sicarii at Masada, but his ideas for raids on the nearby towns were too reckless even for those daring men. Now he was gathering adherents in the desolate hills south of Jerusalem. Like John himself Simon was a skillful demagogue, and at a time when Rome had repossessed most of Judaea and the Jews seemed to lack imaginative leaders, many men no doubt found him inspiring. He promised slaves their freedom; he promised plunder for those who would follow him. His band swelled to an army. Whether he was more a patriot or a robber would be difficult to determine, but he was successful. Having defeated John's Zealots outside Jerusalem, he marched south into Idumaea, which he ravaged, then north again. According to Josephus, he had forty thousand followers by this time. Some Zealots ambushed him at a pass and kidnaped his wife, but in his anger he created so much ruin outside Jerusalem, killing elderly people and generally raising havoc, that the Zealots gave the woman back to him.

In Jerusalem the Zealots were now tyrannizing the more moderate citizens, robbing the rich and raping the women. Many of these Zealots, though so called, were Galileans who had escaped from Gischala with John over a year before. Josephus says that some of them for variety put on women's clothes, doused themselves with perfume, and tripped through the city with braided hair and painted eyelids, seeking whom they might attract and then suddenly killing for sport. For this reason perhaps, and from general disappointment at John's sanction of violence as well as pure envy of his power, the Idumaeans who had not left Jerusalem attacked John's followers in the spring of 69 and chased them into the Temple. With the endorsement of the more conservative inhabitants, they also invited Simon and his horde into the city.

Simon's army, joined by ordinary citizens, laid siege to John and his forces at the Temple. The Zealots built four towers from which they could send missiles down at Simon's soldiers. They also set up catapults to hurl down stones. But it was time for the confusion to be compounded: a priest named Eleazar split from John and formed a third faction. John seems to have been making himself increasingly unpopular at this period. First the Idumaeans had separated from him and now Eleazar had broken off, with a band that included several very influential Jews.

Since John controlled the porticoes that encircled the top of the Temple hill, Eleazar could not have gotten past him and down into the city if he had wanted to. Eleazar therefore took a portion of the Temple away from John: the inner area of the sacred enclosure, the highest and holiest part of the vast complex, including the Holy of Holies itself. He and his men apparently had food up there, and plenty of consecrated wine to drink.

A selfish, senseless, impious, mutually suicidal war ensued among Eleazar, John, and Simon—a war without reason, without achievement, and even without progress. From the heights of the Temple terrace Eleazar's men, the fewest in number but the most advantageously placed, shot javelins down every day on John's men in the Temple's outer courts; John's men put stones and darts in their machines and shot them up at Eleazar's men, and also threw missiles down at Simon's men in the city below; and Simon's men repeatedly attacked the Temple hill and were repeatedly repulsed. Sometimes John's men made a foray from the outer Temple into the parts of the city around the hill, struggled with Simon's men, and burned some of the storehouses where the citizens had put large quantities of grain in preparation for the siege by the Romans. After driving John's men back up the hill, Simon's men would burn more storehouses in pique —until the area at the foot of the hill was a black ruin and most of the food supplies so carefully gathered had dissipated in smoke. Through it all, pious Jews would climb the hill to offer sacrifices in the Temple as usual, even though the holy structure was now polluted with the dead. John and Eleazar were sufficiently good Jews to let them come but frisked them for weapons anyway. If a battle happened to be going on, a man at sacrifice was likely to end up with an arrow in his chest, fired perhaps by one of Eleazar's adherents.

Several months after learning that Galba was emperor—not until toward the end of the year 68 in fact—Vespasian sent Titus to Italy to congratulate Galba. Titus probably contemplated the trip with a sense of duty rather than a sense of pleasure. Life proved attractive in the East, and besides he thought he had fallen in love there. Since King Agrippa was with his father much of the time, he had gotten to know this man's sister Berenice very well; it was with Berenice that he thought he was in love.

If their racial and religious differences troubled him, he tried to dismiss them as irrelevant for the present. She allured him; that was that. Even though she was about forty, ten years older than he, her animation had not begun to flag and her beauty had not yet decayed. Her maturity only made her more captivating. She had had three husbands and had functioned as her brother's queen for many years; she had helped her brother through the mazes of Oriental politics, had been whispered about as being his mistress, and had been insulted by the procurator Florus and by her fellow Jews at Jerusalem. In other words, she was a woman of experience, not a naïve, nonsensical girl. Titus—a solid soldier like his father, schooled in Roman politics and Roman war, and already married twice himself—appreciated Berenice's maturity.

Agrippa traveled with Titus toward Rome, since he had business of his own there, but Berenice did not make the party a trio. She stayed in the East, where she put her experience to use by pleasing Vespasian. She loved the son passionately, and that was all the more reason for her to charm the father.

By January of 69, Titus had gotten as far as Greece; but at Corinth he learned that Galba had been assassinated in the Roman Forum and that young Otho, who had managed the assassination, was the new emperor. The sybaritic Vitellius, however, had been proclaimed emperor by his legions on the German frontier and was marching south to dispute the title with Otho. Titus decided that it was not yet time to congratulate anybody; his commission from his father, besides, had been only to congratulate Galba. Leaving Agrippa to continue on to Rome, he turned back toward the East and Berenice. He sailed past the Greek and Ionian coasts and stopped at Paphos on the island of Cyprus to visit the celebrated Temple of Venus, goddess born of the sea foam.

In the great temple, rich with the gifts of kings, Venus was worshiped in the form of a cult image—a conical stone. Titus presented male animals for sacrifice at the altar in front of the temple, whereon pure fire burned and no blood from victims was allowed to fall. The priest consulted the entrails: they were favorable for a great undertaking. Having said this much, he added that he would like to speak to Titus privately.

When Titus emerged from the private interview he did not reveal what the priest of Venus had told him, but he did not look at all displeased. Perhaps the man had suggested that Titus would conquer the Jews, or watch his father become emperor, or even become emperor himself some day. He continued his voyage eastward.

Near the end of spring in 69, Vespasian moved in the direction of Jerusalem and his general Cerealis reduced rebellious Idumaea. Inside Jerusalem the three factions snarled and fought and bit at one another while the ordinary citizens looked on aghast, suffered, and worried about what would happen when Rome laid siege. But Vespasian let the city alone: he was not willing to commit himself to a siege of the great metropolis quite yet. He set up a garrison at Bethel ten miles to the north, however, and another at Ephraim northeast of Bethel, and his cavalry stamped out whatever resistance remained in the immediate environment of the holy city.

Then he returned to Caesaraea, where he got the news that the sybaritic Vitellius was emperor. Vitellius' legions from Germany had beaten Otho's forces in northern Italy; and Otho, though not accustomed to heroic acts, had committed suicide in a noble Roman manner, leaving his troops to weep.

It seemed that a man could make himself emperor if he had a strong enough army. Vespasian had three devoted legions, and there were, besides, the prophecies of Josephus and others, saying unequivocally that he would be emperor. For quite a while he had intermittently played with the idea of making a bid for the imperial throne; now the time seemed right. At Caesaraea his soldiers were muttering that their general deserved to rule the Roman world—not the ludicrous, luxurious, gluttonous Vitellius. In addition to his own men Vespasian could count on three legions under the command of Mucianus, governor of Syria, who very much wanted him to be emperor. He could also count on the two legions under the command of Tiberius Alexander, the Jewish renegade and friend of Rome, once procurator of Judaea but now governor of Egypt. He could count on Oriental kings such as his friend Agrippa, and on other troops, Roman and mercenary, throughout the East. He could count on the Egyptian, Syrian, and Pontic fleets. The legions on the Danube frontier were reportedly disgusted with Vitellius and wanted an emperor they could respect. Of course the Jewish business was not yet over, but only Jerusalem remained to be conquered, and again the siege could be delayed.

If Vespasian lost, he would also lose his life, like Galba and Otho. It was assuredly a risk—but it was a well-calculated one. Vespasian wrote to Tiberius Alexander, who had the two legions in Alexandria proclaim him emperor on July 1, 69. A couple of days later his own legions swore fidelity to him as emperor. Cities all over the East followed suit, and so did the five legions in the Danube region. At Berytus he received the homage of cities and potentates, and here he held a council of war.

At Berytus he also set Josephus free. Josephus had, during a captivity that by now amounted to almost two years, been a model prisoner. He had even married the person whom Vespasian had chosen for him, a girl from Caesaraea. But he was still in chains, and life was still very uncertain. Vespasian, it seems, now remembered Josephus' prophecy and thought highly of him for it; and Titus suggested that, to signify that he had been unjustly put in chains, the bonds should be cut through with an axe rather than just unfastened. The girl from Caesaraea left him, but that was a small matter. Josephus placed, in front of his own now-Latinized name, the name Flavius—the *nomen* of the house to which Vespasian belonged; and since he could not go back to Jerusalem, he stayed with his patron. The major difference was that he followed him around as a free man rather than as a chained man.

From Berytus, Vespasian went to Antioch, where he dispatched Mucianus, governor of Syria, across Asia Minor to Italy with a considerable army to defeat Vitellius. Vespasian himself would refrain from participating in the war. He eventually sailed with Titus and Josephus to Alexandria to make sure that the great Egyptian grain supply did not go to Italy.

The news from Europe continued to be good. The prefect of the imperial fleet at Ravenna defected from Vitellius and joined Vespasian's forces. Before Mucianus could get even close to Italy, the Danubian legions went ahead on their own and started toward Italy full of enthusiasm for Vespasian. Their precipitancy could have hurt Vespasian's cause, but it did not: they crushed the Vitellian legions outside Cremona and sacked and burned the city. The legions in Spain, Gaul, and Britain now swore fidelity to Vespasian. The Danubian army, fresh from its Cremona victory, marched toward Rome. Vitellius did little except vacillate, act pusillanimous, and stay supine, and his demoralized troops north of Rome surrendered without a fight.

At Rome itself the prefect of the urban cohorts happened to be an elderly brother of Vespasian named Flavius Sabinus. He did not want any bloodshed in the capital; he preferred to negotiate with Vitellius, who was in his palace. And Vitellius, tired of it all, preferred to abdicate, hoping that then he would be able to retire to a life of wine, indolence, and family matters and let somebody else rule the world. But he still had many loyal subjects at Rome, and they would not hear of abdication. They prevented him from depositing his insignia of imperial office in the Temple of Concord on December 18 and chased him back to the palace. Rome still contained soldiers as well as civilians who were loyal to Vitellius, and the aged Flavius Sabinus began to worry. With a few senators and soldiers favorable to Vespasian and with a noble lady who wanted to watch a bloody fight, he ensconced himself in the Temple of Jupiter Optimus Maximus on the Capitoline Hill, just as the Jewish partisans had ensconced themselves in the Temple of God at Jerusalem.

The Temple of Jupiter Optimus Maximus meant almost as much to Romans as the Temple at Jerusalem did to Jews. According to Tacitus, the original building had been begun by the Etruscan kings in the sixth century B.C. The present one had been dedicated in 69 B.C. and much embellished by Augustus. It was the house of the king of the gods, chief of the Roman Pantheon and protector of the Roman state. It was also the place where the archives concerning Rome's relations with foreign powers were stored. New consuls offered sacrifice here. The great triumphal processions celebrating victories over Rome's enemies made this building their destination. Much more than any other structure it symbolized the greatness of Rome.

When the Vitellian forces attacked, the band under Flavius Sabinus ran out on the roof of an old colonnade that projected from the temple and threw stones and tiles down on them. The Vitellians threw up pieces of burning wood, which set the colonnade on fire. Then they burned the gates and prepared to enter the temple itself, but Flavius Sabinus stopped them by tearing down the statues of Rome's heroes and piling them up every which way as a barricade. The attackers climbed onto the roofs of the tall buildings next to the temple. Somebody—probably Flavius Sabinus' men in an effort to dislodge the attackers—set fire to the roofs. The fire spread; it jumped to the wooden supports, representing Roman eagles, that held up the roof of the temple itself; then the whole building blazed and crashed and crumbled. Almost at the moment of Vespasian's victory this great, impious mistake had cast shame over his bid for the throne.

The Danubian legions entered Rome soon afterward and put an end to Vitellian resistance. Vitellius himself was dragged through the streets and murdered, and on December 21 Vespasian was acknowledged emperor. But the infuriated mob had already stabbed Vespasian's elderly brother to death, mutilated his corpse, and cut off his head for permitting the Temple of Jupiter Optimus Maximus to burn.

With the Empire now fully secured, Vespasian deputed Titus to finish off the Jews and sailed from Alexandria for Italy. Titus marched to Caesaraea, taking along Josephus, detachments from the two legions stationed in Egypt, and the prefect, or governor, Tiberius

Alexander, whom he had appointed chief of staff. In accepting such a position this man (Philo's own nephew) had receded about as far as he could from his race and heritage. Having already governed Judaea as procurator for the Romans, having sent Roman soldiers to massacre his fellow Jews during the Alexandria riots of 66, and having been the first man of influence to hail the conqueror of Galilee as the new Roman emperor, Tiberius Alexander was now committed to helping Titus overcome Jerusalem. Six years before, he had served Nero's general Corbulo well as chief of staff in a campaign against the Parthians. His knowledge of the geography and customs of the land of his ancestors would help him serve Titus well.

At Caesaraea during the early months of 70, Titus gathered troops, and other troops joined him on the march eastward to Jerusalem. He had his own legion, the Fifteenth—the one he had brought from Alexandria at the beginning of the war—plus the Fifth, which Vespasian had stationed at Emmaus, and the Tenth, which Vespasian had stationed at Jericho and which had caused the end of Qumran. These legions had been depleted to fill the army that Mucianus conducted through Asia Minor to fight Vitellius; but they were now replenished, partly from the detachments that Titus took along from Egypt and partly from forts on the Euphrates, so that they were presumably at their full complement of over five thousand men each. Titus also had the Twelfth (the Thunderbolt), the legion that had retreated from Jerusalem four years before under Cestius Gallus, but that was now reconstituted and eager to erase its shame. With the cavalry units, the mercenaries, and the auxiliaries furnished by Agrippa and the other kings, the whole force amounted to about sixty-five thousand men— more than Vespasian had had when he descended on Jotapata.

In the early spring of 70, Titus began his march. The troops passed many parties of Jews on the road. Nearly all of them were going to Jerusalem too—not for war but for religion, since the time of Passover was approaching. The Romans did not disturb them, but some of the soldiers probably thought that they would be seeing these Jews later on.

Protected by ravines on the east, west, and south sides, Jerusalem was pregnable only from the north. Unfortunately for Titus, its northern side was protected by a wall, begun by Agrippa I when he was king of Judaea over a quarter of a century ago. He had erected it to enclose the suburban area that had sprung up north of the city proper, and although it had been left unfinished until the start of the war and then finished in a hurry, it had ninety square towers and was a formidable barrier. A second wall with fourteen towers stood between the northern suburban area and the more northerly part of the city proper; and a third wall with sixty towers cut through the city itself from Herod's palace on the west across the Valley of the Cheese-makers to the Temple hill on the east. Titus stationed most of his forces on an eminence called Scopus ("the Lookout"), in the stony fields outside Agrippa's wall, and he placed some of his troops farther north than that. But he put the Tenth Legion, the legion from Jericho, on the Mount of Olives, beyond the ravine that edged the city on the east. In other days Christ and his disciples had sat and talked on the Mount of Olives, looking over the valley toward the city and its gleaming white Temple. Now Eleazar still held the most sacred parts of the Temple, John still held the outer portions of the enclosure, and Simon still held most of the city; and they still fought.

They managed to combine, however, just in time to disconcert Rome. The united Jews swarmed out of the city, into the ravine, and up the mount, itching to stick swords into Romans after all the nervous months of waiting. The Tenth Legion, busy setting up camp, was caught off guard; many of the men did not even have their weapons handy. It took Titus to save them from a very embarrassing defeat. Rushing to the Mount of Olives with some chosen followers, he rallied the legionaries and gave them a demonstration of personal bravery as he struck and slashed at the Jews from his great horse. At last the Jews were driven off, but it was not a very brilliant victory for the Romans.

The armies had come to grips and the siege was on, but it was Passover. The city was choked with pilgrims by this time, come to thank God at the Temple. For the present the pilgrims' main concern, and the main concern of thousands of ordinary citizens, was not the Roman siege but Yahweh. The unleavened bread must be eaten, the sacrifices must be performed, the ritual must be kept. John took advantage of the holy time to pull off a low trick on Eleazar. He disguised some of his soldiers as pious worshipers and sent them into Eleazar's part of the Temple, where the animals were sacrificed. There they suddenly threw off their robes, whipped out their weapons, and attacked Eleazar's men. The worshipers ran around the sacred precincts screaming and getting in the way; and some were clubbed, and some received swords in their bellies. Eleazar's men crowded into the Sanctuary itself, seeking safety in the small rooms where the sacred treasure was stored. Outside in the Court of the Priests the people who had come to worship hid behind the rough-hewn altar, screamed in pain and terror, and bled over the sacred pavement. At last it was over. John granted a truce and let Eleazar's men out of the Sanctuary. From then on there were only two factions splitting the city: Eleazar's party was a party no longer. The Jews resumed the celebration of Passover.

Abandoning the hill called Scopus, Titus moved in closer until his troops were right outside the wall built by Agrippa I. He even sent Josephus to invite the Jews to a parley on surrender; but he could not have sent a man less wanted and more hated, except perhaps Tiberius Alexander. The Jews would have nothing to do with Josephus or his invitation.

At this stage in the siege many of the Jews were fairly confident. Some of course listened to the prophet who still wailed through the streets, and some remembered Rome's reputation for invincibility or thought that even if Jerusalem should somehow triumph in the end, the period in between would be one of horror. But others told themselves that although the City of David had fallen to the Babylonians, the Seleucid Syrians, and Pompey's Romans, it would not fall to Titus. The two factions, it was true, were at odds within the city, but much of the population belonged to neither faction and just wanted to kill Romans. It was shameful that John's forces occupied the Temple and even more shameful that the holy precincts had been violated by war among Jews; but John was a fiery leader and Simon inspired valor, and the two men could do the Romans much harm if they tried. The worst problem was the diminishing food supply (John and Simon had not left a great deal when they burned the storehouses), but there was plenty of water, which the Romans were reportedly short on. Jerusalem the Holy was God's city and would not be entered by the foreigners unless God wanted it to be. The majority of the Jews assumed that God intended to protect Jerusalem; Josephus thought otherwise.

When Titus was ready, he attacked Agrippa's wall in force at what he considered its weakest point, in its western side. He used machines for firing arrows and javelins, machines for propelling hundred-pound stones, and battering rams. John and Simon decided that the situation was grave enough for a truce with each other. John sent his men down from the Temple to help Simon's men guard the wall, and Simon promised that his own men would not molest them. The Jews fought bravely, even dashing out of the city in an attempt to set the Roman entrenchments on fire, but the Romans finally forced them back; Titus killed twelve all by himself. The legionaries constructed three wooden siege towers cased in iron and moved them up on ramps until they stood flush against the wall and overlooked the city. While men in the towers sent arrows, spears, and stones down at the Jews, other soldiers hammered at the wall with the hugest battering ram—affectionately nicknamed Victor by the troops because it always broke down what it came up against. Victor succeeded as usual, and while the wall crashed and the Romans advanced through, the Jews withdrew to the middle wall—the one separating the suburb from the northern part of the city proper. The whole suburb now belonged to the Romans. It was late in May, and the siege was fifteen days old.

Titus next attacked the middle wall, aiming his blows especially at its central tower. Sometimes the Jews would venture through the wall into the suburb that had so lately been theirs and throw javelins at the Romans, who would throw javelins back. Among the Romans as among the Jews, a few men were eager to distinguish themselves by acts of extraordinary courage. A soldier named Longinus was as hot for distinction as any. He jumped out of the Roman ranks, ran toward the advancing Jews, plunged his javelin into one of them, yanked it out, plunged it into another one, and ran back to his own army, untouched and glorious. His comrades congratulated him on his successful bravery, but sensible Titus was less impressed. According to the general, bravery should not be confused with foolhardiness. A war was a practical matter, and personal heroics had no place in it.

Five days after breaching Agrippa's wall Titus breached the middle wall, and his men moved forward into a part of the city where wool shops, metalworkers' shops, and clothiers' shops crowded for room. Josephus says that Titus, with a restraint rare in conquering generals of ancient times, directed his troops not to kill anybody and not to set any buildings on fire. He hoped that by this extreme leniency he would make the Jews ashamed of themselves and would hasten surrender. But they only attacked his troops instead, slaughtering them in the narrow alleys, so that he had to retreat behind the middle wall. It took him four more days to break through the wall a second time, but this time he stayed through.

There remained the most critical wall: the one extending from Herod's old palace on the west to the Temple hill on the east and protecting a major area of Jerusalem—the Upper City, or southwestern quarter. There also remained the Temple itself (which protected the Lower City, or southeastern quarter) and the Antonia, until four years ago the headquarters for the Roman garrison in Jerusalem—high on the terrace above the northwest corner of the Temple enclosure. In other words, Titus' work had only begun. He had his legions construct four earthworks in the form of ramps, two of them against the wall of the Upper City, the other two leading up' to the Antonia. He also had Josephus proceed along the wall suggesting surrender, but the Jews only discharged stones and arrows at the Romans trying to finish the ramps. The Jews had built forty machines for firing stones and three hundred for firing arrows.

Famine now harassed the city, which was crowded with Passover pilgrims who had not been able to leave. More and more people suspected that God favored the Romans after all. The physically strong or the well-armed invaded the homes of the weak and helpless to search for food. A house that was shut tight was most promising: somebody was probably eating inside. People traded valuable possessions for a little wheat—or for barley, which was cheaper—and sat in remote corners gnawing at the grain, or ground it and baked it into bread and swallowed it in a hurry, praying that no one had smelled the sweet odor.

The rich did not fare much better than the poor. A false informer could usually be hired to testify before John or Simon that a man of wealth was a collaborator or was contemplating desertion, in which case he was executed and his property was seized. Some citizens of means did manage to desert—just as some Romans, according to the historian Cassius Dio, deserted to the Jews. The Jewish deserters must have been by far the more numerous. They converted their property into cash, swallowed the gold coins, and then stole out to the Roman camp, where natural processes or a good cathartic restored their wealth to them.

Many citizens, most of them poor, kept themselves from deserting because they were afraid of what John or Simon would do to their families. But in insistent hunger they would creep past the Roman guards on the wall at night and scout around for food—vegetable matter that the Romans did not need, decaying meat that the dogs and jackals had not yet found. Then they would try to sneak back into the city and eat this offal or share it with their famished wives and children. The Romans caught some of them, and Titus decided that to impress the Jews with a sense of Roman severity and to hurry along a surrender, all those caught must be crucified. Josephus says that five hundred or more were crucified every day, in plain view of citizens looking over the wall. If Josephus is not exaggerating unconscionably, the large number of victims suggests that a considerable proportion of Jerusalem's population was out foraging at night, and also that the Roman soldiers spent the nights combing the area around their camp for hungry Jews. Both conclusions may be justified. After a while, according to Josephus, the Romans grew so tired of crucifying Jews that they started fastening them to the crosses in picturesque poses.

By the middle of June, after more than two weeks of labor, the Romans had completed the earthwork ramps. But the two that were set against the Antonia did not last long. Directed by John, Jews had been digging tunnels underneath them and propping up the tunnels with wood. When the command was given, the Jews set the wooden props on fire, and the earthworks above them collapsed into the conflagration.

The Romans still had the two ramps constructed against the wall, and a couple of days later they succeeded in moving war engines up them. But the Jews in the heroism of despair streamed onto the ramps and set the war machines on fire; the fire spread to the ramps themselves; and the Jews charged straight on to the Roman camp. The camp guards did not draw back but died in place, because according to Roman discipline they would be executed if they left their posts for any reason. When the Romans finally rallied under Titus, the Jews were driven back into the city, but if they had had enough to eat they could have celebrated a victory. The labor of the legions had been rendered useless: the ramps and the war engines were ashes. The Jews, tortured by hunger, had shown that they could still confound Rome.

XVII

JERUSALEM THE HOLY

Titus listened to and rejected the suggestions of his officers. The only way to conquer Jerusalem, he decided, was to prevent foragers and deserters from leaving the city, and food from being smuggled into it, by encircling it with an airtight earthen siege wall. This would aggravate the famine and slowly squeeze the life out of Jerusalem, and the soldiers could enter a limp city. The officers did not contradict the opinion of so competent a general who also happened to be the emperor's son, with an excellent chance of becoming emperor himself when his father died. As for the soldiers, they reacted with enthusiasm. Each unit was assigned a certain sector to build, and unit competed with unit so that the construction was almost a game. In three days it was finished: a great, ugly earthen rampart, almost five miles in circumference, coiling around the city, far enough away to be out of the range of missile fire but near enough to be constrictive. At intervals along it, thirteen garrisons sheltered troops. Titus' soldiers came really close to the Jewish-held part of the city at only one point —the Antonia, which faced the northern portion of the siege wall. They built four new timber-and-dirt ramps at the Antonia, since this great fort would have to fall before the city could be taken.

Inside Jerusalem the children's bellies swelled with hunger, and their elders fell in the alleys or crumpled at home. If the dead could be buried in time, they were buried, but many sprawled in the streets. Sometimes the living grinned as they walked past the corpses: the more people died, the more food would be available. Husbands fought wives for food, and sons fought mothers. People searched sewers for cow dung. Armed men still broke into houses, in most cases finding nothing edible now but perhaps finding money, clothes, or ornaments that would mean a profit for them if normal life ever returned to Jerusalem, and if they had not died by then. The authorities —John, Simon, and their associates—ordered the dead interred at public cost in the hope of reducing the pervasive stink of the corpses. But later the bodies were just thrown over the walls into the ravines that were supposed to protect the city, and the dead lay there in clammy heaps and oozed into one another and sent up their smell.

Jerusalem might have admitted defeat if John's party and Simon's party had not provided a strong backbone for the resistance and intimidated weak souls. Men who were able even went on sallies outside the city and fought the Romans, although the piles of corpses over which they had to march made it difficult to get out of the city and in again. Many persons still believed that Yahweh would not permit the fall of Jerusalem the Holy; others said that Yahweh was punishing the Jews for their transgressions, for forgetting the right ways. Josephus continued to come over from the Roman lines and shout up at the wall that Jerusalem should surrender. Although he was serving Rome, he must have felt he was also trying to serve the Jews. It was useless for them to extend the agony and multiply the deaths; if the Jews did not open their gates soon, this home of his people and his God would be a charnel house.

But Josephus was well fed and petted by the Romans, so the men on the wall called him a traitor, ordered him away, and threw things at him. One time he was hit on the head by a stone and knocked unconscious, and the Jews rushed out to capture his body; but before they could drag it into the city, some of Titus' soldiers rescued it. Watching the Romans carry the body off, the Jews assumed that Josephus was dead and whooped the glad message through the streets. At the Roman camp, however, Josephus recovered, and he came back to shout in their faces that he was still alive and would have his revenge on them for hitting him.

Some of the citizens, perhaps influenced by his frequent exhortations or perhaps unable to stand this city surrounded by the smell of death, defected by jumping from the walls when they got a chance, or pretended to join a sally and then ran fast for the Roman lines. Many, when they reached the Roman rampart, ate too fast and died. A few, like the earlier deserters, swallowed gold coins before fleeing from the city. This method of conveying one's wealth was not original with the refugees from Jerusalem but was an ancient practice. Eventually Titus' soldiers discovered that the Jews were using it: a Syrian mercenary came across a deserter fingering his own excrement for gold. The news spread quickly. Auxiliaries from Syria and Arabia sprang on deserters, slit their bellies open, and rummaged for coins, and some of the legionaries were soon doing it too. In most cases of course no coins were found, but enough soldiers made a profit so that the practice continued. On one night, according to Josephus, two thousand Jews were opened up for money.

Titus thought he should set an example by executing those who were guilty, but so many were guilty that he would have ended up executing half his army. He therefore made a speech expressing his indignation and threatening future offenders. The search for gold diminished somewhat after that, but it still went on clandestinely. The auxiliaries would watch for deserters, venture out to meet them before the legionaries had spotted them, and go to work.

About the night of July 24 the Romans succeeded in taking the Antonia. John's forces, stationed within this palatial fort on the highest point of the Temple hill, had put up a gallant defense during the preceding two or three weeks—trying, for instance, to set the Romans' four dirt-and-timber ramps on fire—but an advance party finally succeeded in scaling the Antonia. After the advance party Titus himself was among the first to invade the great structure. Gradually the Jews were forced back into the Temple. More Roman soldiers, taking advantage of the tunnel that John had dug to undermine the earlier ramps, penetrated the holy complex. Then John's men and Simon's men united in rage to keep the pagans out. It was close combat, sword against sword, with the fighters stepping on the fallen and stumbling over them. Back and forth the Jews and the Romans pushed each other; but the Jews were fighting for their Temple, and the thought of Romans in it could not be borne. They forced Titus' soldiers to retreat into the Antonia.

Then a centurion named Julian almost took the partial victory

away from the Jews with no help from anybody. He had been standing with Titus on the Antonia, watching events; but he was a man
with the strength of a giant and a great deal of skill in battle, and he
could not watch any longer. He dashed down the steps of the fort;
sprang at the Jews, brandishing his sword; dove into them like a warrior demon, striking and killing; and chased them back into the Temple precincts—until the hobnails in his boots made him slip on the
slick pavement and he crashed to his back in a clatter of armor. The
Jews were on him then, and the Romans looking on from the heights
of the Antonia groaned. He lay on his back, working his shield to
fend off the swords and spears; but no Romans came to his rescue,
and the watchers on the Antonia finally saw the Jews lug off his
body.

Titus had the Antonia torn down and ordered the construction of a
broad roadway by which his army could mount to the top of the hill
to attack the Temple. Many of the Jews, however, still refused to believe that God would render His Temple to the Romans, and in some
ways they were not sorry to see the Antonia go. Built by Herod,
named for his Roman friend Mark Antony, and used during the past
two generations to house the Roman garrison at Jerusalem, it was associated in their minds with tyranny.

On the seventeenth day of the month Tammuz in the Hebrew calendar (about August 5) a terrible thing came to pass. For generations at every dawn, when the silver trumpets sounded from the holy
hill, and again every evening, the priests had sacrificed to Yahweh at
the Temple. Even the conflict between Eleazar and John did not
break the daily chain of sacrifice. But on the seventeenth of Tammuz
no sacrifice was offered. Either there were not enough men to perform it or there were not enough lambs. And on the days that followed also, God did not receive His due offerings. The effect on the
Jews was extremely demoralizing; they were ashamed.

Titus considered this a good time to send Josephus to John with
another proposal for surrender and, according to Josephus, with the
suggestion that if John still wanted to fight, the battle should be held
outside the city so that Rome would not be obliged to harm the Temple. And so the two enemies faced each other as they had faced each
other in Galilee, except that this time John was no longer a rising agi-
tator and Josephus represented Rome. According to Josephus' account, John defiantly repeated the affirmation heard so often in those

days—that God would not let His city be captured. But it was beginning to sound hollow, and Josephus replied sarcastically that God might not want to save a city where His sacrifices were no longer performed.

One night Titus deputed thirty men out of each one hundred to attack the Temple. The battle was a draw, but the Jews knew that more assaults on the Temple would come. Titus also had his troops build earth-and-timber ramps up to the northern and western porticoes, close to the razed Antonia. The Jews themselves placed on the Temple roof their own engines for throwing stones and darts, converting the outer portions of the sacred building into a fort. They also burned and cut away the part of the northern portico that had adjoined the Antonia, since if it remained standing its roof might provide a place from which the Romans could shoot down on them.

Many legionaries, too impulsive to wait for orders, did climb on ladders one day to the broad, flat roof of the western portico. They had seen the Jews busy in this area earlier in the day, but the Jews had now gone away, looking tired and easy to beat. It was of course a trick. What the Jews had been doing was packing dry kindling wood, pitch, and asphalt between the rafters and the ceiling of the portico. When the roof was crowded with legionaries, the Jews set the packing on fire—perhaps by shooting flaming arrows or spears into it, although Josephus does not say. In a moment the roof was red and the Romans were dancing and rolling around on it, screaming and shrieking as their bodies burned, jumping off to fall on the Roman side, plunging into the midst of the Jews in front of them so that they might die by sword rather than by fire. Titus, watching the whole performance from a part of the Antonia that had evidently been preserved as an observation post, rushed back and forth in agitation, wanting the soldiers to be saved even though they had climbed onto the roof without orders; but nothing could be done for them.

Although the Romans had been fooled in this instance, some of the defenders of the Temple could not help regretting the cost. A large portion of the western portico—the triple row of great columns underneath which they had so often walked, perhaps looking up at the gold-leaf ornamentation and the paneled cedarwood ceiling almost thirty feet above—now lay a tangled black wreck. But the portico after all was not the Temple; it was an external, Greek-style elaboration that Herod had wanted. Even the pagan and the unpurified could promenade in it, and the destruction of this part of it or any other part was certainly worthwhile if the Temple itself could be preserved. The Court of the Priests, the rough stone altar of sacrifice, and above all the Sanctuary containing the Holy Place and the Holy of Holies —these were the things that the Romans must not touch.

By this time the people of Jerusalem and the pilgrims who had not yet died in the city were gnawing their leather belts and shoes and swallowing dry grass. Among the most famous stories in Josephus is one that he heard in the Roman camp during these days, and it concerns the hunger. Some Zealots smelled the sweet and foreign odor of cooked food and traced it to a house not far away. Ravenous, they broke into the house and confronted an aristocratic young lady named Mary, who had fled to Jerusalem from her home across the Jordan some time before, perhaps when Vespasian's general Trajan was devastating the area.

They told her to hand over whatever food was left.

She said she had saved part of it for them, and brought out half of her baby. She had just eaten the other half, roasted.

Although she urged them to participate, they edged toward the door in revulsion. She explained that she had killed the baby herself, adding that if religious scruples prevented them from eating her child she would finish the meal alone. She also called them weaklings— men afraid to do what a mother had done. But they left in spite of her taunts, and she presumably finished the meal alone.

In its essentials the story may be true; Josephus says that even Titus believed it. He tells it as a horror story, but the baby, squawling incessantly for food that the mother could not give, would certainly not have survived the siege. The mother had ended its agony and allowed it to prolong her life.

Titus' troops, having completed the broad roadway up to the top of the Temple hill, now occupied the outer court of the Temple area —the vast open space bordered by the partly demolished porticoes; and the Jews were relegated to the Temple proper. The Romans brought up their siege engines against the Temple but failed to crack its heavy walls; the battering rams were useless against the massive stones that Herod had used. Titus decided to have his men climb ladders to the roof, but the Jews were there waiting for them. The Zealots pushed the invaders off screaming, stabbed them as they stepped from the ladders, and toppled the ladders themselves so that Romans on their way up plummeted to the pavement and lay in twisted heaps of dead and injured. Titus saw that the assault on the Temple was not a success so far.

He had another plan, however. He ordered his men to set fire to the enormous gates, of wood sheathed in metal, that admitted people to the outer courts of the Temple building such as the court in which women were allowed—though they did not give access to the court in front of the Sanctuary itself. Under the terrific heat the ornamental silver casings melted and ran down the wood, and the fire licked the wood, until those grandiose gates of which Herod had been so proud were giant torches. The fire spread to a single row of columns lining the courts and licked them away too, burning the rest of that day and through the night. The Jews stood back from the heat and watched the blaze lighting the darkness red. It was terrible to see, but the Sanctuary itself was still safe—for the moment.

The next day Titus had the flames put out. In council with his officers he discussed what should be done with this holiest of Jewish structures. Josephus says that some of the officers favored burning it but that Titus himself said it should remain, even if the Jews used the Sanctuary as a fort against the Romans. The question of whether Josephus is telling the truth here has been asked many times and is unanswerable. Since he wrote the *Jewish War* partly for the benefit of his patrons Vespasian and Titus, it is natural to suspect that he tried to make Titus appear very generous and noble-minded, crediting him with a sensitivity that the man did not really have. There certainly were excellent reasons for destroying the Temple. It was already in a sense an enemy fort, and such places were customarily razed. It was also the supreme symbol of Jewish resistance to Roman control and the focus of a religion that refused to recognize the gods of Rome. Burning it would be of tremendous psychological advantage; while it stood the Jews would not really be defeated. On the other hand there was no strictly military necessity for burning it even if the Jews did try to use it as a fort. In addition Titus was perhaps superstitious enough to wonder whether this Yahweh of the Jews might avenge so impious an act. Titus also had friends among the Jews—for instance, Tiberius Alexander, King Agrippa, and most of all Berenice—and he may not have wanted to distress them.

In the inner part of the Temple the Jews had just about stopped hoping. How long could they hold God's house against the Romans? Perhaps God Himself wanted it destroyed: it was at about this same time of the year, in the days of the kingdom, that He had let the Babylonians destroy Solomon's Temple. The Roman road now led up the hill, giving the legionaries and auxiliaries easy access. The northern portico and much of the western portico around the Temple area no longer stood. Fires still glimmered and smoldered at the demolished gates of the holy structure itself and at the single row of pillars. Roman soldiers—smart, businesslike, and uniformly lethal—camped in the great outer courtyard, where Gentiles were permitted, it was true, but where the Roman presence still constituted a gross offense. Down in the sepulchral city the living starved and could not bury the dead.

About August 29 the defenders of the Sanctuary sallied into the outer courtyard and fought the Romans there—fought them with the ferocity of desperate men who had gone beyond courage and wanted only to kill their tormentors. The Romans, closing their ranks, formed a solid wall of locked shields, but the Jews dashed against the shields and killed where they could, and Titus himself had to lead select cavalrymen against them. The horsemen were too much for the defenders; but even so, whenever the Romans retired, thinking that the battle was won, the Jews like pugnacious little dogs turned around and went after them again.

It was several hours before the Jews could be driven back into the Temple, and after a little while they were out once more. Titus meanwhile had gone to his tent. According to Josephus, he did not plan a full-scale assault on the Temple until the next day. But the Jews brought things to a head by engaging the Roman forces in the first courtyard of the Temple itself. This time the Romans chased them all the way back to the Sanctuary—and it was the last time that the Sanctuary was used for anything.

Josephus' account is the only circumstantial one we have. He says that a Roman soldier seized a piece of wood from the part of the Temple that was still burning (presumably one of the gates or the single row of columns) and, as an act of devilment, threw the burning wood through a door or window in the northern part of the Sanctuary. Either the gates and columns had stayed afire for about two days, with the Romans trying to put the fire out all that time, or the soldier was really carrying a firebrand and had been instructed to toss it into the Sanctuary. In any case it landed somewhere in the chain of small storage rooms that surrounded the Holy Place. In a short time the little rooms were blazing, and the fire was consuming the treasures accumulated in them. Some of the Jews ran around in agony, unable to do anything, crying that the end had come; others just stood in shock and heard the fire roar above the yells; and others, insane, slashed with their swords at any Roman within reach.

Somebody on the Roman side ran to Titus' tent to report what was happening, and Titus hurried to the scene, followed by his officers and many legionaries. Once the legionaries saw the blaze they realized that this was a great day for Rome. The Holy Place itself had not yet caught fire and the Holy of Holies beyond it was still untouched; but the flame, the smoke, and the hellish heat from the surrounding chambers were intense and excited the soldiers to a frenzy. They fell on the Jews, mobbed them, and killed them in the ardor of hate—the Jews shrieking and howling and running through the holy courtyards, the legionaries letting out their battle cries and charging and striking, clogging with bodies the steps of the terrace on which the marble Sanctuary stood, heaping dead defenders around the rough Altar of Burnt Offerings in the court below. They also surged into the chambers surrounding the Sanctuary to grab the treasures stored there, the money and the gold objects. Jerusalem was almost won, and it was time for the joy of plunder.

According to Josephus, Titus tried to save the Holy Place but could not prevail against the rage and greed of the troops. Someone threw a torch beyond the great gold entrance doors, and this room of God that only priests could enter turned into an inferno. From the Holy Place the smoke must have drifted past the veil into the Holy of Holies itself, choking the small, bare room where God had lived.

Below in the city the hungry Jews gazed up at the volumes of smoke, heard the clamor of death, and wandered helplessly. God had abandoned Jerusalem. God in His wrath had left His people to wail and His house to burn. The Temple had been famous and beautiful, the glory of the East. Jews throughout the world had looked to it. They had nothing to look to now. The gates of bronze and silver, the great golden doors, the veil of four colors, the massed treasures, the splendor and the mystery—all were gone. There would be no more high priest, no more morning and evening sacrifices. No more crowds would come to Jerusalem for Passover, traveling from far lands to praise Yahweh at the Temple. The heritage of Aaron was taken away. Only memory remained, and lamentation.

Not quite all the Jews on the Temple hill had perished. Five days later some priests who had not died, and who were starving, appeared before Titus to implore safety. But Titus sententiously replied that it was not right for priests to outlast their temple, and they were executed. The leaders of the revolt, John of Gischala and Simon bar Giora, had not died either: with a number of adherents they had made their way through the confusion and down the hill into the city. At least the major part of the city, the whole area from Herod's palace eastward to the Temple and southward to the Valley of Hinnom or Gehenna, still belonged to the Jews and was still protected by the innermost of the three walls. But how long it could hold out was problematical, and John and Simon asked Titus for a conference. He met them in the southwestern part of what had been the spacious preliminary courtyard, where a bridge connected the hill with the city. According to Josephus, he offered them pardon if they surrendered, but they requested permission to pass the rampart of earth that he had thrown up around the city and go out into the desert with their followers and their followers' families. In the wilderness they could start a new life and worship their angry God undisturbed. But Titus, indignant that these defeated people should propose terms to him, ordered the city entered and sacked.

There is not much more to say about the siege of Jerusalem. Titus threw his forces against the southeastern half of the Jewish-held city first—the part lying south of the gutted hill—and it was pillaged and set on fire. The Jews apparently did not put up a resistance. Then Titus attacked the southwestern half, the Upper City. This assault required earthworks, which the legionaries raised against the wall and its towers. Jerusalem's spirit was dead. While the earthworks were being built, thousands of Jews deserted to the Romans. A priest, in return for a promise of protection from Titus, presented the Romans with two seven-branched lampstands like those in the Sanctuary, gold bowls, gold platters, the gold table for shewbread that had been used in the Sanctuary, and the jeweled vestments that the high priest had worn on the Day of Atonement.

In two and a half weeks the earthworks were finished. It was about September 26. The Jews on the wall fought in the knowledge that fighting was useless. When the battering rams shattered parts of the wall they gave up. Some of them ran to tunnels and sewers under the city, to wait there or die there. They even abandoned the strong defensive towers of Herod's palace: there was nothing left to defend. The legionaries raised their military standards on the towers and swarmed into the streets, burning and looting. The generations of suffering and provocation, the generations of underground resistance against foreign ways, the mounting anger against Hellenization, Romanization, Pompey, Herod, Pilate, Florus, and all the rest, had come to this. In many houses the soldiers found no loot but only corpses.

XVIII

TRIUMPH

Tacitus in his *History* says that the population of Jerusalem at the beginning of the siege was about six hundred thousand. Josephus says that during the five months of the siege eleven hundred thousand died; but this figure includes the pilgrims who had crowded into Jerusalem for Passover in the spring and could not get out. Josephus' figure apparently also includes the Jews killed in the mopping-up operation after the city had fallen. The soldiers got rid of any aged and infirm people still in existence, although Titus had specified that only people carrying weapons should die. Both Tacitus' and Josephus' estimates are probably much exaggerated, but the toll must still have been tremendous.

As for the prisoners, they were herded into the ruins of the Temple, where a friend of Titus divided them into various categories. Those who had been agitators were executed. The best-looking young men were saved for the triumph that Titus expected to stage at Rome. The rest were sent in chains to Egypt to labor in the mines, sold as slaves (if they were young enough to have a future), or distributed to various provinces of the Empire, if they were strong enough to be used in gladiatorial combats or pitted against beasts in the arena.

There were still some Jews hidden in the tunnels and sewers, and the soldiers went in to ferret them out and kill them. Most of them, however, had already died. In the narrow passages the stench of the decaying corpses was almost unbearable, and only the hardiest legionaries had the stamina to stay in the sewers long enough to look for loot.

Josephus tells us that he requested pardon for his brother and some of his friends, and that Titus graciously granted the request. Titus also allowed him to enter the prison yard in the remains of the Temple. There Josephus walked among his countrymen as they lay in rags and wailed. Eleven thousand of these captives starved to death, he says, either because the guards refused them food in a hatred that would not die, or because the Jews themselves in hatred refused to eat. The prisoners included many women and children, all packed together in squalor and pain, all hopeless now after the long struggle. With Titus' permission, when Josephus came across people he knew he pointed them out and they were set at liberty. He says he freed about one hundred ninety acquaintances and friends of former days.

But he does not disclose his own thoughts and feelings as he searched for people he recognized among these abject fellow Jews. He does not say whether he regarded them as proofs of God's anger, as foolish folk too obstinate to believe that God had gone over to the Romans, or as poor, tragic victims of demagogues such as John and Simon. Perhaps he congratulated himself for having gained the favor of Vespasian and Titus, or despised himself in the midst of this suffering. He may have yearned to save more of these people and pitied them all with an ineradicable, deep, and heavy sorrow. All he says is that Titus was kind enough to let him have some sacred books.

Titus ordered most of the city leveled to the ground. He deputed the Tenth Legion and some cavalry and infantry units to keep watch over the place. In an impressive ceremony he thanked his troops for their gallantry, called up to his own official platform all the men who had fought with exceptional distinction, and gave each of them a gold crown, a gold chain for the neck, a miniature gold spear and silver standard, some of the gold and silver and costly clothing that had been turned in as loot, and a promotion. Then he sacrificed oxen to the gods for the victory, and a Roman banquet followed.

Later he went to Agrippa's capital, the inland town of Caesaraea Philippi, and presumably Agrippa was there to greet him. One would suppose that Berenice was too. Here Titus watched games in which some of the Jewish prisoners were chewed up by animals or made to fight one another. Josephus does not comment on whether the king and his sister, descendants of Herod and of the Hasmonaeans, also watched these displays, but they can scarcely have avoided doing so.

Titus received acclaim at Berytus, at Zeugma on the Euphrates, and at Antioch, where he denied the citizens' request that the Jews be driven out of the city, explaining that they now had no place to go. The Antiochenes next asked him to abolish the Jews' civic privileges, and he denied this request also. Then he set off for Egypt, since he was to take ship at Alexandria for Rome. He passed through Jerusalem on the way, and felt sorry for it.

By June of 71, Titus was back in Rome, and at the end of the month occurred the triumph—the combined parade, pageant, and sacred festival that provided citizens of the capital with one of their most impressive spectacles. As victorious generals both Titus and Vespasian had been granted triumphs by the senate, but they had decided to hold a joint one, demonstrating to the people the unity within the imperial family. Before dawn the streets were jammed with the Roman citizenry, standing wherever they could, jostling, squeezing in, packing tight to watch the show. The soldiers were drawn up at the Temple of Isis and Serapis in the Campus Martius, since Vespasian and Titus had spent the night there. Crowned with the laurel wreaths which Rome awarded her victorious generals, and robed in purple, father and son stepped from the temple at dawn. In front of the colonnade called the Porticus Octavianae a platform had been set up. From it the two generals received the acclamations of the troops and the praise of the senators, knights, and magistrates. The enthusiasm was deafening; Vespasian raised his hand for silence. Then he and Titus, their heads mantled, prayed to the gods of Rome. The soldiers ate the breakfast that the emperor and his son had furnished; Vespasian and Titus themselves did not eat until they reached the Gate of Triumph. Here they offered sacrifices, and from here the parade started. It would end at the destination of all triumphs: the Temple of Jupiter Optimus Maximus on the Capitoline Hill, now in process of rebuilding after the impious fire of a year and a half ago.

The custom in triumphs was to display as many spoils from conquered countries or tribes as possible; the more spoils there were, and the more expensive and exotic they were, the more glory redounded to Rome and the victorious general. This particular triumph was an extravagant piece of propaganda for the emperor and his house. Babylonian tapestries, jeweled crowns and objects of gold, of silver, and of ivory were carried past the cheering crowd. It seemed as if Vespasian and Titus had brought home to Rome all the gorgeousness of the East. Oriental animals, caparisoned like the favorites of kings, were led past by trainers in purple and gold. Floats three and four stories high went by, made of ivory and depicting in tableaux and tapestries an assortment of scenes from the war—Romans slaughtering Jews, military engines knocking walls over, Romans pouring into cities and setting everything on fire. Ships also formed part of the procession; and so of course did the specially selected young Jews, the tallest and most handsome to be found when the war was over, dressed in lavish costumes for the occasion. John of Gischala and Simon bar Giora were there too, but Simon was hauled out of the parade to be killed at a prison in the Forum. Of all the displays the most important consisted of the sacred objects from the Temple: the gold table for the unleavened bread set out for Yahweh, the gold plates, one of the gold seven-branched lampstands, the silver trumpets that had announced the morning and evening sacrifices, and a copy of the Torah. The crowd jabbered, hooted, and cheered.

Soon after these spoils came Vespasian and Titus themselves, each in a triumphal chariot drawn by four magnificent horses, accompanied by Titus' younger brother Domitian on a splendid charger. When the people saw them coming, they went wild.

In Judaea, however, the war was not over. Although Jerusalem and most of the land hardly breathed, three palace-fortresses in the dry southern region still held out: Herodium, the fortified tomb of Herod; Machaerus, east of the Dead Sea, where John the Baptist had spoken against Antipas and Herodias; and the rock of Masada, west of the Dead Sea and close to Qumran. Bassus, who had been appointed military governor over Judaea, subdued Herodium and Machaerus before he died. That left Masada to face the Roman world.

The new military governor, named Silva, moved against Masada in the year 72 with a force numbering perhaps as many as fifteen thousand men. He encircled it with a wall to prevent its defenders from escaping and set up eight camps around it. Supplies and even water for the camps had to be brought with difficulty across the dusty, rocky, sun-tortured land. He used defeated Jews for this purpose.

On top of the great, flat rock about nine hundred sixty Jews were living. Many of them were Sicarii, brought here in 66 at the beginning of the revolt, when they massacred the Roman garrison and took over. Some may have been votarists who fled from Qumran when Vespasian's Tenth Legion came there in 68. Others may have been refugees from Jerusalem and other desolated places. There were women as well as men, and there were children, a number of whom had no doubt been born on Masada and had never been down to the world below.

The people on the rock did not live poorly. They had two Herodian palaces, an ingenious water system, ritual baths, and a synagogue, plus living quarters within the turreted double wall of stone around the edge of the plateau. An arsenal held enough arms for ten thousand men. Storehouses were well supplied with grain, beans, dates, oil, and wine. Not only the military equipment but much of the food and drink too had been put there by Herod about one hundred years ago. Although he had never needed it, the king had looked on Masada as a place to flee to early in his reign, in case his subjects revolted or Cleopatra attacked. Everything, even the food, was still in a state of excellent preservation, ready for use. This was Herod's unintentional gift to the Jews.

Its sheer rock face made Masada almost totally inaccessible. Only two tracks led all the way up. One, appropriately called the Snake, wound tortuously back and forth on the eastern side, inching toward the top. It was narrow and perilous; if a man missed a step his body crashed on the rocks below. This track was of no value to an army. The one on the western side was more feasible, but at its narrowest point a strong tower stood in the way of further progress. From the tower defenders could pick off soldiers filing upward until the track was clogged with the dead. Even with the rest of Judaea conquered and a Roman army busy down below therefore, those on Masada must have felt relatively secure.

But behind the tower a spur called the White Cliff jutted out to a considerable distance. In the spring of 73, Silva managed to occupy this promontory. He was still several hundred feet below the top of the plateau, but there was room on the spur to build a ramp. His soldiers constructed one about three hundred feet high, and on top of it they erected a stone platform about seventy-five feet across and seventy-five feet tall. This brought the Romans up to the double stone wall rimming the top of Masada. Siege engines similar to those used against Jerusalem were hauled up on the platform. There were a battering ram and an iron-sheathed tower at least ninety feet high, from which the Romans fired missiles at the defenders on the wall.

Inevitably the Romans caused the double stone wall to crumble; but that did not give them access to Masada. Behind the wall the Jews had built another one, made of dirt sandwiched between two rows of beams. This barricade was resilient: it bent to the blows of the battering ram but did not shatter. There was only one thing for Silva to do. He ordered his men to fire torches at the wooden beams.

The wind, however, was blowing wrong for the Romans: it flung the flames back in their faces and almost ignited their own siege engines. The defenders must have hoped that Yahweh might save Masada after all.Then suddenly the wind shifted and the wall began blazing, and the Jews knew that their time was nearly up. The Romans would be on them tomorrow, killing the men, making the women and children slaves, and looting systematically.

The Jewish chief, Eleazar ben Ya'ir, now addressed his countrymen. According to Josephus, he described the sole way to outwit the Romans and preserve freedom. The Jews must set fire to their personal possessions and to the palace that some of them were using as a fort, so that the Romans would be disappointed in their hope for plunder; but they must leave their supplies intact, so that the Romans would realize they were not pinched for necessities. They must also kill one another.

Ten men were chosen by lot to be the instruments of death. In the Herodian palace husbands lay down beside their wives, children beside their parents, all waiting to die by Jewish hands; and the ten men slew. Again by lot the ten now chose the one who would kill the other nine and finally himself.

The excavations of Professor Yigael Yadin, who has opened the citadel to modern eyes and established the veracity of Josephus' account, unearthed small pieces of pottery that may well be the lots used by these men. Each of the shards of pottery bore a name. One name was Ben Ya'ir.

The Romans broke into Masada the next morning, armed to the

full, wary and ready for a fight, and encountered solitude and silence. Only the flames moved. The soldiers shouted through the ghastly stillness—and two women and five children, who had hidden in some water tunnels while all the rest were dying, emerged and told the story. In the smoldering palace lay the dead. The Romans put out the flames. Judaea was conquered.

Almost nineteen centuries later, in the course of the excavations conducted by Professor Yadin between 1963 and 1965, the remains of twenty-seven dead were discovered. Some were men, some women, some children. No other remains have come to light. According to Professor Yadin dogs and vultures may have fed on the other corpses, or the Roman soldiers may have disposed of the bodies as prejudicial to health. On July 7, 1969, the twenty-seven dead were given a military funeral by the state of Israel. Near Silva's ramp they were buried as religious martyrs.

XIX

AFTER THE END

Rome treated her vanquished province sternly but not brutally. Judaea continued under military governors such as Silva. Caesaraea was of course the capital. The governor had at his disposal the Tenth Legion, which was stationed at Jerusalem, probably on the assumption that this place though in ruins still constituted the major area of irritation. Some of the land was farmed out to Gentiles, and some restored to Jewish aristocrats who, like Josephus, had not sided with the rebels. A pagan city named Flavia Neapolis was founded as a Roman colony in Samaria close to the former town of Shechem, where the aged Joshua had delivered God's message to the twelve tribes of Israel in the days of old. A colony for eight hundred veterans, with land to farm, was established at Emmaus, northwest of Jerusalem; and Emmaus became Nicopolis, "City of Victory." This colony plus the legion at Jerusalem would keep central Judaea in check. Hardest to bear was the tax that Rome substituted for the annual Jewish tribute to the Temple. The money now went to Rome rather than to Jerusalem, and it was used for the rebuilt Temple of Jupiter Optimus Maximus on the Capitoline Hill.

Throughout the Empire anti-Semitism increased, since the Jews were held responsible for so much trouble. Besides, the destruction of the Temple, the total defeat of the Jews, the triumph at Rome, and the appearance of Jews as gladiators and as meat for beasts in provincial arenas deprived Judaism of much of the dignity it had recently possessed for Gentiles. Idealistic Roman youths and religiously inclined Roman ladies would no longer be eager proselytes. It was now more natural for them to laugh or to spit.

But even so, things could have been worse. Most of the land in Judaea was still controlled by Jews. Although the specter of poverty stalked the streets and fields, there were still rich Jews in the province (even if many of them were collaborators), and business gradually revived. Friends and loved ones who had died in the war were not forgotten, but the present and the future began to occupy people's thoughts too. Rome did not in any way proscribe the practice of Judaism, and with governmental approval new synagogues were built. The people could still read the Torah and live by the Law. They could even keep hoping for a Messiah, and some of them did.

Although Judaism was now a religion without a temple, without priests, and without the ancient ritual of sacrifice, it acquired a new center and new vitality. While the factions had been battling in Jerusalem before the siege, one of the prominent Jews who deserted to the Romans was the rabbi Johanan ben Zakkai. The Midrash contains the story that he escaped from Jerusalem disguised as a corpse. Although from the Zealots' standpoint he was a renegade, he was also a pious Jew, and he obtained from Vespasian the promise that he and his Pharisaic followers could study the Law undisturbed at the city of Jamnia near the coast, a property of the emperor. After the war more Pharisees joined his group, and Jamnia became a school for the reading, interpretation, and expounding of Scripture. Learned, devout, intense, sensible, and rational, the scholars there carried on a rabbinical tradition of Biblical exegesis that enriched the life of the ordinary Jew.

Jewish favorites of Rome did not do badly in those years. King Agrippa, who continued to enjoy the esteem of Vespasian and Titus, retained possession of his Eastern dominions until his death in the year 100. He spent much of his time at Rome, where he received the rank of a praetor, or judge. His sister Berenice lived with Titus at Rome for a while as his mistress and hostess. Titus, however, had to send her back to the East because the Romans would not tolerate her. The fact that she was a Jewess may have bothered some of them, even though she and her brother had so strongly opposed the revolt. The fact that she was Oriental and seductive no doubt bothered others. Titus, already a hero, would presumably become emperor after Vespasian's death, and he must not be allowed to fall prey to an Eastern woman. In 79, when his father's strong and businesslike reign was over, Titus did become emperor; and Berenice rejoined him but was again dismissed, regretfully but finally.

Josephus sailed to Rome with Titus in 71 and prospered. Vespasian lodged him in the house where he himself had lived before becoming emperor, made him a Roman citizen, and assigned him a pension. In addition to the pension Josephus enjoyed an absentee income from land in Judaea that Titus had given him. There was a tense period soon after the war, when a minor Jewish rebellion broke out in Cyrenaica in northern Africa and its leader, a vulgar weaver by trade, named Josephus as one of the men who had furnished him with money and weapons. But Vespasian investigated the case and discovered that a certain Catullus, governor in Cyrenaica, had persuaded the weaver to implicate Josephus and other influential Jews. According to Josephus, Catullus had not dealt fairly with the northern African Jews and did not want eminent Jews in other parts of the Empire to expose him. Soon afterward Catullus' bowels dropped out and he died. Vespasian gave Josephus a large piece of land in Judaea as compensation for the strain he had been through.

Continuing to live at Rome, Josephus saw the Temple of Peace erected by Vespasian in 75 to commemorate the end of the Jewish war; and he saw the triumphal Arch of Titus, one of the noblest monuments left to us from imperial Rome, completed and dedicated after Titus' sudden death in 81. On the arch was depicted in relief the splendid triumphal procession of ten years before, with people blowing the silver Temple trumpets and carrying the seven-branched lampstand. Before Vespasian's death presumably, Josephus finished writing the *Jewish War* for the emperor and Titus, first in an Aramaic version and then in a Greek version.

Titus' younger brother Domitian came to the throne in 81, and although Domitian's reign was notorious for cruelty Josephus does not seem to have suffered. In fact Domitian exempted Josephus' Judaean estates from taxation and punished people who tried to malign him. Writing must have occupied a great deal of his attention in these years. The *Jewish Antiquities,* a lengthy work tracing the history of

the Jews from the Creation to the last procuratorship, appeared during Domitian's reign. It was followed by the treatise *Against Apion,*
in which Josephus, still pious at heart in the midst of his Roman
prosperity, sturdily defended Judaism in the face of anti-Semitic attacks. Finally came the *Life.* The date of his death is not known, but
he probably lived on into Trajan's reign as a highly respected citizen
of the capital of the world. Rome even set up a statue in his honor.

Not long after the war's end some desperate refugees from Judaea
tried to incite rebellion among the Jews of Alexandria, but influential
Alexandrian Jewish moderates did not want any trouble and the refugees were turned over to the Romans. Throughout the remainder of
Josephus' lifetime the Jews of the Diaspora, remembering what had
happened in Judaea, stayed subdued. They chafed no doubt, and
took insults from the pagans, and wept for their homeland, and met
in the synagogues and discussed the Torah and preserved their way of
life; but they did not try to fight Rome. About the year 110, when Josephus was almost certainly dead, there was trouble between the
Greeks and Jews of Alexandria. Both groups sent envoys to Trajan,
but the affair was evidently settled amicably.

Then in 115, while Trajan was at war against Parthia, fierce Jewish
insurrections suddenly broke out in Cyrenaica, in Egypt, and on the
island of Cyprus. Gentiles were massacred mercilessly. The Jews of
northern Africa elected their own king. In 116 the revolt spread to
Mesopotamia. Judaea also seems to have been in rebellion at this
time, although the records of the whole affair are meager. We know
that Trajan tried vigorously to suppress the Jews, but it appears that
there was still sporadic fighting in 117, when Hadrian came to the
throne. Jewish tradition calls him Hadrian the Cursed.

During the early part of Hadrian's reign the Jews were quiet
enough on the surface, though resentment and the urge to strike back
at their oppressors must have been strong underneath. Then the
emperor did one thing, or possibly two, that they could not stand for.
On a visit to the East about the year 130 he may have ordered that
Jerusalem be converted into a pagan city containing a grand temple
to Jupiter. At about the same time or perhaps earlier, in confirming
an edict against castration that Domitian had issued many years before, he added that circumcision was a form of castration and that
anybody practicing it must be killed. The edict was not aimed

specifically at Jews, who were by no means the only Eastern people to practice circumcision. Hadrian's intention was surely to do away with what he considered a barbaric mutilation of the human body and to force on Oriental men the more enlightened ideas of Graeco-Roman civilization. But to the Jews of course the prohibition was unthinkable.

The result was the second great revolt of Judaea, lasting from 132 to 135. We know little about it, since there was no Josephus to record it, but recent archaeological finds, especially in the region south of Jerusalem, have added a great deal to our knowledge. Unlike the earlier revolt this one had a strong leader: the man called Simon bar Kokhbah. His real name was Simon bar Kosiba; the nickname Bar Kokhbah, or "Son of a Star," was a Messianic allusion. Some of the ordinary population of Judaea may have thought that in him the Messiah had finally come, although many of the rabbis opposed him and, punning on his name, called him "Bar Koziba"—"Son of Lies."

He definitely had some Messianic qualifications: he was a great warrior and a dynamic leader. If anybody could overcome the Romans, he could. He brooked no opposition; he defied Romans and detractors alike; and for the most part he was backed by the tremendous enthusiasm of people who, whether or not they regarded him as the Messiah, looked to him as their true ruler and general, the savior of Judaism from the Empire of the unjust.

But his victories could not last, and the Romans methodically encroached on the territory he had won from them. He had to withdraw to the dry land south of Jerusalem—the area of Herodium, Masada, and Qumran. When the Romans attacked his fortified hill of Bethar, he was killed.

After the second war so many Jews were sold into slavery that the market price of Jewish slaves fell sharply. Throughout the known world Judaea came to be called Palestine, in memory of the Philistines who had once possessed its coast; the implication was that the province was not really the land of the Jews. Rome ran ploughs over what had been Jerusalem, wiping it away. On its site a new city arose—a magnificent pagan center named Aelia Capitolina, after the man called Aelius whom Hadrian had adopted as his heir. A statue of Hadrian on horseback decorated Aelia Capitolina, and a temple to Venus, the obscene fertility goddess whom the Greeks worshiped as Aphrodite and the Canaanites had worshiped as Ashtoreth, was erected. On the site of the Temple of God, whose holy ground had not so far been disturbed, the Romans raised a great temple to Jupiter. According to Roman law any Jew setting foot in Aelia Capitolina would be put to death.

Jewish resistance to Rome was over forever. A long time would elapse before Jews lived again in what had been their holy capital. Eighteen centuries were to pass before they could regain control over the land that Yahweh had given to their ancestors.

BIBLIOGRAPHY

I. Ancient Sources

The principal ancient source, and for many events the only one, is of course Josephus. Faith in his reliability is not strengthened by the fact that when he narrates the same incident in two works, the two versions are likely to contain important discrepancies. He is probably more trustworthy on matters unrelated to himself than on those with personal significance. His own Hasmonaean ancestry, for example, may induce him to treat Herod too critically and Mariamne too ideally, and his accounts of his activities in Galilee are certainly colored by what he wants his readers to think about himself. Even when his personal feelings or motivations are not involved, he may err from the truth by depending on erroneous sources.

On the whole, however, he is as credible as most ancient historians. Although he may possibly present a slightly biased view of Herod, surely no one would ever call Herod a kindly king. The popular Jewish leaders both under the procurators and during the revolt may not all have been quite the robbers, frauds, and unprincipled demagogues that Josephus in self-justification makes them out to be, but it would be very difficult to defend them as high-minded heroes. The recent excavations on Masada under the direction of Professor Yigael Yadin have shown Josephus' descriptions of Masada to be painstakingly accurate and suggest that a strong commitment to truth characterizes his historical writings in general.

The Apocrypha According to the Authorized Version. London, New York, and Oxford, n.d.

Dio, Cassius. *Roman History*. With English translation by Earnest Cary. (Loeb Classical Library.) 9 vols. Cambridge, Mass., 1961.

Josephus, Flavius. (Loeb Classical Library.) 9 vols. Cambridge, Mass., New York, and London, 1926–1965. Includes the following:

> *Against Apion*. With English translation by H. St. J. Thackeray. Vol. I, 162–411.

> *Jewish Antiquities,* Books XII–XVII. With English translation by Ralph Marcus. Vols. VII and VIII.

> *Jewish Antiquities,* Books XVIII–XX. With English translation by Louis H. Feldman. Vol. IX.

> *Jewish War*. With English translation by H. St. J. Thackeray. Vols. II and III.

> *Life*. With English translation by H. St. J. Thackeray. Vol. I, 3–159.

————. *The Jewish War*. Translated with an introduction by G. A. Williamson, Baltimore, 1959.

————. *Life and Works*. Translated by William Whiston. Introduction by H. Stebbing. New York, n.d. (first published in 1737).

The Mishnah. Translated and with an introduction and notes by Herbert Danby. London, 1944.

The New Scofield Reference Bible. Edited by E. Schuyler English *et al*. New York, 1967.

Nicolaus of Damascus. *Historiarum excerpta et fragmenta quae supersunt Graece* (*Excerpts and Fragments of Histories Which Remain from the Greek*). Edited by J. C. Orellius. Leipzig, 1804.

Philo. With English translation by F. H. Colson and G. H. Whitaker. (Loeb Classical Library.) 10 vols. and 2 supp. vols. Cambridge, Mass., New York, and London, 1929–1962. Includes the following:

> *Embassy to Gaius* (*Legatio ad Gaium*). Vol. X, 3–187.

> *Every Good Man Is Free* (*Quod omnis probus liber sit*). Vol. IX, 1–101.

> *Flaccus* (*In Flaccum*). Vol. IX, 295–403.

> *Hypothetica: Apologia pro Judaeis*. Vol. IX, 405–443.

————. *Legatio ad Gaium*. Edited with introduction, translation, and commentary by E. Mary Smallwood. Leiden, 1961.

Pliny the Elder. *Natural History*. With English translation by H. Rackham, W. H. S. Jones, and D. E. Eichholz. (Loeb Classical Library.) 10 vols. Cambridge, Mass., and London, 1938–1952. Vol. II (Books III–VII), translated by H. Rackham.
Plutarch. *Lives*. With English translation by Bernadotte Perrin. (Loeb Classical Library.) 11 vols. Cambridge, Mass., 1962.
Strabo. *Geography*. With English translation by Horace Leonard Jones. (Loeb Classical Library.) Vol. VII. London and New York, 1930.
Suetonius Tranquillus, Gaius. *The Lives of the Caesars*. With English translation by J. C. Rolfe. (Loeb Classical Library.) 2 vols. London, 1920.
Tacitus, Cornelius. (Loeb Classical Library.) 4 vols. Cambridge, Mass., and London, 1962. Includes the following:
The Histories. With English translation by Clifford H. Moore.
The Annals. With English translation by John Jackson.

II. Suggested Modern Readings

The following list is no more than representative; works on the Dead Sea Scrolls alone would furnish an extensive bibliography. It is, however, intended as a guide for the man who is interested in a more complete picture of Judaea in the first centuries B.C. and A.D. For an extremely readable and informative history of the Herods, the reader is referred to the two volumes by Stewart Perowne. In my remarks on Masada I have relied largely on the published research of Yigael Yadin.

Abel, Félix Marie. *Histoire de la Palestine depuis la conquête d'Aléxandre jusqu'à l'invasion Arabe*. 2 vols. Paris, 1952.
Aberbach, M. "The Conflicting Accounts of Josephus and Tacitus Concerning Cumanus' and Felix' Terms of Office," *Jewish Quarterly Review*. Vol. XL (1949–1950), 1–14.
Allegro, John Marco. *The Dead Sea Scrolls and the Origins of Christianity*. New York, 1957.
———. *The People of the Dead Sea Scrolls*. Garden City, N.Y., 1958.

———. *The Treasure of the Copper Scroll.* 2d rev. ed. Garden City, N.Y., 1964.

Avi-Yonah, Michael (ed.). *Jerusalem.* Preface by Izhak Ben-Zvi. New York, 1960.

Bernstein, Leon. *Flavius Josephus: His Time and His Critics.* New York, 1938.

Bevan, Edwyn Robert. *The House of Seleucus.* 2 vols. New York, 1966 (first published in London, 1902).

———. *Jerusalem Under the High Priests.* London, 1924.

The Cambridge Ancient History. 12 vols. New York and Cambridge, 1923–1939. Vols. VIII–XI, edited by S. A. Cook, F. E. Adcock, and M. P. Charlesworth. Note especially the following contributions:

   Bevan, E. R., "The Jews." Vol. IX, 397–436.

   ———, "Syria and the Jews." Vol. VIII, 495–533.

   Longden, R. P., "The Wars of Trajan." Vol. XI, 223–252.

   Momigliano, A., "Herod of Judaea." Vol. X, 316–339.

   Stevenson, G. H., "The Year of the Four Emperors." Vol. X, 808–839.

   ———, and A. Momigliano, "Rebellion Within the Empire." Vol. X, 840–865.

   Tarn, W. W., and M. P. Charlesworth, "The Triumvirs." Vol. X, 31–65.

   ———, "The War of the East Against the West." Vol. X, 66–111.

   Weber, W., "Hadrian." Vol. XI, 294–324.

The Catholic Encyclopedia. Edited by Charles G. Herbermann *et al.* 15 vols. New York, 1907–1914.

Charlesworth, Martin Percival. *Five Men: Character Studies from the Roman Empire.* Cambridge, Mass., 1936.

———. *Trade Routes and Commerce of the Roman Empire.* Cambridge, 1924.

Cross, Frank Moore, Jr. *The Ancient Library of Qumran and Modern Biblical Studies.* Garden City, N.Y., 1961.

The Dead Sea Scriptures. In English translation. With introduction and notes by Theodor H. Gaster. Garden City, N.Y., 1956.

Downey, Glanville. *Ancient Antioch.* Princeton, 1963.

Dupont-Sommer, A. *The Essene Writings from Qumran.* Translated by G. Vermes. Cleveland and New York, 1962.

The Encyclopedia of the Jewish Religion. Edited by R. J. Zwi Werblowsky and Geoffrey Wigoder. New York, 1966.

Farmer, William Reuben. *Maccabees, Zealots, and Josephus: An Inquiry into Jewish Nationalism in the Greco-Roman Period.* New York, 1956.

Ferrero, Guglielmo. *The Greatness and Decline of Rome.* Translated by Alfred E. Zimmern and H. J. Chaytor. 5 vols. New York, 1909.

Grollenberg, L. H. *Atlas of the Bible.* Translated and edited by Joyce M. H. Reid and H. H. Rowley. Foreword by W. F. Albright and H. H. Rowley. Preface by Roland de Vaux. London, 1963.

Gross, William J. *Herod the Great.* Baltimore, 1962.

Guignebert, Charles. *The Jewish World in the Time of Jesus.* New York, 1959 (first published in 1935; first published in English in 1939).

Harding, G. Lankester. *The Antiquities of Jordan.* Rev. ed. New York and Washington, 1967.

Harrison, R. K. *The Dead Sea Scrolls: An Introduction.* New York, 1961.

Henderson, Bernard William. *Civil War and Rebellion in the Roman Empire A.D. 69–70.* London, 1908.

————. *Five Roman Emperors: Vespasian, Titus, Domitian, Nerva, Trajan—A.D. 69–117.* Cambridge, 1927.

Jackson, F. J. Foakes. *Josephus and the Jews.* London, 1930.

The Jewish Encyclopedia. Edited by Isidore Singer *et al.* 12 vols. New York and London, 1901–1906.

Jones, A. H. M. *The Cities of the Eastern Roman Provinces.* Oxford, 1937.

————. *The Herods of Judaea.* Oxford, 1938.

Kraeling, Carl H. "The Episode of the Roman Standards at Jerusalem," *Harvard Theological Review.* Vol. XXXV (1942), 263–289.

Kraeling, Emil G. (ed.). *Historical Atlas of the Holy Land.* Chicago, 1959.

Laqueur, R. *Der Jüdische Historiker Flavius Josephus.* Giessen, 1920.

Macurdy, Grace Harriet. *Vassal-Queens and Some Contemporary Women in the Roman Empire.* (Johns Hopkins University Studies in Archaeology, No. 22.) Baltimore, 1937.

Marijnen, P. A. (ed.). *The Encyclopedia of the Bible.* Translated by

D. R. Welsh, with emendations by Claire Jones. Englewood Cliffs, N.J., 1965.

Mattingly, Harold. *Coins of the Roman Empire in the British Museum*. 3 vols. London, 1965–1966 (first published 1923–1930). Includes the following:

Augustus to Vitellius. Vol. I.

Vespasian to Domitian. Vol. II.

Nerva to Hadrian. Vol. III.

Mommsen, Theodor. *The Provinces of the Roman Empire from Caesar to Diocletian*. Translated by William P. Dickson. 2 vols. New York, 1899.

The New Catholic Encyclopedia. Edited by William J. McDonald *et al*. 15 vols. New York, 1967.

The New Century Classical Handbook. Edited by Catherine B. Avery. New York, 1962.

Nilsson, Martin P. *Imperial Rome*. New York, 1962.

Nock, Arthur Darby. "The Roman Army and the Roman Religious Year," *Harvard Theological Review*. Vol. XLV (1952), 187–252.

Noth, Martin. *The History of Israel*. Translated by Stanley Godman. New York, 1958.

Oesterley, W. O. E. *A History of Israel*. 2 vols. Oxford, 1932.

———, and Theodore H. Robinson. *Hebrew Religion*. London, 1933.

The Oxford Classical Dictionary. Edited by M. Cary *et al*. Oxford, 1949.

Parker, H. M. D. *The Roman Legions*. Oxford, 1928.

Parrot, André. *The Temple of Jerusalem*. Translated by B. E. Hooke. London, 1957.

Perowne, Stewart. *The Later Herods: The Political Background of the New Testament*. London, 1958.

———. *The Life and Times of Herod the Great*. London, 1956.

Pickl, Josef. *The Messias*. Translated by Andrew Green. St. Louis and London, 1946.

Pritchard, James B. (ed.). *Everyday Life in Bible Times*. National Geographic Society, 1967.

Raphael, Chaim. *The Walls of Jerusalem: An Excursion into Jewish History*. New York, 1968.

Reifenberg, Adolf. *Ancient Jewish Coins*. 2d ed. Jerusalem, 1947.

———. *Israel's History in Coins from the Maccabees to the Roman Conquest*. London, 1953.

Ricciotti, Giuseppe. *The History of Israel.* Translated by Clement della Penta and Richard T. A. Murphy. 2 vols. 2d ed. Milwaukee, 1958.

Richards, G. C., and R. J. H. Shutt. "Critical Notes on Josephus' Antiquities," Part I, *Classical Quarterly.* Vol. XXXI, Nos. 3 and 4 (July–October, 1937).

————. "Critical Notes on Josephus' Antiquities," Part II, *Classical Quarterly.* Vol. XXXIII, Nos. 3 and 4 (July–October, 1939).

Rostovtzeff, M. *The Social and Economic History of the Roman Empire.* 2 vols. 2d ed. Revised by P. M. Fraser. Oxford, 1957.

Roth, Cecil. *The Dead Sea Scrolls: A New Historical Approach.* New York, 1965.

Schürer, Emil. *A History of the Jewish People in the Time of Jesus Christ.* Edinburgh, 1885–1890. Includes the following:
   Division I. 2 vols. Translated by John MacPherson.
   Division II. 3 vols. Translated by Sophia Taylor and Peter Christie.

Schwarz, Leo W. (ed.). *Great Ages and Ideas of the Jewish People.* New York, 1956.

Shutt, R. H. J. *Studies in Josephus.* London, 1961.

Smallwood, E. Mary. "The Chronology of Gaius' Attempt to Desecrate the Temple," *Latomus.* Vol. XVI (1957), 3–17.

————. "The Date of the Dismissal of Pontius Pilate from Judaea," *Journal of Jewish Studies.* Vol. V (1954), 12–21.

————. "Some Notes on the Jews Under Tiberius," *Latomus.* Vol. XV (1956), 314–329.

Smith, George Adam. *Atlas of the Historical Geography of the Holy Land.* London, 1915.

————. *The Historical Geography of the Holy Land: Especially in Relation to the History of Israel and of the Early Church.* 2d ed. London, 1894.

————. *Jerusalem: The Topography, Economics and History from the Earliest Times to A.D. 70.* 2 vols. London, 1907.

Tarn, William Woodthorpe. *Hellenistic Civilization.* 3d ed. Revised by the author and G. T. Griffith. London, 1952.

Tcherikover, Victor. *Hellenistic Civilization and the Jews.* Translated by S. Applebaum. Philadelphia, 1959.

Thackeray, Henry St. John. *Josephus: The Man and the Historian.* New York, 1929.

Vaux, Roland de. *Ancient Israel: Its Life and Institutions.* Translated by John McHugh. New York, 1961.

The Westminster Historical Atlas to the Bible. Edited by George Ernest Wright and Floyd Vivian Filson, with an introduction by William Foxwell Albright. Rev. ed. Philadelphia, 1956.

Williamson, G. A. *The World of Josephus.* Boston, 1965.

Yadin, Yigael. *Masada: Herod's Fortress and the Zealots' Last Stand.* New York, 1966.

————. "The Temple Scroll," *Biblical Archaeologist.* Vol. XXX, No. 4 (December 1967), 135–139.

Zeitlin, Solomon. *The History of the Second Jewish Commonwealth: Prolegomena.* Philadelphia, 1933.

————. *The Rise and Fall of the Judaean State.* Philadelphia, 1962.

INDEX